AMERICA

The Men and Their Guns That Made Her Great

AMERICA

The Men and Their Guns That Made Her Great

Edited By
Craig Boddington

 Petersen Publishing Co.

Petersen Publishing Co., 8490 Sunset Blvd., Los Angeles, CA 90069

Library of Congress Catalog Card Number: 81-82704
ISBN 0-8227-3022-7

Printed in the United States of America

Graphic Design By Larry Brown
Cover Illustration By Leon E. Parson
Special Historical Consultant, Phil Spangenberger

CONTENTS

INTRODUCTION

A S THE HISTORY of civilized mankind goes, this land we now call America has had but a brief tenure. As these lines are being written the 205th anniversary of the signing of the Declaration of Independence has just passed. To us as individuals, 205 years is a long time indeed, but in the history of nations it is insignificant, whether we speak of modern times or the great nations of antiquity.

However juvenile America may be considered in the annals of the human race, insignificant she will never be considered. These stormy two centuries have seen a loose collection of runaway colonies weld together and spread across a great continent. They've seen vast acreage cleared for the plow, and arid wastelands turned green with irrigation. They've witnessed the rise of industrial capability never seen on this planet, and they've seen the spread of American influence throughout the globe.

The rise of a great nation has never been easy, nor ever totally peaceful, and that has certainly held true with this land called the United States of America. Force was first required to build an independent nation, and then to keep it free. Force was required to open the vast wilderness to the west of the Appalachias, and later it was required to keep the Union under one flag. In different times from ours, when different values prevailed, force was also used to expand the influence of a growing nation testing her wings. And force has been required to preserve the sovereignty of other nations allied with the suddenly powerful United States.

Today there are many who prefer not to recognize the part that firearms have played in the forming of America. This, perhaps, is regrettable. Violence, to be sure, is not pleasant to contemplate, but it has always been a fact of man's existence. To deny that, or to ignore it, is a disservice to our forefathers. The freedoms and the standard of living we enjoy today were hard-won, and Americans have fought hard to keep them. And, regrettably, it is entirely likely that someday we shall have to fight for them again.

It is important that we keep in mind that firearms were among the tools that forged our nation. Like any tool, the gun is only as good or as bad as the man who uses it. Had we not had many men who used these tools well in the last two centuries, then the thirteen colonies would not have become the United States of America, nor would those United States have remained free.

The thought behind these pages, then, is to remember the gun as the important tool that it was, and still is. However, this is not primarily a book about firearms. Rather, it's a book about America, as seen through Americans who found need of that most essential tool—and used it well when the need arose.

Within these pages are Americans whose names are household words—heroes that will always be remembered. Names like Theodore Roosevelt, William F. Cody, Alvin York, J.E.B. Stuart, and so many more. On the other hand, there have been outstanding Americans who measured up at a critical time, but whose names are largely forgotten. Some of them will be included within. Timothy Murphy, Samuel Walker, Elfego Baca, Frederick Russell Burnham—such names will not be known to all, but perhaps they should be.

Firearms have been used to cause violence, it is true, and that may be seen in these pages. But they have also been used to prevent greater violence, and that also will be seen. They have even been used as a tool to promote America's good will abroad, as when Annie Oakley performed before the crowned heads of Europe.

There have been so many heroes and heroines in

American history, and so many incidents in which fire-arms played a major role, that the planning of this book became difficult. Many appropriate situations were not included because of a wealth of material already published pertaining to them. Some other widely documented incidents were included simply because the book would be incomplete without them.

We did not attempt to encompass the whole of American history; such would be impossible in one book. As a starting place, we went to the beginning—the Revolution. Out of the wealth of heroes and the legend of the Kentucky rifle, one name stood out—Timothy Murphy, who turned the tide of the Battle of Saratoga and perhaps the entire war with the marksmanship of the backwoodsman. We then went on through the periods of the development of America—the emergence of the Republic, the first pioneers into the Shining Mountains, the opening of the frontier, the tragic War Between the States, the era of the buffalo hunter and of the cattle drives, and our early fumblings of imperialism in Mexico and the Philippines. The First World War seemed a fitting place to end this volume, for America emerged from that struggle as a world power, a position she still maintains. And what could be more fitting for the final chapter than the saga of Alvin York, a revolutionary frontiersman cast into the hell of a modern war and surviving through his skill with a rifle.

Some chapters, you will find, deal with a particular American and his involvement with a particular firearm. Others deal with a particular type of firearm and the effect it had upon America and the Americans who used it. All are factual, all were written by recognized authorities in their fields, and all offer good reading. For what can be more exciting than a panorama of the vast United States of America panned across two centuries, and what people can be more interesting than our own forebears, the ones who created this land?

We make no apologies for the use of firearms in this book, for they are as much a part of our heritage as the Americans who have used them. And those Americans, were they here today, would affirm that they were glad their guns were there when they needed them. It is to be hoped that they always will be.

Craig Boddington
Los Angeles
July, 1981

Artist C.A. Risley depicted the typical uniform and equipment of Dan Morgan's Riflemen. (*Courtesy I.R. Miniatures, Inc.*)

CHAPTER ONE

TIMOTHY MURPHY— REVOLUTIONARY RIFLEMAN

By Joe D. Huddleston

ON THE AFTERNOON of October 7, 1777, an American rifleman fired a shot at a British Major General, mortally wounding him. This single act by a soldier may have changed world history. Neither Private Timothy Murphy nor the rifle he used with such deadly skill were what you would normally expect to find in the ranks of the Continental Army. The American frontiersman and his longrifle were themselves a breed apart from what the world had ever seen. So much so that the buckskin-clad frontiersman, popularized in book and film, has captured the imagination of the world, and the "Kentucky" longrifle has been proposed as a national symbol. The image varies from the truth somewhat.

At the time of the Revolution, the personality of the frontiersman had evolved over 150 years of being on the cutting edge of advancing civilization. These people, man and woman, were stoic pragmatists, intimately familiar with violence, and exposed to the almost constant threat of disaster in all its forms; Indian attack, accident, disease, hunger, and border war. He had adapted to the wilderness by assuming a mixture of ways from his European heritage and survival techniques learned from the Indians. He would not hesitate to take scalps, shoot prisoners, or fight by deception and treachery if he saw it as necessary. He viewed the American Indian as a rival for the necessities of life, and often as less than human.

The frontiersman possessed a hardihood difficult to comprehend in today's world. He frequently was in marginal health, with a poor, monotonous, seasonal diet contributing to malnutrition. His habit of treating most ailments with calomel—a mercuric compound—rotted his teeth. While his brothers in the towns and villages of the eastern seaboard lived in comfort equal to that of the

cities of Europe, the family at the foot of the Appalachians lived in dark, cramped log cabins or brush lean-tos. All hands labored to clear land, plant and harvest, hunt and trap, and gather food in the forest. Water was considered an adequate drinking beverage at best, and the normal drink from childhood was homebrewed cider and beer. Most adults consumed homemade whiskey at a rate about four times today's national average.

Timothy Murphy, born in 1751 near the Delaware Water Gap in New Jersey, was raised in this society. His parents were young Irish immigrants. When Tim was about eight years old, the family moved west to Shamokin Flats, now Sunbury, in east central Pennsylvania. It appears that here he was indentured or apprenticed to the Van Campen family, and moved with them northeast to the Wyoming Valley in Pennsylvania. This 20 mile stretch of the Susquehanna River valley between Pittston and Shickshinny was the heart of the frontier. Here, Murphy would have worked, fought, and played as any frontier teenager might, and grew to manhood.

Frontier recreation involved those skills needed for survival. There were contests of strength and agility, such as foot and horseback races, and of skill with tools such as the axe and rifle. Doubtless here Tim would have begun to show skill in the two areas in which he later excelled—running and shooting. He was short, five feet six to five nine, stocky and powerful, and a fast and long-winded runner. His complexion was dark, his hair black, and he had a forceful set to his features.

It was during this period that Tim's reputation as an Indian fighter began, and at this time he acquired the longrifle with which he became so famous.

A rifle was a very personal thing to the frontiersman. He used it almost daily, and it supplied many of his

The Battle of Saratoga, October, 1777, was the first major American victory and has been regarded as the turning point in the Revolution. Timothy Murphy has always been credited with firing the shot that felled British General Fraser, demoralizing the British and eventually leading to their surrender. Painting by H. Charles McBarron Jr.

needs. It provided food, hide for barter or clothing, protection from Indians and animals, and furs for sale. A young man would deal with the local gunsmith whose work he most admired, and together they would agree on the essentials: caliber, length, weight of barrel, and amount of decoration. In the early 1770's a rifle made in Pennsylvania would have been around .50 caliber, with a barrel 42–44 inches long, and would have weighed eight to eleven pounds. Its stock would have been maple, either straight or curly grain, with a simple brass patchbox. It might be scantily carved and lightly engraved. This arm had evolved from the German Jaeger rifle over the period 1720–1770 to meet the needs of its changed environment. It was well-made, considering that it was handcrafted in crude shops on the fringe of civilization.

The American frontiersman was probably more intimately familiar with his personal arm than any other individual in the world at that time. His frequent use of it made him aware of the rifle's capabilities, and he was able to shoot it under all conditions of wind and weather. He certainly had more opportunity to practice, and greater need for accuracy, than the soldiers of the armies of the world. Even his standing in the local community rested, in some degree, on how well he performed in the frequent shooting matches. This expertise, combined with a determined personal independence and intimacy with violence, made the frontiersman perhaps the most deadly combination of man and firearm in the world. He had the will to kill without hesitation, and the skill to do so efficiently.

Tim Murphy would have gone through the process of discussion with the gunsmith of his choice, and the specifications of the rifle to be made established. It is here that the legend of Tim Murphy begins to evolve. He was an independent and free-thinking man, as his later experiences were to prove. This expressed itself at this stage by the type of rifle he chose. He had made or purchased a double-barreled rifle. It may have been a side-by-side type, but was probably the more usual

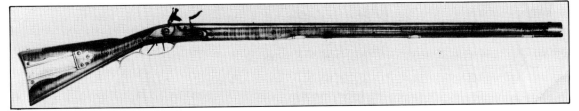

This Pennsylvania longrifle was made by Jacob Dickert of Lancaster, who worked from 1769 to 1822. In .50 caliber, with set trigger, it is similar to rifles that Dan Morgan's men brought to war. *(Photo courtesy George Shumway)*

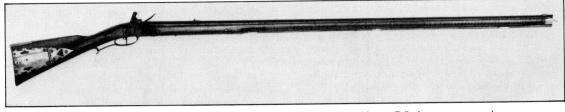

This ornate longarm by John Newcomer, also of Lancaster, is a .51 caliber smoothbore. Rifled arms were surely more accurate, but also slower to reload, and more difficult to manufacture. *(Photo courtesy George Shumway)*

swivel-breech. A gun of this style had one barrel mounted above the other. When the top barrel was fired, a latch was activated and the barrels rotated by hand to place the unfired one under the hammer, or cock. Double-barreled rifles were never common, and anyone using one was sure to attract attention. This, combined with Tim's exceptional marksmanship, gave him an immediate reputation.

In the spring and early summer of 1775, the American colonies were swept with the story of the British Lexington-Concord expedition. The British were surrounded and held in a state of siege in Boston by New England Minutemen. On June 14, the second Continental Congress voted to raise six companies of riflemen from Pennsylvania, two from Maryland, and two from Virginia. Thus began the American Army.

One of the Pennsylvania companies was formed in Northumberland County by Captain John Lowden. Timothy Murphy, age 24, his brother, John, and presumably his friend and constant companion, David Elerson, enlisted on June 29, 1775. The company left almost immediately for Boston.

The rifle companies arrived too late to participate in the Battle of Bunker Hill. However, Tim and his companions quickly taught the British pickets to keep their heads down with their sniping. During this period of siege Murphy is credited with one act of marksmanship. In September a party of British soldiers or marines were moving about in a barge planting buoys and taking soundings. Supposedly it was Tim who opened fire on them at a range approaching half a mile. The first shots caused such panic that the British lost control of their boat, and slowly drifted toward shore on the

tide. The riflemen continued to fire until virtually the entire crew was killed or wounded. When the survivors managed to paddle back to Boston, they had to be carried ashore on stretchers.

Boredom soon set in, however, and the riflemen chafed under camp discipline until the British evacuated the city in March of 1776. George Washington had taken command of the Continental Army, and he moved his main force to New York City after the British evacuated Boston.

In order to protect New York City from the high ground across the East River, Washington sent a strong force over to Long Island. Here, on August 27, his forces suffered a defeat. Murphy was among the riflemen that fought that day, and was evacuated with them a few days later to Manhattan Island.

For most of the balance of 1776, Washington's forces suffered defeat after defeat. They lost Manhattan Island, barely escaping with their army intact. They fought a disastrous retreat across New Jersey and finally stopped on the Pennsylvania side of the Delaware River. Here, Tim and his companions were among the force Washington took across the Delaware on Christmas night and they fought in the stunning victory in Trenton, New Jersey, the following morning.

On January 6, 1777, the Continental Army went into winter quarters in Morristown, N.J. While there, Murphy and his fellows underwent the novelty of being inoculated for smallpox. The riflemen were almost certainly used in the vigorous patrolling activity Washington maintained against the British in northern New Jersey. The British complained of the harassment, and were incensed by the fact that the Americans would be so insensitive as to fight when they should be resting.

In April, 1777, Washington caused to be formed a corps of 500 picked riflemen, under the command of Colonel Daniel Morgan. Tim Murphy and David Elerson were among those chosen.

As the new organization was being completed, Washington wrote Morgan to outline how he intended to use them:

> The corps of rangers nearly formed, and under your command, are to be considered as a body of light infantry, and are to act as such. . . .
> It occurs to me that, if you were to dress a company or two of true woodsmen in the Indian style, and let them make the attack with screaming and yelling, as the Indians do, it would have very good consequences, especially if as little as possible were said or known of the matter beforehand.[1]

Morgan's men sharpened their claws on the British during June and July. Henry Knox, Washington's chief of artillery, credited them thus:

> We had a large body of riflemen, under Colonel Morgan, perpetually making inroads upon them, attacking their pickets, killing their light-horse . . . .[2]

A modern historian, Lynn Montross, states ". . . events of 1777 were to prove Washington had created the best regiment of the Continental Army. . . ."[3] On August 17, Washington sent Morgan and his men north, to help stop an invasion.

For several months, the majority of the British northern army had been working its way south from Montreal. The intent was to join with the southern army in the vicinity of Albany, New York, effectively splitting New England from the rest of the colonies. By the time Morgan's men arrived to join the American defenders, several battles had been fought, and a number of forts and outposts taken by the British. General Horatio Gates, commander of the Americans, put Morgan's men to work against the British, under General "Gentleman" Johnny Burgoyne, almost the moment they arrived. Morgan's force, now down to 400, was used to harass, screen, and annoy the British advance. Combined with a select force of 300 light infantry under command of Major Henry Dearborn, Morgan quickly sent Burgoyne's Indian scouts packing for home. These were followed shortly by the bulk of the

Canadians and Tories. Murphy and his companions volunteered repeatedly for raids along the fringes of Burgoyne's force, delighting in a little legal Indian killing. When the riflemen first brought an Indian scalp back into camp, Major Dearborn probably spoke for all his New Englanders when he said it was ". . . a Rareety with us."[4] It was certainly no "Rareety" to the hardy frontiersmen.

With his scouts and Indians driven off by the riflemen, Burgoyne was denied his eyes and ears. He groped to the Hudson River, and, on September 15, made the fateful crossing, effectively cutting his communications with Canada. He now turned south along the Hudson until he realized he faced a major American force in fortified positions on a ridge known as Bemis Heights.

On September 19th, still without knowledge of the disposition of the American forces, Burgoyne moved out on a reconnaissance in force with three probing columns. General Benedict Arnold, a major commander under Gates, finally gained Gates' permission to advance with Morgan and Dearborn against the center column. All went well at first, as Murphy and his fellows routed the British advance party in a piece of newly-cleared land belonging to a farmer named Freeman. As the riflemen raced pell-mell across the field, they struck the force of the British main body and scattered. Morgan was discovered a few minutes later by one of Gates' aides calling his men back together with a turkey call. Reinforcements were sent up, and the battle became general, with Morgan's men taking to the trees as snipers. The battle swept back and forth across Freeman's farm for several hours, until the other British columns could be brought to bear, and the Americans retired behind their earthworks.

While Burgoyne was the victor and retained the field of battle, he was in a desperate situation. He was short of supplies, had suffered a large number of casualties, still did not know the American dispositions, and had given up hope of receiving help. The morale of his soldiers had taken a plunge, for Tim and his companions had killed a large number of officers, artillerymen, and artillery horses. The Americans had proven they were willing and able to stand up toe-to-toe and slug it out, which the British had not thought likely.

Meanwhile, it was not just a shortage of supplies that wore on the British nerves. The riflemen were still sniping and harassing. They could not even sleep well. At night, packs of wolves prowled the no man's land between the lines, howling, snapping and fighting as they fed on human and horse flesh discovered on the battlefield.

During this three-week lull, Murphy and Elerson

---

[1] Sparks *The Writing of George Washington*, Vol. VII, p. 461.

[2] Quoted in Commager and Morris *The Spirit of 'Seventy-Six*, p. 537.

[3] Montross *The Story of the Continental Army, 1775–1783*, p.187.

[4] Dearborn *Journals of Henry Dearborn, 1776–1783*, p. 5.

stayed busy. They became known for their daring. On two occasions they ambushed British foraging parties, killing or dispersing the British and returning with the supplies. One night they captured a sentinel, and extracted the password from him. While Elerson took the sentinel back, Tim entered the British camp using the password, and caught an officer alone in his tent. With a little gentle nudging from the point of Tim's scalping knife, the officer walked out of camp as a prisoner without alerting the sentries. Tim hastily hustled his prize back to Bemis Heights and safety.

It is little wonder his reputation was growing.

On the morning of October 7, Burgoyne personally led over 2,000 of his men forward on another reconnaissance in force. After advancing almost a mile, his main body of troops stopped in a field. With each flank resting in the woodline surrounding the field, the troops sat at ease while their officers tried to see what lay ahead through their telescopes, and foragers cut desperately needed hay from the field.

While the British were thus disposed, Gates directed a subordinate, "Order on Morgan to begin the game." With this vague directive, it appears that Morgan devised the tactics used to begin the battle. The riflemen, with Dearborn's light infantry, would attack through the woods on the British right flank and rear while another column attacked the opposite flank. Finally, after the British had shifted to meet these blows, a third column would attack the center.

This phase went pretty much as planned. The riflemen hit the Hessian mercenaries manning their portion of the line in flank and rear, and as they shifted in response, Dearborn hit them in front. Meanwhile, the other American columns were also successful. The British line began to collapse. Burgoyne sent one of his aides, Sir Francis Clerke, forward with an order to withdraw to the fortifications. Tim Murphy is credited with wounding Clerke at this point, causing his capture, and finally his death later that night.

As a result of Sir Francis Clerke's failure to deliver his message, the British, and particularly the Hessian mercenaries, continued to fight from their exposed positions, taking heavy casualties as they were forced back. The reconnaissance force lost all 10 of the cannons it had brought forward. The failure to retire in good order while they had time cost the British dearly.

Major General Simon Fraser, "the darling of the British Army," began to bring up fresh troops and prepare delaying positions. It was at about this point that General Arnold arrived on the field, and seeing Fraser's actions, called to Morgan, and pointing out the magnificently uniformed officer on his big grey gelding, said:

That officer upon a grey horse is of himself a host, and must be disposed of—direct the attention of

some of the sharpshooters among your riflemen to him.[5]

Accordingly, Morgan gathered a handful of his best shots, including Timothy Murphy, about him, stating:

Do you see that gallant officer? That is General Fraser—I respect and honor him, but it is necessary that he should die.[6]

The riflemen went to their duty. Tim climbed a tree on the field. According to one participant:

Immediately upon this, the crupper of the grey horse was cut off by a rifle bullet, and within the next minute another passed through the horse's mane a little back of his ears.
An aid of Fraser, noticing this, observed to him, "Sir it is evident that you are marked out for particular aim; would it not be prudent for you to retire from this place?"
Fraser replied, "My duty forbids me to fly from danger."[7]

Moments later Fraser was shot through the abdomen, and removed from the field. Before he died, he stated he had seen the man who shot him, and that man had been in a tree.

A British Lieutenant, William Digby, gives an idea of the effect of the fall of Fraser:

Fraser was mortally wounded, which helped turn the fate of the day. When General Burgoyne saw him fall, he seemed to feel in the highest degree our disagreeable situation. . . . Our cannon were surrounded and taken, the men and horses all being killed . . . it evidently appeared a retreat was the only thing left to us.[8]

The British finally retreated to their fortified positions. Arnold, in a frenzy, gathered troops from the field and attacked at several points, always to be repulsed. Finally he moved to the Hessian redoubt on the extreme right flank of the British line, where he found the riflemen were in the process of isolating the position. He led Morgan's men in a successful assault, but was wounded in the process. Nightfall ended the battle.

With the Americans holding the key ground on his

5Quoted in Commager and Morris *The Spirit of 'Seventy-Six,* p. 593.

6Thatcher *Military Journal of the American Revolution,* p.102n.

7Quoted in Commager and Morris, *The Spirit of 'Seventy-Six,* p. 593.

8Quoted in *ibid.,* p. 597.

right, there was nothing left for Burgoyne but retreat. He retired to the village of Saratoga during the night, and surrendered his force on October 17th.

The effect of the defeat of the British invasion force was far-reaching. The French, influenced by the victory, proposed an alliance with the Americans in January 1778. The result was open French military and naval support for the Revolution, and the use of French forces both in America and the British West Indies. The British had to reduce their forces in North America in order to defend the Indies, and the remaining British faced a much stronger American-French force on land and the French Navy at sea. Historians agree the victory at Saratoga was a turning point in the war, if not the most significant engagement of all. Little of this did Tim Murphy realize when he pulled the trigger on Sir Francis Clerke and General Simon Fraser.

In the meantime, General Washington had been anxious to have Morgan's riflemen returned to him. Gates released them and sent them south after Burgoyne's surrender. The riflemen were engaged in several skirmishes after rejoining Washington, and then moved with the Army into Valley Forge for the winter. Here, they were reorganized into the 11th Virginia Regiment.

Because of the need of the British to supply forces to

Captain Dan Morgan, later a general, organized his company of riflemen on the order of the Continental Congress. *(Courtesy George Shumway)*

the West Indies, the forces in North America had to consolidate. This meant that the British in Philadelphia had to march, bag and baggage, across New Jersey to join with the forces in New York City. While making this march, Washington engaged them at Monmouth. The riflemen, in a flanking position, were not a part of the battle. The following day, Murphy and Elerson were among a party that captured a British general's elaborate coach while scouting the rear of the retreating British.

Monmouth was the last major battle in the northern theatre of the war. This did not mean, however, that the war in the area was over. Along the frontiers, there flowed a particularly brutal guerrilla warfare between patriot and Tory, with a liberal sprinkling of British and Indian mixed in. As a result, Morgan sent three companies of his riflemen, including Murphy and Elerson, to protect the settlements west of Albany. Here Tim Murphy was to have some of his most hair-raising experiences.

As Sergeant of Captain Gabriel Long's Company, Murphy was stationed at what is now Middleburgh, New York, in the Schoharie Valley. This valley opens on the Mohawk River 25 miles west of Albany, and runs from there southwestward toward the Pennsylvania border, along the northwestern edge of the Catskill Mountains. West of Schoharie was little but wilderness all the way to the Great Lakes. Out of this wilderness bands of Indians and Tories raided the settlements. To protect themselves, the residents of the valley had constructed three fortified strongholds. The northernmost was the lower fort, because it was on the lower end of the Schoharie Creek. Next came the middle fort, now Middleburgh, and still further southwest, the upper fort, now Fultonham.

One of Captain Long's first assignments was the capture of a notorious Tory of the region, one Christopher Service. Long's force moved to its task, with Tim scouting ahead. As they neared Service's home, Tim intercepted a courier bound for Service. From a message he carried, it was learned a party of Tories was moving toward Service's house, where they hoped he had provisions for them. Captain Long turned aside to intercept the party. The ambush was successful. The Tory band was dispersed with several killed and wounded.

Captain Long returned to his original purpose. The unit surrounded Service's house, and took him without incident. As they escorted him out of the house, he made a desperate grab for an axe, and Elerson shot him dead. The result of this little excursion was a considerable dampening of Tory activity in the valley for a time.

Raid and counter-raid continued through the fall of 1778. Thayendanegea, a Mohawk war chief known to the whites as Joseph Brant, raided German flats (Herkimer, NY) from his base in the town of Unadilla,

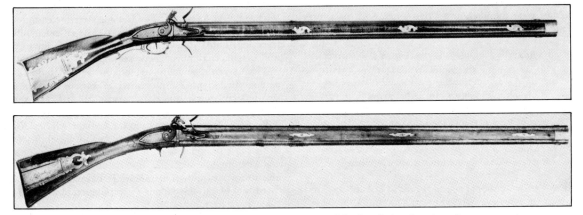

It is not known how uncommon double-barreled rifles were at the time of the Revolution, but several prime specimens survive. The top rifle by N. Boyer is .47 caliber; the bottom, in .51 caliber, is by William Antes. Both date approximately from the 1780's and are similar to the rifle Timothy Murphy is believed to have carried. *(Top photo courtesy George Shumway; bottom photo courtesy Kansas State Historical Society)*

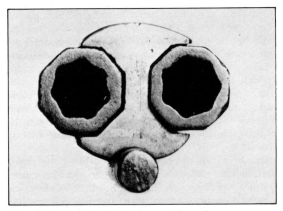

Most double-barreled flintlocks carried one hammer, two frizzens, and two sets of sights. After firing one barrel, the second barrel was swivelled into place by hand, the hammer recocked. *(Courtesy George Shumway)*

on the upper Susquehanna River. A punitive expedition was formed that included the riflemen. Tim and his unit raided and burned Unadilla and surrounding villages from October 2 until they returned to the middle fort on the 16th. Brant and the hated Tory leader, Captain Walter Butler, retaliated with a raid on Cherry Valley that was termed a massacre. Murphy and the Schoharie riflemen went to the settlement's relief.

A short while later, Tim and a scouting party killed several Indians in the Mohawk Valley. They were in turn ambushed and scattered, and Tim had to run for miles to outdistance his pursuers.

During this time in the Schoharie, Tim developed a love for Peggy Feeck, and eventually was to marry her, to the distress of her well-bred Dutch family. To them,

Tim was nothing more than a hard-drinking, hell-raising Indian fighter, hardly fit to enter the family of a well-to-do planter.

The spring of 1779 opened with another series of British-inspired raids. In one a white girl was captured, and Tim pursued the party alone. He trailed four warriors and the girl all night. He ambushed them over breakfast, and after a deadly game of hide-and-seek, killed all four Indians and returned with the girl.

From May to November, Tim and David Elerson were involved with a major punitive expedition under the command of Major General John Sullivan. This combined force of 4,000 men was charged by General Washington with the "total destruction" of the Iroquois orchards, crops and towns in western New York. Tim's woodcraft and marksmanship made him the most famous scout in Sullivan's army. Major Moses Van Campen wrote that he was one soldier "who never missed his aim."

The Campaign saw no large battles, but Tim and Elerson were engaged in the most famous incident of the expedition on September 13th. Lieutenant Thomas Boyd was sent to reconnoiter the Indian town of Chinesse. Contrary to his orders to take only five or six men, he formed a detachment of 26. Moving at night they missed the trail and at daybreak struck the wrong town. They killed and scalped two Indian defenders, while the rest fled. During the return the party encountered more Indians, and killed two of them. While pursuing the rest, the party was almost surrounded by several hundred Indians. Only the scouts and flankers escaped, Tim and David among them, but Lieutenant Boyd and 15 others were surrounded. All were killed but Boyd and a rifleman named Parker, who were taken to Chinesse, where they were tortured. Their bodies were found the next day when Sullivan's force entered the town. Sullivan reported to Congress:

It appeared that they had whipped them in the most cruel manner, pulled out Mr. Boyd's nails, cut off his nose, plucked out one of his eyes, cut out his tongue, stabbed him with spears in sundry places, and inflicted other tortures which decency will not permit me to mention; lastly, cut off his head and left his body on the ground with that of his unfortunate companion who appeared to have experienced nearly the same savage barbarity.[9]

It was such occasional acts of brutality that led the frontiersman to believe the Indian was an animal to be exterminated.

While the Sullivan expedition did little to remove the Indian, it had devastated them. An estimated 160,000 bushels of corn, many acres of vegetables and orchards, as well as 40 towns were destroyed. They did such damage that the six Iroquois nations never recovered. The coming winter was a time of Indian dependence on British charity.

In the fall of 1779 Tim's enlistment with Morgan's riflemen expired. He returned to the Schoharie, where he enrolled in Captain Jacob Hager's Company of the Fifteenth Regiment of Albany County Militia, commanded by Colonel Peter Vrooman.

As soon as winter eased, Tim began scouting to the westward, in anticipation of Indian raids. The Indians, in close dependence with the British all winter, were expected to be afoot in strength to avenge the destruction done by Sullivan's expedition. While on one such scout, accompanied by Captain Alexander Harper, the two of them were surprised and captured by a band of eleven braves. They were bound, and hastily marched toward the Indian camp at Oquago, now the town of Deposit, which was about 60 miles away. That night the captors, knowing they were safe from pursuit, posted no sentry. Murphy and Harper managed to untie one another, and without waking the Indians, they gathered all the firearms and hid them a short distance away. They then methodically began to knife and tomahawk the sleeping Indians. To have left them alive would have meant pursuit. Sometime during this gory work, the survivors awakened, but by then it was too late. Only one of the eleven escaped with his life. Tim and Harper returned to the Schoharie with news of the Indians massing at Oquago.

Colonel Vrooman mobilized his Militia, and sent one company of riflemen west to cover the frontier. Tim went along as guide and scout. The company encountered a party of Indians near Harpersfield and a

pitched battle developed. The Indians were forced to retreat, leaving 30 dead in their wake. The riflemen suffered four killed. The "Battle of Harpersfield" rang up the curtain on another bloody season.

Tim's reputation continued to grow. He single-handedly rescued another captured white woman, and led a small party in the successful rescue of two captured Schoharie farmers.

By now, Tim was known to the Indians who raided in his region of New York. It appears that his ability to fire a rapid second shot without reloading had the Indians crediting him with the supernatural power of being able to shoot rapidly indefinitely. To have killed or captured him would have made the reputation of any warrior who accomplished it.

In the meantime, a force of between 800 and 1,500 British regulars, Indians, and Tories were gathering under Sir John Johnson for a determined raid on the Schoharie. On the night of October 15, 1780, Johnson led his forces past the upper fort and worked his way down the valley toward the middle fort, burning patriot farms as he went. Early the next morning he approached the middle fort, driving back a 40-man reconnaissance party sent out by the post's commander, Major Melancthon Woolsey. Murphy, naturally enough, had been among the members of the reconnaissance. Now he found himself besieged with 200 comrades, under command of the very timorous Major Woolsey. They faced an enemy that outnumbered them at least four-to-one, and who had artillery. The scene was set for Tim's most famous exploit.

For hours the two forces exchanged fire. The Tories and Indians continued to scatter through the valley, burning and destroying. In the fort, Major Woolsey was putting on quite a performance, according to legend. At first fire, he had been found cowering among the children gathered in the fort, and when the derision of the defenders had driven him to the parapets, he still crawled on all fours. Therefore, when Sir John sent forward a white flag, it was assumed that it was to negotiate the fort's surrender, and the Major's response was a foregone conclusion.

Murphy was not ready to surrender. In violation of all the honors of war, and in open mutiny, he raised his double rifle and fired a shot that sent the bearer of the white flag scurrying for cover. The Major was furious, but he could not discover the culprit. The general action continued, then the white flag reappeared. Again Tim drove the bearer to earth with a near miss. This time Woolsey had been watching. In a rage, he threatened to kill Murphy, but the militia closed ranks around their hero. Thus thwarted, Woolsey ordered the fort's flag struck in surrender. Tim replied that he would kill the first man who tried it.

While conditions inside the fort were in this pre-

9Quoted in Albert Wright *The Sullivan Expedition of 1779*, Part I, p. 47.

carious state, Sir John sent the flag of truce forward again, and for a third time Tim drove it away. By now Sir John was becoming unsettled at the delay. He did not know the strength of the fort, but all it had shown was defiance. He led his men away, on down the valley. He passed the lower fort, still burning as he went. Those Tory homes he spared were quickly torched by the patriots.

The fertile valley, which had supplied Washington's Army with over 80,000 bushels of grain, was laid waste. So much so that it was never seriously threatened again. Had it been, its defenders were intact and ready to fight because of the determination of one man, Timothy Murphy.

Tim's enlistment in the militia expired that fall. In early 1781 he enlisted in the Pennsylvania Continental Line, under General "Mad" Anthony Wayne. As a member of this unit, he fought in Virginia and was present at the surrender of Lord Cornwallis at Yorktown, which effectively ended the war.

Tim returned to New York and the Schoharie. Here, he became a farmer and solid property owner. His beloved Peggy bore him five sons and four daughters before her death in 1807. His second wife, Mary Robertson, bore him four additional sons. He rose in status as time went on, becoming a local political power. He died in 1818 at the age of 67, of cancer of the throat.

Tim Murphy was a legendary hero for most of his life, and continues to be one today among those who know of him. A small man, he emerges from history larger than life, the finest known example of the tough, individualistic soldier and Indian fighter that helped make the United States and the way of life we are fortunate to enjoy today.

Both Aaron Burr, left (portrait by John Vanderlyn), and Alexander Hamilton, right (portrait by John Trumbull), were leading figures in American politics at the time of their 1804 duel. Burr was Vice President under Jefferson; Hamilton had been Secretary of the Treasury under Washington. *(Courtesy New York Historical Society)*

CHAPTER TWO

THE BURR-HAMILTON DUELLING PISTOLS

By Merrill Lindsay

HAVE YOU EVER looked at a fine antique pistol and wondered what tales it could tell if only it could talk? Tales of bravery, perhaps of violence, even death will run through one's mind. There is no need to guess about the history of the pair of single-set trigger Wogdon duellers safe in their original case in the underground vaults of the Chase Manhattan Bank in New York City. These are the very pistols which were used in the duel between the founder of the Chase Bank, then the Manhattan Company, Aaron Burr, and Alexander Hamilton, founder of the Bank of New York and the Bank of the United States.

Burr's successful campaign to get a charter for the Manhattan Company toppled Hamilton's banking monopoly and was a major factor leading to the famous duel. Business tactics haven't changed much in nearly 200 years. Hamilton saw to it that his brother-in-law was a stockholder in Burr's company so that he would be able to report back on the activities of the enemy company. Burr's method of getting around the Hamilton monopoly was to apply to the state of New York for a charter, not for a bank, but for a water company. The state could hardly refuse a charter for a new water company which would provide fresh clean water to New York. A deadly epidemic of cholera which had killed hundreds of Manhattanites had been correctly attributed to the water supply, the source of which was the old Collect Pond now buried under a network of streets south of Canal Street. Collect Pond, as the name indicates, collected the runoff from pastures and farms in the Wall Street area and could have been contaminated from dozens of sources.

Burr's Manhattan Company did in fact do what was granted in the charter. The company brought clean water from the lakes in the Central Park area, then a clean virgin forest north of the city. Water pipes made of hollowed out cedar logs led to the populous southern tip of the island. Excavated lengths of these wooden water mains still survive in the Chase Manhattan Company's own museum.

Water, however, was not what was on Aaron Burr's mind. In the small type of the charter the Manhattan Company was empowered to "exchange monies," and not a week had passed since the granting of the charter when the Manhattan Company opened its first bank, thus breaking the back of the Hamilton monopoly. Competition in business was not the only source of conflict between the two men. They had had two duels in the political arena, once when Burr tied with Jefferson in his run for the Presidency and again when Burr campaigned for the Governorship of New York State. The conflict reached the point where Hamilton was impugning Burr's morals and had disparaging remarks to make about Burr's beloved daughter, Theodosia.

The Manhattan Company opened its first bank in competition with Hamilton in 1799. It was no coincidence that the very day that the Bank of the Manhattan Company opened, at a dinner given to celebrate the opening of the new bank, Hamilton's brother-in-law, John B. Church, a professional dueller who had killed his man in England, insulted Burr. The insult was so deliberate and obviously planned and issued in front of Burr's friends that Burr, who could not have relished fighting a professional, felt required to challenge Church. The duel, fought with Church's pistols at the ferry landing in Hoboken, resulted in Burr having a button shot off his vest.

Five years and more political, legal and financial rivalry between the two men led Hamilton, who was notoriously hot headed, to abuse Burr in a public

The Burr-Hamilton pistols were made by British gunmaker Wogdon for Hamilton's brother-in-law, John B. Church. They possess several characteristics not found on any other duelling pistols of that era, including weighted bronze forestocks, adjustable sights, inordinately large caliber (.54), and the fatal (for Hamilton) single-set trigger.

gathering. Again Burr challenged and again a duel was fought with Church's pistols, this time in Weehawken. Hamilton claimed that he never intended to fire his gun but that it went off in the air. The truth is that the pistol in Hamilton's hand did go off harmlessly in the air and struck a tree in back of Burr twelve feet off the ground. I am sure I know the reason why.

The pistols which Hamilton provided for the duel were trick pistols with concealed hair triggers, or what today's target shooter would call a single-set trigger. Using these trick pistols, Hamilton, whose brother-in-law had had the pistols made in London by a well-known British maker by the name of Wogdon, could set his hair trigger without anyone noticing. This gave Hamilton a theoretical advantage by allowing him to shoot faster and easier than Burr. Burr's gun had the same trick trigger but it would have been of no help to Burr unless Hamilton had told Burr of the concealed setting device.

Hamilton owned a fine pair of correct English duelling pistols made by Nicholson in London, given to him by his father-in-law, old General Philip Schuyler, after the Battle of Saratoga. These pistols, which are well documented, turned up in a private collection in Middlefield, Connecticut, as a result of recent publicity about the pair used in the duel. Hamilton owned these

pistols which would have been legitimate for the duel. Instead he elected to borrow the trick pair from his brother-in-law Church. So one has to choose between what Hamilton said and what he did.

The advantage that Hamilton thought he had with Church's pistols was that by pushing his trigger slightly forward, which set the hair trigger, he could fire his pistol with a bare half-pound pull. One of the same pistols in Burr's or Hamilton's hand without the trigger set, could not be fired in a conventional manner with less than a 10 to 12-pound pull.

What happened to Hamilton is very simple—he booby trapped himself. He set the hair trigger of his own pistol intending to have the edge over Burr in speed and accuracy of fire. Understandably, with the tension of the duel, Hamilton held the gun a little too firmly and unconsciously squeezed the hair trigger a little too hard. As he lowered the gun on its target he was holding too tight and the shot was accidently fired up into the air before he had Burr in his sights. Burr, who had no idea that these were trick pistols, squeezed hard and slow and put an aimed shot into Hamilton. The lead .54 caliber ball found Hamilton's liver and he died within thirty-six hours.

How do I know this? I have booby trapped myself many times shooting target guns with single or double-

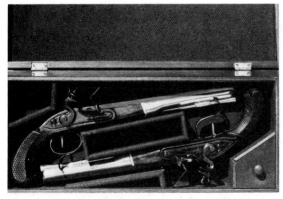

The cased Wogdon pistols still reside in the vaults of the Chase Manhattan Bank, founded by Aaron Burr.

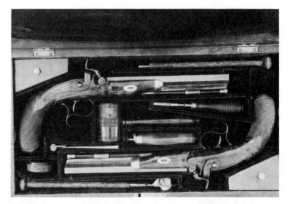

These American-made duellers by Vallee of Philadelphia are sparsely decorated in keeping with their intended use.

Duelling was an affair of honor bound by strict rules and conventions well known to both Burr and Hamilton.

set triggers, and my only excuse was the tension of a competitive target match. No one was pointing a loaded gun at me, but before I could bring my gun to bear on the target I squeezed a little too hard and blew my chance of winning by throwing away one shot high in the sky.

A friend of mine, Harry H. Sefried, invented the Winchester "Miracle Trigger" which is an adjustable detent or set trigger. Harry personally adjusted my own Winchester with the lightest pull possible. The gun could be discharged by blowing hard on the trigger. It was a "miracle" that I didn't shoot myself in the foot before I persuaded Harry to make the pull harder . . . and I think of myself as knowing something about guns.

It is hard to know the intent of the dying Hamilton who said that he had no intention of shooting at Burr. He was either trying to make Burr out to be a cruel coward, which he succeeded in doing, or he was trying to divert attention from the pistols themselves, realizing that it would do him no credit to be discovered to have provided trick pistols for a duel.

Actually, the Church pistols by Wogdon have several unusual characteristics which disqualify them for use in duels. The pistols, which today reside in the vaults of the bank which Burr founded, have not only concealed set triggers, but weighted bronze forestocks, adjustable front and rear sights and a .544 caliber bore. While some of these features could be found on a cased pair of gentleman's pistols, none of them would appear on a proper set of duelling pistols nor would a gentleman in either England or France consider employing them in an affair of honor.

The caliber of duellers had been established at .50. Fifty caliber is big enought to do plenty of damage and .54 caliber is heavy enough to shoot horses with. Proper duelling pistols do not have adjustable sights, at the most they have a fixed front sight and a bead for approximate aiming. The theory of duelling with pistols was that you brought your arm down and pulled the trigger when your index finger was pointed at your antagonist. You were not a meat hunter at a target range where you could take cold-blooded aim and, allowing for windage and elevation, drill your quarry.

Finally these unusual pistols have solid bronze forestocks soldered directly to the barrels for greater muzzle weight, in accordance with a theory that extra muzzle weight makes the arm steadier and more accurate. This theory is still around in shooting circles and guns are made today with adjustable weights which can be hung on the muzzle end of the barrel of a target pistol. Such pistols are used in the Olympic matches, but this is the *only example* of an Eighteenth or early Nineteenth Century flintlock pistol with such a weighting device.

Although I have seen lots of flintlock pistols, I did not rely entirely on my own judgment. I asked Clay Bedford, who owns over a thousand pairs of English flintlock pistols, how many of them had bronze forestocks. The answer was "no bronze forestocks." This left me with the only possible conclusion; that John Church

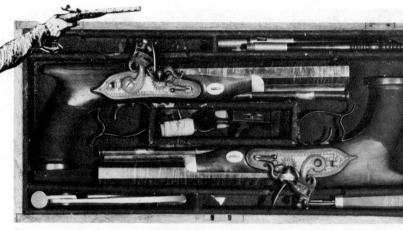

This cased pair of flintlock duelling pistols belonged to Andrew Jackson, a participant in several duels during his stormy lifetime. Accessories included bullet mold, cleaning rod, mainspring vise, and screwdrivers. *(Courtesy Smithsonian Institution)*

Duelling pistols were designed to be fired as though they were an extension of the hand pointed and aligned rather than aimed.

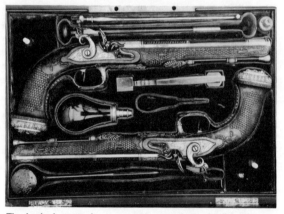

The high degree of ornamentation on these duelling-type pistols marks them as intended for presentation rather than actual use on the field of honor.

had had the bronze forestocks made in New York to replace the original walnut full-stocks. There was no other answer as Church had had these pistols made or finished to his specification by Wogdon when he visited London in 1797 and had brought the pistols directly to New York.

I then sought the opinion of Harold Peterson, Chief Curator of the museums of the National Park Service and an author and authority on American-made arms. My questions to him were, "How many bronze forestocks have you seen on American-made pistols or put on as an addition on British arms?" "Are they very common?" The answer from Harold was, "Not very many, I have not seen or heard of a single one except for the Burr-Hamilton pistols." Since then I have found a single example in the Winchester Gun Museum.

This leaves only one question unanswered. How can we be sure that these pistols are indeed the ones that Burr killed Hamilton with? The Chase Manhattan Bank headed by David Rockefeller has done research in the archives and documents connected with this bit of their and the United States' early history. They have established that these very pistols were used in three duels. The first, I have noted, was between Church, the owner, and Burr. The second time that they were used

was in a duel between Alexander Hamilton's son and a George Eacker in which duel the son, Philip Hamilton, was killed. This was in 1802, two years before the Burr-Hamilton affair.

After the third and final duel, the pistols were returned to Colonel John B. Church by Hamilton's second, a young lawyer, Nathaniel Pendleton. The fatal duel took place on July 11th and the return of the pistols to Church is noted in a letter written by the surgeon, Dr. David Hosack, who attended the duel. His letter was written a month after the duel, on August 17, 1804.

What would have happened if Hamilton had had better control of his pistol? Both men might have been killed as had happened in many a duel with pistols. Let us suppose, however, that Hamilton's planned advantage had worked and he had gotten off the quicker shot. Would Hamilton have been indicted for murder in New Jersey and made a virtual exile in New York? I think not. Hamilton's father-in-law, General Philip Schuyler, was both wealthy and influential. The Schuylers were related by marriage to the Van Rensselaers, the Van Cortlandts and other members of the old New York Dutch aristocracy. Schuyler would have turned heaven and earth to prevent his daughter's husband from being called a murderer. At worst he would have been called a headstrong West Indian, which he was, and exonerated as having fought a duel of honor. A year or two in Washington, where he was quite at home, would have caused people to lose interest and the duel would have been forgotten. Hamilton had had an important hand in the creation, the adoption and the defense of the United States Constitution. His ambition was enormous. Even though he lacked public appeal and support, the step from Secretary of the Treasury under Washington to President of the United States was a distinct possibility until Burr's bullet cut him down. Now all one can do is speculate . . .

History has long placed a black mark against Aaron Burr for killing Hamilton in the duel; the author's investigation indicates that history needs to be rewritten.

The Winchester rifle has long been known as the "gun that won the West." That may or may not be accurate, but there's no question that it was the early mountain men and fur traders with their St. Louis Hawken's rifles that opened the vast West and showed the way for countless prospectors, settlers, and farmers.

CHAPTER THREE

THE HAWKEN SAGA

By Arthur J. Ressell

A S THE LOW slow-moving snow clouds squeezed the last remaining flakes from their midst and scattered them haphazardly over the little valley, the first hint of day lazily erases the ghostly illuminated darkness, leaving the slowly spreading lightness of daybreak. The stillness was in itself as profound as the roar of a cannon. The gentle breeze of morning had not yet awakened to rearrange the new fallen snow, shooing it gently from the treetops to drop silently to earth, leaving its little snow tracks upon the forest floor.

Snuggled back in the protective bosom of a narrow earthen outcropping, made even more secure from falling snow or chilling wind by an overlacing of pine boughs, squats huddled over the last glowing traces of a tiny fire, a lone sentinel.

The warmest of wooly undergarments cover our trapper's skin, covered thereover by the most durable elk hide shirt and pants; loose fitting for comfort and air circulation, but every seam tightly and lovingly stitched with sinew, forming an everlasting marriage of the skins. His feet bound in lightweight rabbit fur are covered over with an outer layer of prime buffalo fur knee boots, secured by wrap-around leather thong. Hudson Bay's finest four point black bar blanket encompasses his torso, in the form of a hooded capote—an excellent choice for warmth, weight and camouflage. Across his lap, cuddled lovingly like a child to a mother's breast, he holds his greatest possession. His friend, his guardian, his provider, his courage, his love—his rifle! *The tool among all the tools of his trade.* In essence, a trusty horse, a trusted rifle and trust in The Almighty, were the big three in every trapper's life. Lucky indeed was the fur-searching explorer whose rifle bore the mark "HAWKEN." For history reveals that this "HAWKEN" name proved its worth so routinely that it became a legend in its own time.

A myriad of books and movies have virtually brainwashed the 20th Century lover of our early eras of nostalgia into assuming that the 1873 Winchester was the "Gun that won the West"—tain't so!

Long before the Winchester was even a gleam in anyone's eye, the St. Louis Hawken was a leader among earlier guns, winning numerous footholds in our westward movement, in the hands of our first foraging fur trappers.

1816 was the approximate year that St. Louis welcomed Jacob Hawken, master gun builder, from a large family of gun builders in and around Hagerstown, Maryland, well known in that area in the 1700's for the quality of their craftsmanship. Jacob proudly carried this expertise to the gateway to the West, plying his trade for a short while with an established gunsmith, John Lakenan, independently for a short while, and then around 1822 establishing the legendary partnership with younger brother Samuel who reached St. Louis by way of Ohio. Like his brother Jacob, Sam sought the challenge to supply arms to the rapidly growing fur trade market centered in St. Louis.

There were no historic "OK Corrals," "Bunker Hills," or "Alamos" to which the Hawken rifle can be related. Its historic heritage was born out of the way it proudly performed in countless one-on-one encounters. Certainly its being related to such outstanding names in America's growth as Ashley, Bridger, Carson, Freemont and many others, shows that the leaders, those outstanding in this specific era of the fur trade, thought highly of its merit.

The earliest of St. Louis-made Hawken rifles in the 1815–1820 period carry the distinct profile of their slightly earlier Maryland ancestors.

In Hawkens of this period, we see a gun amazingly like the New England-style guns of the Golden Age

The earliest known St. Louis Hawken, in .36 caliber, was made between 1816 and 1822 and bears strong resemblance to a Pennsylvania rifle. It has been converted from flint to caplock. *(Photo by Steve Smith)*

1700's period. Long, slender, graceful and well balanced even in its apparently cumbersome length. A trapper's gun, with smallbore of .36 caliber, well suited to the smaller game of our fur-trapping pioneer. The large forged iron triggerguard and small triggers, are easily accessible to the winter trapper's gloved hand.

"J. Hawken, St. Louis" is the barrel marking on the earliest known of St. Louis marked Hawken guns, placing its birth somewhere between 1816 and 1822. Originally made in flintlock, as no doubt numerous other Hawken rifles were, it has seen a late shortening (about two inches) and conversion from flintlock to the revolutionary caplock ignition. Quite a few known St. Louis Hawken rifles bear converted flint-type locks. Some obviously began their existence as flintlock guns. Others of later design carry converted flintlock lock plates, but the entire gun probably never saw usage as a flintlock. It was common practice to utilize a less desirable and less expensive flintlock in this period of growing popularity of the percussion system of ignition, and convert it to the new system rather than fabricate or purchase the newer-style percussion lock. An original "Hawken" St. Louis rifle has yet to be found in original flintlock.

In the ensuing years the lightweight Eastern styling, gave way to a more rugged stature capable of the endurance necessary to the day-in day-out usage demanded of it. This type rifle, still showing a striking resemblance to its ancestors, begins to take on a more "classic" plains' rifle appearance. The triggerguard scroll (originally an English design) is more defined; with solid long bar triggers and elongated tang to reinforce a relatively slender wrist for such a weighty gun.

The mountain men were a solitary breed, with few witnesses to their exploits and practically no written records. If they survived to old age—and few did—they had luck as well as courage and skill with their Hawken rifle. In Jack Hines' oil painting, the Hawken's one shot may not be enough.

This fullstock Hawken from the 1830's exhibits a larger caliber (.50), and a somewhat shorter barrel. Though many were made in flintlock, a Hawken in original flintlock has yet to be found. *(Photo by Steve Smith)*

Twelve to fifteen pounds of functional firearms stress the "Man" in Mountain Man. Wear marks may be and were seen on the under forearm area of a number of surviving specimens, evidence the fact that many of these guns and their half-stock descendents were right at home across the pommel area of the Santa Fe saddle!

Just as the Hawken rifle was a most important tool-of-the-trade to the early fur trapper, it was doubly true of the fur hunter, that rugged individual who breathed historic significance into the name "Mountain Man" whose trapping and hunting exploits ranged from the 1830's up through the 1850's when the buffalo robe became as important as the beaver hat!

Like any other tool, however, the rifle could also be put to evil use. Both pathfinder and psychopath outfitted himself in St. Louis before starting his westward trek. As a result it was a Hawken rifle that earned the grisly reputation for one of the greatest murderers in American history.

It was in November of 1846 when English adventurer George F. Ruxton rode into the city of Chihuahua in northern Mexico and was appalled to see that "opposite the principal entrance, over the portals which form one side of the square, were dangling the grim scalps of over one hundred and seventy Apaches, treacherously and inhumanely butchered by Indian hunters in the pay of the state." Ruxton was looking at the handwork of one James Kirker, Irish/American who had found scalp hunting a more diverting and profitable trade than running a New York City grocery store.[1]

Kirker arrived in St. Louis in 1817 and after several years of mercantile business joined the Ashley-Henry expedition to the fur country of upper Missouri in 1822.

During this period, Kirker was companion to such notables as Jedadiah Smith, Thomas Fitzpatrick, James Clyman and William Sublette and saw his first bit of Indian fighting against the Arikaras who had attacked Ashley's party.

For the next 16 years Kirker spent his time trapping in the area of New Mexico to such a tremendous success that he was eventually denied trapping rights by Governor Norbain of Santa Fe. Stripped of his trapping rights, Kirker for a time served as guard to the many supply wagons of the prospering copper mines of the area. Constant attack upon these lines as well as numerous Mexican villages by the ruthless Apache led to Kirker forming his own band of Indian fighters to repel the Apache. Among his band were numerous Shawnee braves as well as a Shawnee Chief, Spy Buck.

Chihuahua City in the 1840's was the metropolitan center of the Southwest for traders and mountain men. Many came through there in search of relaxation and entertainment at one time or another.

It was in the summer of 1843 when a war party of Apaches attacked a mule train belonging to J. Calistro Porras, a millionaire Chihuahua merchant. Porras' mule train consisted of about 80 mules loaded with merchandise headed for Chihuahua directly from the St. Louis port. The train had nearly made it all the way

In the early days of photography a hunter had to drag his game into the studio along with his prized Hawken.

[1]Leroy Haten (ed.) *Ruxton of the Rockies*—Autobiographical writings by the author of *Adventures in Mexico* and *The Rocky Mountains* and *Life in the Far West* (Norman: University of Oklahoma press 1950)

.54 caliber "plains style" rifle by Samuel Hawken exhibits the classic half-stock design that is considered the Hawken hallmark. This rifle dates from the 1840–1850 period. *(Photo by Steve Smith)*

back to Chihuahua, when a dozen or so miles short of home, a band of Apaches struck it, took everything and killed all but one of the crew. The sole survivor came running into Chihuahua City and finally quieted down sufficiently to tell in detail what had happened. Porras immediately sought out Kirker and offered him the mules and half of the merchandise if he could overtake and punish the thieves.

Kirker, already on commission to the Governor for bounty on scalps, could earn a fortune in this campaign, so Jim took his force on the trail, accompanied by Shawnee Chieftain, Spy Buck. Picking up the trail from site of the attack, within four miles they came upon a dead mule, abandoned and lanced by the Apaches when it gave out. The trackers moved steadily onward for the rest of the day. By dark, they reached the campsite the Indians had used the first night after the attack. It was littered with coffee, rice and sugar, which was gathered up and sent back to Porras. Kirker and his men were gone by sun up, and by noon they came across another 10 mules that had fallen by the wayside and had been lanced to death. Jim and the men stripped these of their cargo, cached it nearby and pushed on. On the third day Spy Buck signaled from his lead position to halt as he stealthily scouted the hostiles' camp less than a mile ahead. He returned to report to Jim that the opposing party consisted of 43 warriors.

After three days, these warriors had imagined themselves out of danger, and since the cargo contained a great number of flasks of imported liquors, the Indians had decided to camp and indulge in a spree. This was a fatal decision! Eighty-six infiltrators under Kirker and Spy Buck entered their camp when they were all in a drunken stupor, and slit the throats of every Apache. The Shawnees scalped them by cutting a circle at the crown of each head, and sitting down with their feet resting on the shoulders of the dead enemy, they grabbed a hand full of hair, leaning back and pushing forward with their feet, until there was a loud "pop." The scalps were then brought to Spy Buck, who sprinkled them with salt to preserve them, and tied their hair to a scalp pole. While the Shawnees prepared the scalps, Jim went out and rounded up all the horses and mules he could find. With the 43 they got from the slain

Irish-American James Kirker was a notorious scalp-hunter, but also a brave frontiersman. He and his Hawken blazed a bloody trail across the Southwest.

Indians, they had in excess of 100. Jim then directed his attention to the wide selection of liquors. He opened up a considerable amount of it and invited his men to a giant bash. Knowing they would get into the booze sooner or later, he had decided to take a day or so off and get it over with. The mountaineers were soon as drunk as the men they had just killed and they remained that way throughout the rest of the day and part of the next.

On the following morning Kirker called a council. As a former War Chief of the Apaches, Jim knew of a large village within a three-day march beside a lake, and inhabited by at least 1,000 Apaches. Here was a fortune in hair. He asked them if they wanted to go on and attack the village by the lake. They said they would. Kirker directed some of the men to cache the Porras merchandise and some of the others he sent to round up the mules and horses. A corral was built and the animals were driven inside. Leaving substantial guard on the stock, Jim sent Spy Buck ahead to scout. Kirker's total number of effectives, not counting those left behind on guard detail, was 150. More than enough to pull off a surprise attack on an Indian village of this size. Kirker and the men hit the trail, and after a couple of days were rejoined by Spy Buck. He had located the village but hadn't taken the time to reconnoiter it completely, so he and Kirker went back together to inspect the situation in detail.

They circled the village except for the small portion butting the lake. It was surrounded on three sides by gentle rising land, and on the other side by water. After their reconnaissance, the two scouts returned to the main body. Jim ordered the horses moved about two miles to the rear into a ravine and arranged for a half-dozen men to remain there and guard them. He cautiously led the rest of the company, now slightly more than 140, to the rim of the hills overlooking the Apache village. It was just at sunset and the various colored lodges, spread out over the heart of the pine growth, gave the whole view a carnival aspect. The lake was about six miles across and the water was calm as a mirror. There was little or no sound in the twilight. After the sun went down, the Kirker men watched a war party of about 75 braves return to the village west from the direction of Sonora, and as they walked around the edge of the lake, scalps could be seen dangling from their belts. They also carried hogs' heads and jugs of liquor captured during their latest raid. The men withdrew a couple of hundred yards and Spy Buck informed him that the best plan would be to wait until the Indians had had time to get drunk and dance most of the night away. Provisions were brought out and the men had a quick meal. They then laid down to sleep until the guard should give the call at three a.m.

When the call sounded, the men arose refreshed by sleep and formed into two companies, one led by Kirker, the other by Spy Buck. About that time, Spy Buck returned from another look at the village and gave the word that all but three or four at the village were dead drunk. Kirker led his company to one side of the camp and Spy Buck to the other side. Dawn was just breaking by this time. Kirker had a special whistle which he was to blow when everything was ready. Then the men were to rush into the camp yelling, shoot all they could with the first discharge, then finish the job with knives and tomahawks. One of the company however, Andy, had loaded a musket with buckshot and was stationed next to Hobbs, second in command of the detail under Spy Buck. Hobbs claimed that he had given Andy specific instructions not to fire until he heard Kirker's whistle, but when an Indian suddenly came out of one of the lodges near Andy, he blazed away, almost tearing the savage in two. Andy was

kicked over backwards by the gun's explosion, the barrel ripped out of the stock. Alarmed, the Indians began to stir, and both parties rushed into the fight without any other signal.

Kirker must have presented quite a ferocious sight with his array of weapons. Routinely he was dressed in the fringed buckskins of the frontiersman, a wide brimmed Mexican hat and huge spurs, embellished and ornamented with other Mexican finery. In addition to the fine Hawken rifle, eloquently mounted with numerous silver inlays, one of which bore his name, "Santiago Kirker," he was also armed with a choice assortment of pistols and Mexican daggers.[2]

At the first onslaught, Kirker's Hawken claimed another scalp and no doubt numerous more along with its owner's knives, pistols and tomahawk.

The Shawnees fought like devils, hoping to take enough scalps to go back to Missouri and retire. They were using their knives and tomahawks as their principal weapons, while the Americans firing both rifles and pistols were pushing a great number of the Apache braves into the lake and pursuing them across the valley. Many of the Apache made it to the nearest mountain and found refuge there while another large number rushed into the lake and were drowned. The Shawnees gave up chasing them and sought out the huge corral containing nearly 1,000 horses and mules, as well as mustang ponies.

Kirker also quickly turned to business. He ordered Hobbs to take 20 men and go at once to the place where they had all their horses and mules corraled. He was afraid the Indians might regroup and try to retake the precious animals. This Hobbs did, untying both herds of horses, and they started the trek back to Chihuahua City at once, leaving many of the men behind to clean up various small chores. The Shawnees finished collecting scalps and many of the others were gathering up things about the camp.

Kirker's victory over Cochise's Apaches produced a totally unexpected dividend; the rescue of a large number of Mexican women and children who had been prisoners of this band. Kirker's men also liberated 300 sheep and goats so Kirker told the freed captives that they could drive the animals back to Chihuahua City and keep them. While these flocks were being rounded up, Dave Allen and a couple of men with him happened upon the remains of what had been a flourishing community, by this time reduced to a heap of ruins.

Quite evident were the foundation stones of a church, complete with a large cross made of Ligum Vitae, a tropical American tree of hardwood. Nearby were the

2Wm. E. Connelley, *War with Mexico 1846-1847*—Doniphaus Expedition and the Conquest of New Mexico and California (Topeka Kansas Author 1907)

remains of a smelting furnace, a huge pile of cinder slag and some droppings of silver and copper. While looking into a hollow portion of a ceramic cup at the site, Allen found a nugget of gold weighing about 10 ounces. This discovery sent the rest of the men flocking to the ruins, and soon they picked up other smaller bits and pieces of precious metal. A messenger was sent immediately to Kirker notifying him of the find. When he came on the scene he called a council to determine their course of action—should they stay and look for more gold, or return to Chihuahua City at once to claim their scalp money, sell off their captured livestock and negotiate with Porras for their share of the retrieved merchandise? Kirker pointed out that even though much of the livestock had been started out ahead, it would be slow work getting them down the trail. He thought they must start at once to be safe, for he predicted the Apaches would soon return with all of their warriors seeking revenge. In short, Kirker called the meeting only to urge his point of view rather than to consider any other course, for he was convinced that if they were to get back with their skins, they should leave within the hour. This certainly was no time to surrender to gold fever. The others, seeing the common sense in his remarks, and respecting his knowledge of the Indians, agreed to start off at once, leaving behind their visions of treasure, promising some day to return.

The going rate for scalps was $100 for braves, $50 for squaws and $25 for a child's, but upon returning to Chihuahua, Kirker was told by Governor Angel Trijas that there was only $2,000 in the treasury, not nearly enough to pay for the 170 scalps brought in. Discouraged, Kirker headed north to El Paso; and joined Doniphaus' ragged army of Missourians as they launched their invasion of Mexico.[3]

No one will ever know how many Apaches and Mexicans fell to Kirker's Hawken. A man of undoubted intelligence and courage, he was also brutal and unscrupulous to a far greater degree than was required by the admittedly savage dictates of his time and place. "The Devil might have been perching in the rafters of the Hawken shop on the day his rifle was made."

At roughly the same time that James Kirker was engaged in his fiendish trade, a devout young Mormon plainsman was carrying a Hawken rifle in the quest for his people's promised land. Never have two men bearing the same weapon presented a greater contrast in character, aims and ideals.

In 1841 a young Tennessee-born, Illinois-bred countryman named John Brown joined the Mormons and after being ordained an elder of their church at its Nauvoo, Illinois, headquarters, embarked upon a series of missionary expeditions in the southern states.[4]

Early in 1845 Brown and his companions left their work in Mississippi to hasten back to Nauvoo where the Mormon militia was mustering in the face of growing local resentment against their church. Brown paused in St. Louis to purchase a Hawken rifle on March 24. It was to remain by his side for the next fifty years as he strove to serve the word of God and the vision of Brigham Young.[5]

Late in 1846 Brown led a band of Mississippi converts westward to a rendezvous with part of the famed Mormon Battalion at Pueblo, Colorado. There the emigrants and soldiers settled into winter quarters and waited to join the general migration to Utah, while Brown struck out to reach Brigham Young in his camp at Kanesville, Iowa, on the banks of the Missouri.

Brown was appointed captain of the "13th Ten" in Young's party, and served as a scout and hunter as the great trek across the plains began in April, 1847. Brown's Hawken saw frequent use, and he was well pleased with it, for he found that the rifle would drop a buffalo handily at 200 yards. Even a man of Brown's experience, however, was not immune to the most common of accidents of plains travel. On April 28 the emigrants were in camp on the banks of the North Platte River when the young scout reached in the back of a wagon to pull out his coat. The garment snagged on the rifle's hammer and the load went off. The ball tore past Brown and killed another man's horse. Such incidents were not uncommon; during this period possibly as many travelers on the plains were killed by similar mishaps than by Indian attacks.[6]

The Mormon caravan struggled on and cleared South Pass before the end of June, and forded the Green River to reach the rugged Wasatch Mountains by mid-July. Brown and fellow scout Orson Pratt ranged ahead to find a suitable wagon route through the high country. On July 19 they topped the crest of Big Mountain and looked down upon Salt Lake Valley and the new homeland of the Mormons. Three days later they led the wagons down into the broad, shining valley.[7]

Brown did not linger in the new settlement for long.

3Segments of *Kirkers Life* from Reprint of Sante Fe Republican 1847—*Story of Raid*—Wm. C. McGaw—*Savage Scene—The Life and Times of James Kirker, Frontier King* (New York Hasting's House publishers 1972)

4Reference file on John Brown, Historical Department, Church of Jesus Christ of Latter-day Saints, Salt Lake City, Utah. Material supplied by Mr. Dale Beecher Senior Researcher.

5Ibid

6Wallace Stegner, *The Gathering of Zion* (New York McGraw-Hill Book Co. 1964) - John D. Unruh, *The Plains Across The Overland Emigrants* and *The Trans-Mississippi West*, 1840–60 (Urbana: University of Illinois Press, 1979)

7Brown file; Stegner, *Gathering*, 165; Dale L. Morgan, *The Great Salt Lake* (New York-Bobbs-Merrill Company, 1937)

Before the year was out he rode back to Mississippi on a mission for Young and returned to Utah in 1848 with yet another emigrant party. Many more such journeys lay before him. Between 1846 and 1869 Brown carried his Hawken across the plains thirteen times.[8]

On February 28, 1849, Brown joined a party of militiamen led by Captain John Scott in the pursuit of a band of Ute cattle thieves. They caught up with them in the mountains east of the Provo River and attacked their sleeping camp at dawn from all four directions. The seventeen Utes fought for several hours along the course of a brush-choked creek, surrendering only after four of the braves in the band fell to the Mormon rifles. Brown and Scott escorted the women and children back to Salt Lake City, where they were fed and released to a band of friendly Utes. The action at Battle Creek was the first of many clashes between the Mormons and Indians in Utah.[9]

Brown, his Hawken, and his faithful black mule, Zeke, got little chance for rest in the years that followed. Late in 1849 and early in 1850 Brown served with Captain Parley Pratt's expedition to explore the southern area of Utah in search of likely sites for new settlements. With 50 men, 12 wagons, and a brass howitzer, Pratt explored the Sevier River area and followed a route roughly paralleling modern U.S. Highway 91 as far south as Parowan, Utah, and beyond to the rim of the southern basin, finally reaching the Santa Clara River.[10]

In 1851 Brown was occupied with patrolling the country between the settlements of Provo and Cottonwood as the danger mounted from Indian raids. By 1852 he was in New Orleans, Louisiana, where he served as "Superintendent of European Emigration." Meeting shiploads of foreign Mormons in the port city, he took them up the Mississippi by steamboat and then led them overland from Keokuk, Iowa, to Salt Lake City. In 1857 he joined Brigham Young in an exploration of the Idaho country that carried them as far north as the Salmon River. When the Mormons clashed with the United States Government in 1857 Brown served as adjutant in Major William Hyde's battalion of militia. Brown's unit helped to bar General Albert Sidney Johnston's army from marching on Salt Lake City through the old emigrant road in Echo Canyon. Johnston refrained from challenging the Mormon snipers

Mormon pioneer John Brown purchased his Hawken in 1845, and carried it for 50 turbulent years.

who dominated the passage, and the war was eventually settled without any great loss of life.[11]

Brown continued to lead a full and active life in his church's service until well into the 1890s. Sixteen months before his death on November 4, 1896, he donated his rifle to the Deseret Museum in Salt Lake City. It had served him well for over 50 of his 76 years on earth.[12]

John Brown's Hawken is currently in the custody of the Historical Department of the Church of Jesus Christ of Latter Day Saints in Salt Lake City. The rifle is full-stocked, 56½ inches long, and weighs 12 pounds. It is fitted with double set triggers and carries a wooden ramrod in the thimbles under its octagonal barrel. "J & S Hawken St. Louis" is clearly stamped on the top barrel flat. The lockplate is marked "Adolphus Meier." Meier, a merchant and gunsmith who was active in St. Louis as early as 1837, supplied quite a few locks to the Hawkens. The percussion lock on Brown's rifle fits snugly against a heavy barrel that is bored to accept "an ounce ball," which translates to a .66 caliber projectile weighing roughly 430 grains. Even with only a moderate powder charge the piece must have spoken with au-

[8]Brown file

[9]Ibid, Peter Gottfredson, (ed.) *History of Indian Depredations in Utah* (Salt Lake City; Skelton Publishing Company, 1919) 18–19; Juanita Brooks, (ed.) *On the Mormon Frontier: The Diary of Hosea Stout 1844–1861* (Salt Lake City; University of Utah Press 1964)

[10]Brown file; Brooks, *Mormon Frontier*

[11]Brown file

[12]Ibid

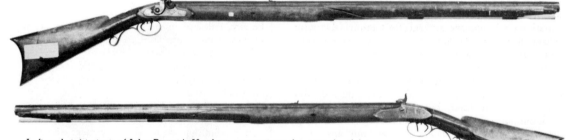

Left and right views of John Brown's Hawken, currently in the custody of the
Church of Latter Day Saints, Salt Lake City. A full-stocked rifle of earlier Hawken
styling, it's a massive .66 caliber firing a one-ounce ball. The lock is marked
"Adolphus Meier," a merchant and gunsmith who supplied numerous locks to
J.&S. Hawken.

thority. It endures today as a priceless link to a past
filled with courage and devotion to an ideal.[13]

While John Brown was stalking Johnston's dragoons
in Echo Canyon, a young Texan named George W.
Baylor was trying his luck in the California gold fields.
He and his fellow prospectors along the Kern River
were continually plagued by the depredations of a
vicious grizzly bear who was known as "Old Buster."
Cattle and horses were swiftly falling prey to the bear,
and he was reputed to have slain and eaten his share of
people as well.

Baylor, tired of losing his stock to the grizzly, resolved to track him down and finish his rampage. He
went on his mission with a complete arsenal. "I had a
good Navy Colt," he related, "I got a light stub twist
German 'doppelbixie,' one barrel a rifle and the other a
shotgun, and I had my Hawkens."[14]

The Texan had a healthy respect for the bear's
strength and ferocity. He rigged a tripwire to the German gun's triggers and mounted it in a brace. Placing
the bait and taking up a safe position at a distance, he
waited for "Old Buster" to spring the trap. The bear
obligingly complied, and received the twin loads of ball
and buckshot. Baylor then finished him with the
Hawken.[15]

George Baylor returned to Texas and compiled a distinguished record as both a Confederate soldier and a
Texas Ranger. After his retirement he became an amateur historian and wrote prolifically. One of his articles
helped to add even more to the lore of the Hawken rifle
in the southwest.

In the 1880s or early 1890s Baylor was living in El
Paso, Texas, when he met an old man named Ferguson
who had captained a train of freight wagons in his

youth. In 1849 Ferguson took a caravan west from St.
Louis to Santa Fe and then struck south to reach
Chihuahua via El Paso. Even in old age he still bore the
stamp of a man used to command and responsibility.
Baylor described him as a "small, wiry Irishman, with
a sharp nose and keen gray eyes that reminded one of a
hawk, and every line of his face showed he knew no
such word as fear."[16]

Ferguson's train had cleared El Paso and was camped
at Berendo Springs near Corralitos, Mexico, when a
large band of Apaches encircled the watering place.
Their chief, whom Ferguson mistakenly identified as

Texan George Baylor, an amateur historian in his later
years, carried a Hawken as a youngster in the great
California Gold Rush of 1849.

13Ibid, Hanson, *Hawken Rifle*

14George W. Baylor "Colonel Baylor tells the Story," El Paso Herald,
December 15, 1900.

15Ibid

Mangas Colorado, demanded that the Americans pay a tribute for safe passage through his territory. Ferguson refused to pay, for he did not trust the Apache's word. The teamsters were much safer circling their wagons around the springs than continuing to drive along the road with the raiders hanging on their flanks. Ferguson could count only ten men besides himself in the train, but "my wagonmaster, Bradford Daily, was a brave man and a good shot, and all my men were armed with a favorite rifle of that day, made by Hawkens, of St. Louis, and all had Dragoon Colt revolvers."[17]

The Apaches laid siege to the wagons for four days. Each day Ferguson would parley with their chief, who repeatedly declared his intention of starving them out and taking their scalps. On the fourth day the chief attacked Ferguson with a knife as they met to talk between the opposing camps. Ferguson stabbed the Indian in the heart after a desperate struggle and then ran for the wagons. The Apaches gave chase and made several futile assaults on the freighters, only to withdraw after their Hawken rifles had killed nine more Indians.[18]

Bradford Daily, Ferguson's lieutenant, carried his Hawken into several more desperate affairs with the Apaches during the next decade. In 1852 he joined a prospecting expedition in company with James M. Adams of San Antonio and veteran frontiersman Jerry Snyder of El Paso. Snyder's slave, Tom, also went along. The four men probed the mountains of the Rio Grande Valley near Dona Ana, New Mexico, in search of gold and silver deposits. Their journey took them into the heart of Mescalero Apache country.[19]

One day they made their noon camp at the head of a draw that branched off from the river. A band of 150 Apaches spotted them and attacked immediately. The outnumbered Texans ran for the draw. A bullet shattered Snyder's thigh and Tom hoisted him on his shoulders while Daily and Adams gave covering fire. When they reached the cover of the draw the Indians hung back, knowing full well the lethal odds involved in trying to storm even a small group of riflemen when they held the best ground.

The Mescaleros settled down to a siege, and kept their enemies on edge by sniping at them by day and howling around their camp by night. The fifth day found Daily and his party in desperate straits. All were starving and crazed with thirst. Snyder's wound was growing worse, although he still made some telling

shots with his rifle. That night an overcast crept across the sky, followed by a slow, drizzling rain. Daily resolved to try to make their escape.

Tom threw his master over his shoulder, while Adams and Daily took a rifle in each hand and led the way into the darkness. They marched 30 miles before dawn and finally reached civilization after an eight-day trek. The Apaches were left to sing over their dead and swear revenge.[20]

In June of that same year Daily survived yet another siege by the Apaches. He was traveling from Chihuahua to El Paso in company with Henry Granger, Dave Rinehart, and a European named Grandjean when they were attacked by 60 Gila Apaches about 45 miles north of Corralitos. All but one of their riding mules were captured by the raiders, and Grandjean was wounded in the leg. The four men took refuge on a piece of high ground. Rinehart and Granger suffered buckshot wounds in helping Grandjean to cover. The Apaches drew off and encircled the travelers' sanctuary as darkness fell.

They tried to rush them at dawn, but "at every charge they met with a deadly and well directed fire from this little band," reported a correspondent for the Missouri Republican. "On the second charge three Indians fell dead and two badly wounded. On the third charge, the Indians came up the mound within pistol range and then the Americans dealt death to them with Colt's army revolvers.[21]

The Apaches broke off the fight until about three o'clock that afternoon, when a fourth charge into the sights of Daily's Hawken netted them only more casualties. They launched yet another attack in a fit of desperate anger. Daily's clothing was riddled with bullet holes but he remained untouched. Granger had placed a carpetbag full of gold and silver coins in part of the rock breastwork he had built around his position. An Indian bullet slammed into it and threw it against his leg. The concussion crippled him.

By now Daily was the only really fit man left in the group, and it fell to him to try and make an escape and bring help back to his wounded companions. Mounting the mule, he had the other men make a diversion while he galloped through the Indian lines. Grandjean had a heavy Swiss rifle that "carried an ounce and half ball at least 1,000 yards." This rifle aided in covering Daily from his pursuers until he had gained a healthy lead over them.[22]

Daily made it to Carrisal, but experienced some difficulty in recruiting any of the locals to aid in the relief of

16George W. Baylor, "How Mangas Colorado Died," El Paso Herald December 23, 1899.

17Ibid

18Ibid

19A. J. Sowell, *Early Settlers and Indian Fighters of Southwest Texas* (Austin; Ben C. Jones and Company, 1900)

20Ibid

21Missouri Republican, August 3, 1852.

22Ibid

This half-stock J.&S. Hawken rifle has a silver cheekpiece inlay inscribed "G.W. Atchison—St. Louis 1836," presumably a fine gift presented to riverboat captain George Atchison. *(Photo by Bill Holm)*

his friends. Late on the night of his departure the desperate Rinehart, Grandjean and Granger slipped past the Indians and struck out for Carrisal. Daily met them on the road with a carriage and drove the exhausted men on to El Paso. Between his Hawken and Grandjean's Swiss cannon they had given the Apaches something to remember.[23]

Daily had already packed quite a few adventures into his 23 years, but he and his St. Louis rifle were to burn even more powder together before the decade was out. In 1853 he signed on as a driver on the San Antonio-El Paso Stage Line. Daily saw service over the entire route which linked San Antonio to Santa Fe via El Paso, and his name crops up frequently in the Texas newspaper accounts of the stage line's operations. His Hawken apparently went with him, for one of his co-workers later recalled that Sharps and "Hawkens" rifles were the most popular longarms used by the expressmen.[24]

On November 14, 1854, Daily was driving the eastbound stage out of El Paso when he met Captain Henry Skillman and the westbound coaches at a waterhole in El Muerto Canyon, located several miles north of modern Valentine, Texas. The 15 whites in the two parties were attacked by 40 Mescaleros. The fighting lasted for several hours, and although none of the expressmen or their passengers were injured, the Apaches kept up a steady fire that killed two mules and wounded several others. Skillman was using a Sharps and made some killing shots at long range. Daily's Hawken also served him well through the encounter.[25]

When the mail service went out of business in 1861 Daily served with the Union Forces in New Mexico, and later became quite wealthy as a merchant and freighter. He died in Las Cruces, New Mexico, in 1875, and the rifle he carried through so many adventures is now unfortunately lost to history books.[26]

We have followed the paths of several men whose unusual exploits were directly Hawken-related. We have also seen that aside from being utilitarian, the Hawken may also be quite exquisite. Kirker's silver mounted rifle we find to be just one of many so made, belonging to other undiscovered notables of the Hawken era. As an addendum to the colorful escapades of Kirker, Brown, Baylor, Ferguson and Daily, I would like to add the following vignettes of three men whose ornate Hawken rifles have recently been "discovered."

Captain George W. Atchison was one of the pioneer boatmen of the upper Mississippi river. His name is listed in the St. Louis directories from the 1830's through the 1850's. As was the common practice in the riverboat business, the captain of a boat was often her designer and builder, so we find many prosperous and influential men in the position of riverboat captains in the early years of the most essential business of water commerce. In an excerpt from Goulds *Fifty Years on the Mississippi*, we find "Captain Atchison often commanded his own boats, in fact, the Irene, Ione, Glaucus, Governor Dodge, Amaranthe and Missouri Belle are all names that will revive pleasant memories in the minds of travelers on western waters in the earlier years of steam navigation. He was one of the most genial and attentive masters to his passengers that was then on the river and few boats were more popular than Capt. Atchison's!"

Atchison's rifle was a magnificent silver-mounted half-stock J. & S. Hawken rifle bearing a cheekpiece inlay engraved "G. W. Atchison St. Louis 1836." This remnant of the middle fur trade era attests to the fact that either the "Hawken's" reputation made it a worthwhile item to be given as a gift or that the owner thought enough of its reputation to outfit himself with the very best. This fancy piece probably never saw more exciting adventure than sporting use up and down the riverbanks of the mighty Mississippi.

Another newly-surfaced Super Hawken is a half-stock J.&S. Hawken elaborately silver inlayed and engraved, bearing a silver cheekpiece inlay inscribed "Moses White."

Moses F. White was born at the lead mine of his fa-

[23]Ibid; John R. Bartlett, *Personal Narrative of Exploration and Incidents in Texas, Mexico, California, Sonora, and Chihuahua, Connected with the United States Boundary Commission During the Years 1850–1853* (New York; D. Appleton and Company, 1854)

[24]Deposition of Charles O. Brown, George H. Giddings vs. United States, Kiowa, Commanche, and Apache Indians (Indian Depredation No. 3873), United States Court of Claims, December Term 1891 1-1V New Orleans Daily Picayune, July 20, 1853, Texas State Gazette, March 7, 1854, San Antonio Ledger, March 2, 1854

[25]San Antonio Ledger, December 28, 1854, Texas State Gazette, January 6, 1855; New Orleans Weekly Picayune, January 10, 1855; Texas State Gazette, April 29, 1854; Western Texian, April 27, 1854

[26]Rex. W. Strickland, (ed.) *Forty Years at El Paso* (El Paso Carl Hertzog, 1962).

Moses White was a prosperous farmer in Saline County, Missouri, and later Jefferson County. His fine presentation grade J.&S. Hawken is one of the best surviving specimens of Hawken rifles. *(Photo by Steve Smith)*

ther, James M. White, at Shibboleth, the family mansion in Washington County, Missouri, in the month of December in 1828. He was raised in Washington and Jefferson counties, the family temporarily resided at Potosi in Washington County in the summer and at Selma in Jefferson County in the winter. His early education was mostly received at Potosi. When about 16 years of age (1844) he was sent to Kemper College at the Episcopalian Institute in St. Louis County of which the building forms the present St. Louis County Court House. From Kemper College he went to the St. Louis University and remained there about a year and a half for the purpose of securing a business education. Leaving school at about 18 he was employed for a month or two at Selma, and then went on the river, his father intending to make him a thorough steamboat man. He obtained a position as steersman under Captain Issai Sellers, a well-known character on the river under whom Mark Twain was trained as a pilot. Mr. White followed the river for about three years, of which time he was nearly always under Sellers' instructions.[27] He learned the river sufficiently to entitle him to the position as a pilot, but river life was not much to his liking, and his tastes were leading him into another direction. As soon as he became 21 years of age, he abandoned steamboating and adopted agriculture. He went into farming in Saline County,[28] Missouri, where a long and rich tract of land had fallen into his possession. He resided in Saline County about ten years, or until about 1859. While living there he was married (in 1852) to Miss Margaret A. Walker, daughter of Nathaniel Walker, one of the pioneer settlers of that part of the Missouri Territory.

The Whites had in all nine children. The farm in Saline County was conducted on an extensive and liberal scale, those being the balmy days before the Civil War when peace and plenty crowned the land and the

Missouri planters, especially those living in a rich county like Saline, could well afford to take matters at their ease. Leaving Saline County in 1859, Moses White and his family came to Jefferson and settled on a farm on the Big River in Township 39 Range 3. White was known as a gentleman of a tender and liberal disposition, and is a man who has seen the world on many different phases.

On the same family tree with Moses White is Ferdinand Kennett.[29] Ferdinand Beauregard Kennett was born in the State of Kentucky in 1813, but when he was a child the family moved to St. Louis where they became active in business and politics and amassed a sizable fortune. One of his brothers was the mayor of St. Louis when Eads Bridge was dedicated in 1874.

Kennett began a journey down the Mississippi River, became acquainted with James S. White at Selma, and decided to locate there. Subsequently he married Julia Dedrick, stepdaughter of James S. White.

He participated with White in both the lead business and the general business enterprises at Selma, branching out later into steamboat ownership and operation, and in a joint venture in lead mining near Joplin with Peter and Henry Blow, both prominent in St. Louis history. He served as representative of this district in Jefferson City for many years.[30]

It may have been through the lead mining enterprises that Kennett acquired the relatively plain fullstock Hawken Rifle bearing cheekpiece inscription, "Ferdinand Kennett from Sam Hawken." This rifle is on display at the Ralph Foster Museum, The School of the Ozarks, Point Lookout, Missouri.

From the number of Hawken rifles owned by local dignitaries, it can be seen that not all of the Hawken production went West. No doubt the future will bring to light other Hawken rifles with prominent St. Louis backgrounds.

So the legend lives on, not only in the adventures and exploits of the mountain men, whose exploits are synonymous with the Hawken name, but in the memory of the early settlers and pioneers—all of whom needed and appreciated the best rifle money could buy.

SPECIAL NOTE*
Narrative on Brown, Baylor, Ferguson and Daily reprinted by permission of author from article in *The Gun Report*, March 1981 by Wayne W. Austerman, historian with Department of History, Louisiana State University, Baton Rouge, Louisiana. Our sincere thanks for this most valuable addition.

27Biographical sketch Moses F. White Jefferson County Historical Atlas, 1875. From the Missouri Atlas of 1876, Jefferson County page 34.

28Moses F. White - probate file #905 estate of John Smith T, Washington County Missouri.

29Probate File #258 estate of Ferdinand Kennett, Jefferson County Missouri

30Valle Higgenbotham, DeSoto Press, DeSoto, Missouri, November 18th, 1963. "Fightingest Missourian."

Sometime in 1830–'31, while serving as a cabin boy on the brig *Corvo*, young Sam Colt whittled the design for a revolving pistol from a block of wood. Sculptor John Massey Rhind was commissioned by Mrs. Colt after Sam's death to do this bronze as a model for a larger monument in Hartford's Colt Park. *(Courtesy Wadsworth Atheneum, Hartford)*

CHAPTER FOUR

MANIFEST DESTINY AND SAM COLT'S REVOLVERS

By R. L. Wilson & Richard Alan Dow

SUMMER 1844. Texas was still an independent Republic, plagued by marauding Mexicans and raiding Indians and defended largely by the quasi-military Texas Rangers, a ferocious but, until this time, poorly armed band. The Indians, particularly, were a threat. Two Texas Rangers later wrote with unqualified admiration, "Those prairie tribes ride with boldness and wonderful skill, and are, perhaps, unsurpassed, as irregular cavalry. They are so dextrous in the use of the bow, that a single Indian, at full speed, is capable of keeping an arrow constantly in the air, between himself and the enemy."

On a July day Colonel John C. Hays and fifteen Rangers picked up the trail of a large band of Comanches near the Perdernales River, north of San Antonio. Following it some distance, it quickly became clear to the Rangers that the Indians had circled back and were now stalking *them*.

When the Indians came into view, some 80 strong, they were clearly confident that this encounter would go like so many previous ones: a volley at long range from the single-shot Mississippi rifles, then, while the puny force hastily reloaded, the Indians could skewer them on their lances at leisure.

But these Rangers acted differently. Spurring their horses directly at the Comanches, urged on by Jack Hays' ringing cry, "Give 'em hell!" the Rangers began to pour a hail of lead at the surprised Indians. In seconds, more than half the Comanche band had been killed or wounded and the rest were in flight.

Sam Colt's revolving pistols had come to the frontier.

Their journey from the East had been difficult, thwarted by far more difficulties than geography. And it would be a few more years before they were firmly settled. Nevertheless, the future of the controversial fire-arms and their entrepreneur inventor was assured from that moment on. Samuel H. Walker, one of the Rangers at the Perdernales, newly arrived in Texas from distinguished service in the Seminole Wars, summed it up in a letter to Samuel Colt two years later: "With improvements I think [the revolvers] can be rendered the most perfect weapon in the World for light mounted troops which is the only efficient troops that can be placed upon our extensive Frontier to keep the various warlike tribes of Indians and marauding Mexicans in subjection."

Walker, who would play an important part in getting Colt revolvers into the hands of frontiersmen, had already experienced the effectiveness of Colt's invention as a private serving in Florida. So too had other giants of the period, including Colonel William S. Harney, who commanded the 2nd Dragoons, and Zachary Taylor, who would lead the U.S. Army into Mexico.

The brash young United States of America was pushing to the limits of its continent under the banner of manifest destiny, the God-given right to conquest, and Colt's invention was giving God a helping hand.

The journey of Colt revolvers to Texas really began on the high seas in 1830–31. A young cabin boy named Sam Colt, bound from New York to India and London in the brig *Corvo*, conceived of a revolving cylinder pistol and carved a model of its basic components from a block of wood with a $1 jackknife. It wasn't really the *idea* of a revolver that was new. Although he naturally denied it in order to protect his patents, Colt almost certainly saw revolving flintlock pistols in use in India or on display at the Tower of London's Armouries. It was Colt's method of advancing and locking the cylinder, coupled with the percussion cap ignition system which was just beginning to supplant flint and steel, that gave him an invention which was to prove highly patentable.

Colt returned from his voyage and, to the chagrin of his father, made it clear that he was quitting the sea to pursue his new idea. He hired gunsmiths in various places to build prototypes, and when borrowed money ran out, set himself up as the famous "Dr. Coult of Calcutta," giving lectures and demonstrations of laughing gas throughout the U.S. and Canada. His profits were poured into his invention.

Among those who worked on the project, the long suffering John Pearson of Baltimore is best known. Working for a pittance (and even at that, seldom paid on time—if at all), Pearson's letters to Colt are a poignant record. Most importantly, Pearson produced the prototype Serial #1 Colt revolver. Made in 1834–35, it was the sample which Colt used to secure investors for his first major manufacturing venture.

In 1835 Colt applied for his U.S. patent, and while this was pending, again borrowed money from relatives and traveled to England and France, securing patents from those major industrial centers which might otherwise have infringed on his U.S. rights. The U.S. patent was granted in February of 1836, and this, along with another for improvements in 1839 and an extension granted in 1849, would assure Colt a virtual monopoly on revolvers until 1857. As events turned out, he needed the time.

In March of 1836 the state of New Jersey chartered the Patent Arms Manufacturing Company, which established its headquarters in the industrial city of Paterson and also opened a sales office and showroom at 155 Broadway, New York City. It wasn't until late in the year, however, that Colt had any production models to show, relying until then on his prototype pistols for demonstrations. And the first revolver off the production line wasn't a pistol at all, but a revolving cylinder Ring Lever Rifle, the Model No. 1.

Uprisings in the South, first with the Creek Indians and later with the Seminoles, who resisted the idea of selling their cattle and moving west of the Mississippi, were involving federal troops in a seeming no-win situation. The guerrilla tactics of the Indians—a feint which forced the soldiers to fire their single-shot firearms with little effect, followed by an attack on the frantically reloading troops, and then a quick disappearance into the wilderness—convinced many of the front line officers that better arms were needed.

Despite a trial of new longarms at West Point in 1837, which proved grossly unfair to the Colt rifle and ultimately disapproved it for military service, Colonel William S. Harney was impressed. He found a way to purchase 50 of the ring lever models, and Colt delivered them personally to Florida. The combat forces reached a far more favorable decision than had the desk bound ordnance officers. In December of 1840, Harney led an

This watercolor drawing was used by Sam Colt in applying for his first patents in the U.S., England, and France. (Courtesy Museum of Connecticut History)

The earliest known photo of the Patent Arms Mfg. Co. in Paterson, New Jersey. The man is believed to be Samuel Colt. (Photo Courtesy Gerasimos K. Livitsanos)

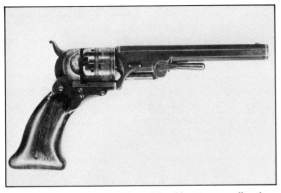

The Model No. 3 Belt Pistol, in .31 caliber, was smaller than the "Texas" model, and was popular with wealthier westbound emigrants. *(Courtesy Woolaroc Museum)*

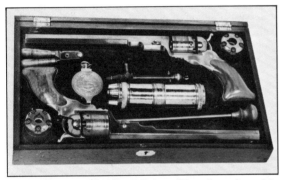

This rare cased pair of No. 5 Holster, "Texas" pistols in .36 caliber with nine-inch barrels, were part of the estate of former Secretary of State William H. Seward.

expedition into the Everglades after the renegade chief Chekika. With 90 dragoons, many armed with Colt's rifles, Harney dispersed the Indians, capturing several and killing their chief. First Sergeant P. W. Henry later wrote to Colt, "... there was not a man in the whole detachment that did not feel himself of five times the force with one of your repeaters, than with the common carbine or musket."

The Seminole War was winding down, and there were some further setbacks. Poor quality control resulted in burst cylinders, and some officers who had formerly praised the revolvers began to have reservations. The rifles proved too high priced for much success on the civilian market—although the pistols, now in four models, were selling well enough. However, Colt was also having problems with his Board of Directors. One, the treasurer John Ehlers, quietly gained a controlling interest in the company and began to liquidate it to his own profit. One of the last major sales of Paterson revolving arms was to the Republic of Texas. Between 1839 and 1841, 180 of the No. 5 Holster pistols, 100

Ring Lever Rifles, and 180 Model 1839 Carbines were purchased, with an unknown number sold to Texas civilians. While not sufficient to save the Paterson operation, these orders were the seeds from which the new Colt era would germinate.

A closer look at the Paterson Colt arms is warranted, for as Colt himself later said, "... a capital of nearly £30,000 was expended without any beneficial result, except in gaining experience, both in the arms themselves and in the machinery required for their manufacture." This is perhaps a disservice to the Paterson models, which were among the finest arms of the time and were proudly presented by Colt and others to heads of state around the world. But they also contained very real flaws, which Colt would correct in his next and successful attempt at manufacturing.

The Ring Lever Rifle, which had begun to interest the military in revolving arms, was of varying calibers, .34 to .44, and this variety produced one of its drawbacks—it required too many different sizes of projectiles for efficient use in the field. It was followed by the No. 2 Ring Lever, in a single, standard .44 caliber; the Model 1839 Carbine, in .525 caliber smoothbore and with an exposed hammer; and the Model 1839 Shotgun, a .62 caliber smoothbore which was probably produced only to compete in the area of military muskets. The total number of longarms manufactured was a meager 1,912.

Colt's first production handgun was the No. 1 Pocket Model (called the "Baby Paterson" by collectors today). In .28 caliber, it was designed to compete with the Derringer, although the latter was both smaller in size and of larger caliber. A total of 500 were made at Paterson. The No. 2 and No. 3 Belt Models were in .31 caliber and differed mainly from each other in the style of the grips. Together they totaled a production of 850. The most important Colt pistol from this period was the No. 5 Holster model, widely sought on the frontier and called the "Texas Arm" by Colt himself. It was in .36 caliber and larger than the other models. A thousand were made, and many had found their way to Texas before the Paterson operation ceased.

A small number of pistols were also made up from existing part inventories after Ehlers took over the Patent Arms Manufacturing Company. About 500 in all, these have been dubbed the Fourth Model Ehlers (.28 caliber) and the Fifth Model Ehlers (.31 caliber).

All told, 2,850 handguns were produced at Paterson.

When Colonel J. C. Hays took on the Comanches (in what is now referred to as the "Hays Big Fight"), he had recently armed his men with the No. 5 Holster pistols, probably received from the short-lived Texas Navy. The Paterson revolvers were five-shot models, and each had a spare cylinder which could be loaded in advance and easily swapped, giving each pistol the capability of firing ten shots in rapid succession. A Comanche chief complained of the Rangers that they "have a shot for every finger on the hand."

The Rangers weren't the only Texans who appreciated the big Colts. E. W. Moore, who had been in command of the Texas Navy, wrote to Colt: "The confidence that your Arms gave the Officers and men under my Command when off Campiche in 1843 and opposed to a vastly superior force is almost incredible but may be imagined when I state what with the boarders of a Sloop of War we could discharge nine hundred and sixty balls in one minute and forty seconds—in short if in command of a Vessel of War again I would not sail if I could possibly avoid it without your repeating arms and I would have none other."

The main complaints about the Patersons from the Texans were the intricacy of their mechanisms, which were sometimes not able to withstand the rough handling on the frontier. The poorly burning powder of the time often clogged the cylinders. And from the viewpoint of the mounted soldier, reloading was difficult as the barrel had to be removed and it was possible to drop both barrel and cylinder in the process. These were some of the improvements that Sam Walker wanted

Colt to consider when he wrote his famous letter in 1846. Colt's willingness to learn, his courage to take on another production effort in spite of earlier failures, and his generosity in crediting Walker's contributions all paid off in the end. Another major conflict was brewing which became the training ground for the Civil War and an entirely new plateau of advances in arms technology. In 1845 war was declared with Mexico, and Sam Colt had a hand in its outcome.

Both Samuel Hamilton Walker and John Coffee Hays, who more than anyone else brought the Colt revolver to early prominence, were physically unprepossessing men compared with their flamboyant and burly Ranger companions, who dressed "as outlandishly as possible, and with their huge beards looked almost like savages." But both were Titans in battle, Walker being called "the thunderbolt of the Rangers" when his exploits during the early stages of the Mexican War brought him to public attention. Lionized both by his men and the press, it was natural that he should be selected to return after his first tour in Mexico to conduct recruiting in the east.

The ever alert Sam Colt had heard of Walker, and an undated letter contains a very typical Colt request for

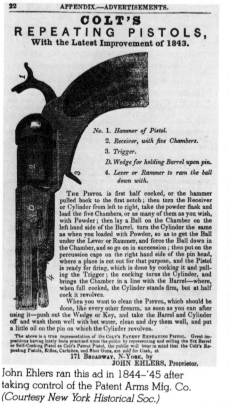

John Ehlers ran this ad in 1844–'45 after taking control of the Patent Arms Mfg. Co. (*Courtesy New York Historical Soc.*)

Captain Samuel Walker, soldier and Texas Ranger, was killed in Mexico before his company was fully armed with the revolvers he helped design. Prior to his death Colt sent him two pistols as a gift.

endorsement of his revolvers and a promise that "Should Col. Hase take the command of the regiment ordered from Texas & desire them armed with my repeaters I have but little doubt that his requisitions would be complied with at once . . . the arm(s) are very much Improved since we first commenced there manufacture & I have no doubt that with the hints which I may get from you & others having experience in there use in the field that they can be made the most complete thing in the world."

It is in reply to this tentative contact that Walker wrote his letter of November 30, 1846, describing the Hays Big Fight and stating flatly "that you deserve a large share of the credit for our success."

Two days later Colt was ready with a written quotation for pistols in lots of 1,000. Subsequent correspondence guarantees to incorporate suggestions for changes in design made by Walker and a pledge to deliver the pistols in three months—all promised by a bankrupt inventor without a cent of capital, without a work force, with no tools, and no factory! When the Ordnance Department agreed to purchase 1,000 pistols on December 7, 1846, Sam Colt began some mad scrambling, prodded at regular intervals by Walker, who wanted the

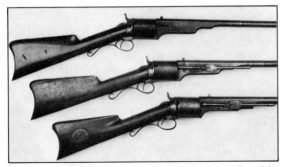

Three variations of the Model 1839 Carbine produced by Colt at Paterson. *(Courtesy Woolaroc Museum)*

Colt commissioned popular artist George Catlin to paint a series of pictures illustrating Colt arms in use; this scene depicts an 1839 carbine in Brazil.

arms for the new company he was raising before returning to Mexico.

The first problem was production, and Colt contacted Eli Whitney, Jr. (son the the famous cotton gin inventor) at New Haven, Connecticut. Whitney was already filling a government contract for muskets, and even though he eventually agreed to take on the pistol project as a priority, Colt lived in fear that the Ordnance Department would find out that their musket orders were being delayed in favor of Colt's pistol contract. Colt tried hard to keep Walker around as the sole government inspector. Walker, who wanted the pistols desperately, was willing to bend the rules and protect Colt's subterfuge. But time was running out. Walker would shortly leave for the south to pick his horses and train his company, and Colt would be at the mercy of a less sympathetic federal inspector.

"I wish you would get orders to spend about one month·with me at the manufactury of thees armes," he pleaded with Walker on January 18, 1847, "it will be to our mutual advantage if you can do so . . . If you do not come on & spend some little time with me & approve the first arms that are finished I know I shall have difficulty with the Ordnance Department.

"They will be more hostile to me than ever when they find out that I have hired the Whitneyvil Ormoury & all the men & mashinery that have been employed making U.S. Rifles for the Ordnance Department."

At the same time, though, Colt kept urging Walker to get the contract increased. Walker, meanwhile, kept trying to convince Colt that he had to have an actual gun to demonstrate—that his description alone was not enough for the short-sighted, unimaginative officialdom. When Walker finally left for Mexico, the first of the new pistols had still not been produced.

The arm that Walker and Colt were collaborating on was as much larger-than-life as the men who would immortalize it. A barrel-mounted loading lever had solved the problems of reloading on horseback. The cylinder capacity had been increased to six rounds. The folding trigger of the Paterson models, extended only when the hammer was cocked and requiring a complex internal mechanism, had given way to a fixed trigger with a square-backed triggerguard. The caliber was a hefty .44. But most impressive was the sheer mass of the pistol—4 pounds 9 ounces of steel and iron with a 9-inch barrel. It could be used as an effective bludgeon if there wasn't time to reload!

Colt planned for the arm to be carried in pairs, with one spare cylinder for each pair. This would give each trooper an effective repeating fire rate of eighteen rounds, or a company of one hundred men a whopping eighteen hundred shots—all of which could be unloaded in a minute or less!

While the army was still waiting for the Walker Colt,

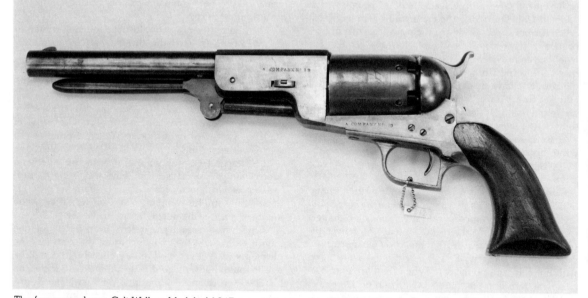

The famous and rare Colt Walker, Model of 1847, was a massive .44 caliber six-shot revolver with a nine-inch barrel, weighing four pounds nine ounces. It shot as far and as accurately as many longarms of the day. Though further improvements would be made, this finally, was the culmination of Sam Colt's dream and the legend of the Colt. This pistol, "A Company No. 19" was one issued to "A" Company, Mounted Riflemen, in the Mexican War.

the Paterson Texas models were in use in Mexico. David Farragut (who would be immortalized during the Civil War with his "Damn the torpedoes, full speed ahead" as he fought at Mobile Bay) planned an attack on Veracruz that would send a vessel close in, allowing 500 Colt armed volunteers to jump onto the city walls from the ship's yardarms. Unfortunately, Veracruz surrendered before Farragut's innovative plan could be carried out.

By October 5, 1847, Sam Walker was at the Castle of Perote, about to begin the march on Puebla. He was still without the Colts for his men, but in a letter to his brother, Jonathon, he reveals, "I have just received a pair of Colts Pistols which he sent to me as a present, there is not an officer who has seen them but what speaks in the highest terms of them and all of the Cavalry officers are determined to get them if possible. Col. Harney says they are the best arm in the world. They are as effective as the common rifle (at) one hundred yards and superior to a musket even at two hundred yards."

Shortly after, Walker, now in command of three companies, set out as a vanguard for General Lane's forces. In the town of Huamantla they encountered 1,600 dug-in Mexicans, and Walker led his 250 men in a sweep through the streets. Although there is no clear account of just what happened, at some point before the Mexicans were successfully driven off Walker received a fatal wound from a lance. The gallant officer who had

survived so many earlier wounds and who had escaped a Mexican imprisonment, died without seeing his dream of a Colt-armed company fulfilled. His gift pistols were saved by his companion, Captain Bedney F. McDonald, and one was returned to Sam Colt. It remained in Colt's private collection, and is today in the Wadsworth Atheneum, Hartford.

Gradually the Walker Colts were issued to the army in Mexico, but apparently never in quantity sufficient to support the kind of lead-slinging charge envisioned by Colt and Sam Walker. But their impact was still felt in lesser ways.

An officer who had served in Mexico would later state, "Such confidence was reposed in those pistols, that whenever I had occasion to send small parties in advance, or to employ express-riders to carry the mails through Indian country, it was always made a condition, that they should be furnished with Colt's revolvers; otherwise they would not risk their lives in such service." And the redoubtable Sam Chamberlain, whose colorful sketches and even more colorful journal have provided a record of the First Dragoons (who were only slightly more tame than Harney's rake-hell second regiment), relates that on July 6, 1847 he was "ordered to report to (Major D. H.) Rucker, who gave me a blessing, swore that I was more trouble than all the rest of the company, and ended by issuing me a Colt's Revolver, one of twelve sent to him for trial." If Sam's chronology is accurate, this dragoon corporal had possession of a Walker Colt months before its co-developer, Captain Sam Walker.

The new weapons proved a mystery to some of the men, as Ranger Captain John S. ("Rip") Ford recalled. "While at Vergara, we drew six-shooters, the old fashioned long-barreled arm. It carried a ball as near the mark, and to a greater distance, than the Mississippi rifle. Many of the men had not used revolvers. Some of them put the small end of the conical ball down first. A single fire usually burst the cylinder. Some let the loose powder trail around the cylinder; six shots would be fired at once. One day a "greeny" was in his tent cleaning his pistol. The adjutant advised him to remove the caps. He said he would. In a minute or two a pistol shot was heard. Greeny had shot his own horse in the head and put himself afoot."

But most quickly found the big pistol devastatingly effective, as Ford further relates: "A skirmish ensued at a little place called San Carlos; Sergeant Major William Hewitt stood in one place and killed three Mexicans with a six-shooter. After the firing ceased the rangers measured the distance, and reported it over one hundred and twenty yards. Hewitt was one of the best shots with a pistol the writer ever saw."

At camp in Encerro, Ford recorded a contest between the Colt pistol and a rifle. "While at this camp the men made a trial between the Mississippi rifle and the six-shooter of Colt's last pattern (the Walker). The six-shooter threw a ball (a) greater distance than the rifle."

Walker had specified that Sam Colt mark the new pistols according to the companies of Mounted Riflemen to which they would be assigned. His own company, C Company, was to be designated first, and these Colts were serialized 1 through 220. So too were A, B, and D Companies. E Company was numbered 1–120. Colt produced an additional 100 pistols for use as gifts and for civilian sales, and these were numbered 1001 to 1100. One of the pair that Sam Walker received and was carrying when he died bore the number 1020, and it is this pistol that was returned to Colt.

The pistols were further marked with "U.S./1847" over the barrel lug, and, in spite of having been made by Eli Whitney at Whitneyville, are inscribed on top of the barrel "ADDRESS SAML COLT NEW-YORK CITY." The cylinders of all the pistols bear a roll-engraved depiction of the Hays Big Fight, showing both Hays and Walker in action. There is a possibility that Walker provided the sketch for this scene, which was executed by W. L. Ormsby, an engraver of Colts during the Paterson days. Appearing as part of the cylinder engraving were the words "COLT'S PATENT" and "MODEL U.S.M.R." (for U.S. Mounted Riflemen).

Response to the Colt Walker had been phenomenal, and Sam Colt immediately set out to improve it, and at the same time to establish his own factory, under his direct control, at Hartford. Using some leftover Walker parts, and incorporating a number of changes, Colt issued a limited production of 240 pistols now called the "Transition Walkers" or the "Whitneyville-Hartford Dragoons." They sold out immediately. The transitional pistol was smaller in size than the Walker, and bore the serial numbers 1100 to 1340.

By early 1848 Colt was already manufacturing the First Model Dragoon, still in .44 caliber, but a somewhat more manageable 4 pounds 2 ounces in weight. The modern revolver was well on the road to development. Colt continued to solicit contracts from the U.S. military which, in turn, continued to maintain an incredibly conservative attitude.

As the Mexican War ended, however, a surge of historic events around the globe, including gold rushes in California and Australia, the Crimean War, a rash of upheavals in Europe, and the continuing problems with Indians and outlaws on the western frontier, provided a ready market for Colt revolvers even without government purchases.

Nothing could now stop the United States from expanding, and nothing could prevent Sam Colt from expanding right along with it. He would become a legend in his own time, and, at his death, one of the wealthiest men in the country—as much a symbol of manifest destiny in the industrial world as westward expansion was in the political.

Like so many thousands of young Southerners, this handsome Virginian saddled his horse and rode off to answer the call for glory. He was a first lieutenant of the Confederate Cavalry. (*Photo Courtesy Herb Peck*)

CHAPTER FIVE

THE CONFEDERATE CAVALRY— RIDERS FOR A LOST CAUSE

By William A. Albaugh III

PEOPLE ARE STILL talking and writing about the unpleasantness of an affair which occurred in the United States some 120 years ago, even though all that, supposedly, is over and done with. When persons from the two sections of our great country get together, it is not hard to start an argument as to who did what to whom, or where and when. It is still a fascinating subject even at this late date of 1981, and as a matter of hard fact, there is still a disagreement as to what caused this fracas, and even what it should properly be called.

It is known by diverse names in different parts of the country. I am of course referring to THE WAR. In the North it is usually termed "the Civil War," but some diehards prefer "the War of Rebellion." We in the South are even more in disagreement. Most, except those soldiers who fought therein and glorified in the name "Rebel," lean to "the War between the States." The hardshells, and there are many, never refer to it other than "the War for Southern Independence," and some such as members of "United Daughters of Confederacy" fondly call it "The Lost Cause." The last is probably the most appropriate term of all. As a matter of fact, it was jolly well a lost cause long before the first shot was fired. However, North or South, there is total agreement in saying, "It was a hell of a war."

Another question is how did the South accomplish the miracle of staying alive for four long years? This question is unanswerable.

In any event, this war was unlike any other before it or after it and was the first real modern and sophisticated clash of arms the world had seen. Despite this, there were numerous examples of pure chivalry, worthy of the days of knighthood. Instances such as the Federals refusing to fire upon a single man entering "no

man's land" whose only purpose there was to give water to fallen friend or foe. There are also many accounts of the other side being given orders not to shoot some individual because he was "too gallant to die."

The War was in a talking stage years before actual hostilities started, but with time, the talk became louder and more strident and hostile. With the advantage of hindsight, many people believed that with wisdom it would have been averted, but it wasn't. There was insufficient wisdom.

Even after it was generally accepted that the war was inevitable, it now seems odd that little preparation was taken on either side to really prepare for the fight. Possibly this was due to overconfidence on both sides as to their own invincibility, plus the universal belief that if indeed the war *did* start, it would be over in a very short time. Still another reason for such apathy might be called the Medical Classic, so well known to doctors. This is where, upon being told of having an incurable disease that could be delayed or cured with proper treatment, the patient never returns for treatment, in the vain hopes it might just go away. But, neither war nor malignancy ever go away through wishful thinking.

After years of smouldering embers of discontent, a crisis (but no fire) was caused by the secession of South Carolina on Dec. 20, 1860. This was hailed with jubilation throughout the South. We gather this joy did not extend north of the Mason-Dixon Line.

This secession caused South Carolina to become not only a sovereign state, but indeed a sovereign nation. As such, she claimed as her own all property within her confines, and in particular, all property that was jointly occupied by all other states and simply called, "Federal property."

A week later, December 26, 1860, the Federal troops in South Carolina garrisoned at Fort Moultrie, on Charleston Harbor and commanded by Major Robert Anderson, U.S.A., stealthily removed from the on-shore fort to Fort Sumter in the middle of the harbor, where it was much easier to defend.

January 9, 1861, the embers were fanned into a definite spark. It was on this date that South Carolina troops fired on the Federal ship, "Star of the West," which had attempted some succor to the Sumter Garrison. The same day, the state of Mississippi seceded, followed by Florida on the 10th, Alabama on the 11th, and then Georgia on January 19th. The next state to leave the Union was Louisiana, January 26. The 1st day of February Texas departed the United States by the same route, and the 4th of this same month saw the birth of the Confederate States of America headquartered in Montgomery, Alabama, and with a provisional Government headed by the Provisional President, Jefferson Davis, and "Little Alex" H. Stephens, its Vice President.

In the North, "Honest Abe" was inaugurated President of the United States, much to the relief of outgoing President Buchanan and chagrin to the Southerners who had hoped that Breckinbridge of Kentucky might have won the election.

April 11 the Confederacy gave Fort Sumter its final demand for its surrender and the following day made good its promise of bombardment. On the 14th, the fort capitulated after Major Anderson obtained permission of the Confederates to parade his garrison, raise the Federal flag, and give the national salute of 100 guns. After the 50th sounded, a gun burst, which killed one private and injured five others. This was the first bloodshed of the war!

The captured troops from Fort Sumter were well received after the surrender, treated with the customary Southern hospitality, then released.

May 6, 1861, the state of Arkansas seceded, as did North Carolina on May 20th, followed by Virginia on May 23rd, and Tennessee on June 8th. These last four states to secede were hastened by President Lincoln's call for troops to be used against seceding states, issued on April 19th. This was unthinkable to any of the three border states of Maryland, Missouri, and Kentucky. Maryland was the only state not to go with the South, but nevertheless her warm sympathies leaned towards her sister southern states, and she was well represented in the Confederate army.

In the fall of 1861 almost the whole of the State of Missouri was in the hands of the federal forces, but what was left of the Legislature that federal General Lyons had driven from Jefferson City met in Neosho near the southwestern corners of the state and did formally secede from the Union to join the Confederacy,

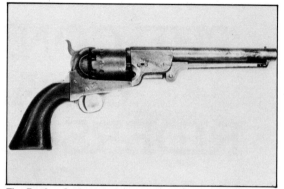

The Rigdon-Ansley revolver, made in Augusta, Georgia, was one of many Confederate copies of the Colt design. (*Photo Courtesy Bruce Kusrow*)

The excellent five-shot Kerr revolver, made in London, was popular with the Confederate Cavalry and was imported by blockade runners. (*Photo by E.N. Simmons*)

being the 12th through so-called "Rebel Legislature."

Kentucky followed the same route, and on Nov. 18, 1861, an irregular convention, composed mainly of Kentuckians serving in the Confederacy, met at Russelville, declaring the independence of Kentucky, and forming a provisional government, and taking steps to secure their admission into the Confederacy. By this time, the war was well under way. The Southern "Stars and Bars" now had 13 stars.

From the time of the first shot in early January, 1861, until the bombardment of Fort Sumter in April, there was a hiatus of actual combat. After this, although there were a few hostile brushes between North and South, such as at Philippe, Big Bethel, and Vienna, all in Virginia, there was nothing that could be called a real fight until the battle of Rich Mountain, in western Virginia, on July 11. This battle was disastrous for the South, and the war finally began in earnest and was to last for four years.

Meanwhile, with the birth of the Confederate States and inauguration of Lincoln, the majority of the southern people realized that in the very near future war would be upon them. Even so, most still thought it

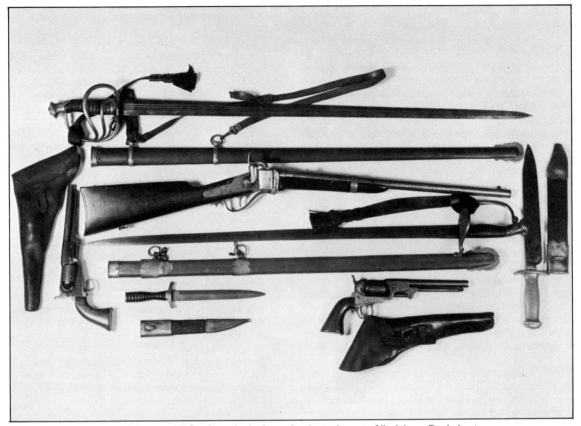

Though totally unprepared for war, the South made the best of its limited assets. All of these Confederate arms were produced in the South, including the copy of the Sharps carbine and the copies of Colt revolvers.

would be of short duration. Nevertheless authorities of the newly founded nation took stock and were appalled at the terrible lack of war material available.

Both parts of the divided nation had advantages and disadvantages. The North boasted a total population of 22,400,000, with 2,486,400 men from age 18 to 45, with a great influx of foreigners every year. Opposed to this manpower, the South had a total white population of 6,343,000 with 3,760,000 blacks and with military potential of 692,000, all white. This of course was an initial advantage for the North.

On the other hand, with few exceptions the people were undividedly in support of the Confederacy. For example, the people of Virginia seceded long before their legislatures made this act legal. Many people of the North had divided feelings, and many thought the South should be able to leave the Union peacefully. This was a plus for the South.

Of the 44 States, 13 seceded, leaving 21 for the North. These 21 contained within their boundaries the industries of 99 percent of the entire nation and also

control of most of the entire country's finances.

While the South was woefully inadequate in its basic supply of arms and factories, this lack might be counterbalanced by the fact that it was an agricultural region. Even though "neighbors" might be separated by many miles, most families had been in the same town or county for many years. They were far closer knit than the people of the urban North. Too, as the companies and regiments were drawn from local sources most soldiers knew the men with whom they were being thrown, and there were few strangers.

PART II
FROM EMBERS TO FIRE

Having once been Secretary of War for the United States, but now President of the Confederate States, Jefferson Davis, after taking office, began to choose the persons who would administer his wishes. For Chief of

Ordnance he appointed Josiah Gorgas, with rank of major, and a very good choice it was.

Gorgas was born in Pennsylvania, attended West Point, and graduated sixth in his class of 1841. His subsequent career had all been in the field of ordnance, mainly in the South. But from 1845 to 1846 he went on leave of absence to study his profession in Europe. He commanded Mt. Vernon Arsenal in Alabama from 1853 until 1856. In December 1853, he married the daughter of ex-governor Gayle of Alabama. In 1856 he was transferred to the arsenal at Charleston, S.C., after a short stint of duty at Kennebec Arsenal in Maine. He also had served in the Mexican War with distinction in the siege of Vera Cruz, and later was in charge of the ordnance depot there.

He resigned from the army in April 1861 with the rank of captain, and he and his family moved to Alabama, where he felt more at home than in the North. It was here that he received his appointment from Davis. He promptly sent Captain Caleb Huse to Europe to procure munitions of war. Huse, a competent, experienced ordnance officer did extremely well, obtaining a contract with the London Armoury for all arms (guns and revolvers of the Kerr patent), after the Royal English contract had expired. This brought the South a large number of Enfield rifles and the well-made Kerr five-shot revolvers.

At home, Gorgas was sending agents to the Northern munition makers, the manufacturers of uniforms, buttons, swords, and cavalry furniture. Even at this late date, these makers of war material were delighted to do business with the South. Gorgas also insisted on using tobacco and cotton to purchase needed arms. He arranged for effective service by blockade runners to carry purchases in Europe back to the Confederacy. Still further, he let government contracts to would-be makers of rifles, guns, revolvers, etc. and etc. He was an exceptionally capable and effective administrator.

In 1895, after his death in 1883, a lengthy account of his Confederate activities was published in *The Confederate Soldier in The Civil War*, edited by historian Ben LaBree.

Therein, Gorgas gave an account of the arms stored in the Southern arsenals at the time of the war. Under the subtitle of "Small Arms," he states the following:

"At the formation of the government, or the beginning of the war;

Small Arms

At Richmond, Va.	(about) 4,000 rifles—no muskets
Fayetteville Arsenal, N.C. . .	(about) 2,000 rifles—25,000 muskets
Charleston Arsenal S.C.	(about) 2,000 rifles—20,000 muskets
Augusta Arsenal, Ga.	3,000 rifles—8,000 muskets
Mt. Vernon Arsenal, Ala., ...	2,000 rifles—20,000 muskets
Baton Rouge, La.	2,700 rifles—27,000 muskets
Total:	15,000 rifles 120,000 muskets

There were in Richmond, about 60,000 old, worthless flint muskets, and at Baton Rouge, about 10,000 old Hall's Rifles and carbines. At Little Rock, Ark., a few stands, increasing the aggregate to say, one hundred and forty three thousand. To add to this, must be added the arms owned by the several states, and by military organizations throughout the country, giving, say one hundred and fifty thousand in all for the use of the armies of the Confederacy. The rifles were of calibre .54, known as Mississippi rifles, except those at Richmond, taken from Harpers Ferry, which were calibre .58; the muskets were the old flint locks, calibre .69, altered to percussion. Of sabres there were a few boxes at each arsenal and some short artillery swords. A few hundred holster pistols were scattered here and there. There were no revolvers."

As steel supplies grew short in the South, arms like the Griswold & Gunnison Colt copy had brass frames and barrels of twisted iron. (*Photo Courtesy Wiley Sword*)

A large number of small iron works such as the Columbus, Georgia, Firearms Mfg. Co. tooled up to meet the South's need for arms. (*Photo Courtesy E.G. Carson*)

The entire report, rather than the fragment given, is very enlightening, showing just how few arms, artillery, and equipment the South had.

In response to a government call for private arms, a good many thousand shotguns and sporting rifles were turned in. These, along with arms purchased from the North and Europe, resulted in a heterogeneous collection of Springfield and Enfield muskets, Mississippi and Maynard rifles, Hall's and Sharps' carbines, and arms of English, German, Austrian and Belgian manufacture, of many different calibers.

In addition to the C.S. Government agents, the individual states also sent their agents North, and abroad, presenting more duplication and competition between the states. It raised already high prices, as the United States government was also competing with them. The Confederacy possessed only two first-class foundries and machine shops—the Tredegar Iron Works in Richmond, and Leeds Factory at New Orleans. However, there were several machine shops of second class. Also there were a number of woolen and cotton mills, some 20 paper mills, and a few small iron furnaces and forges, but with very meager production. Skilled mechanics were rare, but there were numerous carpenters and blacksmith shops. In other words the potential for maintaining a war effort was small.

Realizing the shortage of guns, revolvers, and swords, the South reverted to weapons first used by primitive man. These were spears (called pikes), with six-foot wooden poles, the tips of which were capped with a foot-long blade of iron. Also, short swords such as gladiators used in ancient Roman days were made and issued. Needless to say the unfortunate men who were thus armed were something less than happy.

To give a concrete idea of the diversity of Southern weapons and uniforms, we quote what an observer of the Battle of Lexington, Mo., (Sept. 1861), had to say: "Scarcely a hundred of the Confederates were uniformed; scarcely two had guns alike—no two exhibited the same trappings. Here went one fellow in a shirt of brilliant green, on his side an immense cavalry sabre, in his belt two navy revolvers, and a Bowie knife, and slung from his shoulder a Sharps' rifle. Right by his side was another, upon whose hips dangled a light medical sword, in his hand a double-barreled shotgun, in his boot an immense scythe, on his heel the inevitable spur, his whole appearance from tattered boot, through which gazed audaciously his toes, indicating that the plunderings of many a different locality made up his whole. Generally, the soldiers were armed with shotguns or squirrel rifles; some had the old flintlock muskets; a few had Minie rifles; and others, Sharps' or Maynard rifles, while all to the poorest had horses."

Regardless of the weapons or equipment, the Mis-

These noncoms of the "Bolivar" troop, 1st Mississippi Cavalry, carry breechloading Maynard carbines. Manufactured in Massachussetts, the Maynard was dependable and prized by troopers on both sides. Though listed as a "standard" arm by some Southern units, it was available only when captured from Yankees. (*Photo Courtesy Herb Peck*)

souri State Troops, fighting on the Southern side under General Sterling Price, CSA, did well in the above battle. Their loss was small, partly due to the rolling of wet bales of hemp, pushed ahead of the troops in final assault on Mulligan's Union force shut up in a fort at the Masonic College. The Southern force captured 3,500 men, besides 3,000 rifles, seven guns etc.

Early in the War it is noted that the 8th Tennessee Cavalry under Colonel George G. Dibrell of the famed Forrest Brigade, was armed with 400 flintlock muskets—this for a cavalry regiment?

Further information as to the Forrest Brigade has it that as late as "the fall of 1862," about one half of the brigade "had no other arms than shotguns and squirrel rifles, which they had brought from home."

Green, of the Kentucky "Orphan" Brigade, claims that at Monterey, Mississippi, there was a blacksmith shop kept busy turning out old-fashioned pikes to arm some of the brigade who had no funds! The affair at Lexington gives an example of the types of arms and uniforms of the Southern Army. This occurred in the far (then) west of the country. Let us now see how things fared in Virginia.

In the month of May 1861, there was an order, obtained through a special application made in person by R. L. T. Beale, to General Robert E. Lee, commander-in-chief of the Virginia forces. Major Carr, at Fredericksburg, Virginia, was directed to muster into service a cavalry company from the county of Westmoreland, Virginia. The officers of this company had given the troops the name of "Lee's Light Horse," in memory of "Light Horse Harry" Lee of the Revolution and who, along with Robert E. Lee, had been born in Westmoreland County.

The company in question numbered a total of 61 men. Most were young, but there were several as old as 45. Thomas S. Garnett was captain. He had attended VMI, and had been a lieutenant in the Mexican War. He later became colonel of the 48th Virginia Regiment of Volunteers. R. L. T. Beale was a first lieutenant at the time, but later became colonel of the 9th Virginia Cavalry and still later a brigadier general of cavalry.

Beale in his *History, Ninth Virginia Cavalry*, recalls that on this day in May, there "was nothing very martial in the appearance of the company. The officers and men were clad in their civilian dress, and their horses with saddles and bridles of every description used in the country. Their only arms were sabres and double-barreled shotguns collected from the homes of the (local) people." This company became "Co. C, 9th Va. Cav.," and the regiment was known as "Lee's Legion." It had 10 companies, but for a time, they did not act in concert with each other; each being more or less on its own, on detached duty.

The following year in April 1862, Beale reports:

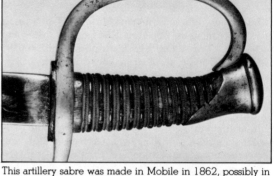

This artillery sabre was made in Mobile in 1862, possibly in a blacksmith shop. (*Photo Courtesy C.J. Pugliese*)

"Near the close of April the regiment reorganized, the privates electing the company officers, and these (in turn) electing the field officers. These elections were general throughout the army, and were regarded as a great political blunder, amounting almost to a crime, in the legislature department of the Confederate Government. The consequences, doubtless, would have been disastrous in the extreme, but for the firmness, energy, and good sense of the military commanders."

Beale was entirely correct in his abomination of this practice. For example, Colonel Richard M. Cary, colonel of the 30th Va. Vols., as of June 13, 1861, declined to run for reelection in April 1862, opposing the principle. Nevertheless he was reelected to colonel but refused to accept the commission due to his "unwillingness to hold an office conferred by those subject to his control." He dropped down to the rank of lieutenant of artillery. This was a loss to the Confederacy, and there were countless others.

In the 9th Va. Cav., its first colonel, John E. Johnson as of Jan. 2, 1862, was dropped at the reorganization and replaced by William H. F. ("Rooney") Lee. Shortly thereafter, all companies of the regiment acted in concert with each other.

At the time of the reorganization, Beale notes that the appearance of the regiment (in April 1862) "was but a slight improvement upon that ascribed to one of the companies the year previous. Three of the companies had been partly armed with inferior carbines and pistols by the counties in which they were raised; most of them were supplied with such sporting guns as could be collected by the officers from the people of the country. The equipment of the horses was of the most inferior kind, and varied with the means of the individual troopers. No regular squad, company, or regimental drill had been generally adopted, and the supply of books on tactics was wholly inadequate to the wants of the officers."

A member of the Texas Cavalry poses with a sabre and Colt 1851 Navy. In .36 caliber, the Colt Navy was a Confederate favorite. (*Photo Courtesy Herb Peck*)

The 9th Va. Cav. was not a regiment drawn from the back woods, but was composed by-in-large by prominent and well-to-do citizens. Its Colonel "Rooney" Lee, was the second son of Robert E. Lee. Young Lee later became a major general of the cavalry, serving in virtually all the campaigns of the Cavalry Corps of Army of Northern Virginia.

This same regiment played a large role in the encirclement of McClellan's Union forces, cutting him off from his supply depot. Obviously, their clothing and "inferior" weapons did nothing to dull their competence as horsemen. This same 9th Cavalry was to join forces with the 1st Va. Cav., whose colonel had been "Jeb" Stuart, but when he advanced to general, Lee took over Jeb's old job.

PART III
FROM FIRE TO HOLOCAUST

When the clarion of war was sounded, far more volunteered (650,000) than the nearsighted Confederacy thought were needed, and far more than could be properly equipped. To the average Southerner, the horse was merely an extension of his own body, and regardless of distance, long or short, a saddle was thrown over

The Cook carbine was made in some quantity in Athens, Georgia. (*Photo Courtesy Claude Coile*)

the back of one of his horses. This was true of his father, and his father before him—there simply were no other ways of getting from point "A" to point "B" except astride a horse. So, when war was declared, old Betsy was saddled up and ridden to the recruiting office, the volunteer expecting to fight as he did everything else, with Betsy. This was his way of life.

Realizing his bare fists would not be sufficient for this fight, he brought with him a hunting rifle, or single or double-barreled shotgun, which until then were used to provide meat or fowl for the family.

He was aghast to learn that he would need a sword. Although his ancestors had been proficient in their use during the Revolution, their expertise of this arm was not an inherited trait. If the recruiting officer insisted, he again saddled old Betsy, and rode back home to get granddaddy's or great grandfather's sabre, which had hung peacefully over the mantle. Up until then, his only experience with edged weapons was the Bowie knife.

To take care of all the horses in the South required a very large number of blacksmiths. As a consequence, there was a shop of this nature at practically all crossroads. In such shops, almost all metals—iron, copper, brass, lead, tin, wood—could be worked individually, or collectively, and fashioned into objects of necessity. The smiths were a great boon to the industrial starved South, which had very few industrial plants compared with the North that had over 100,000.

At the smithy were produced: buckles, canteens, Bowie knives from scythe blades, and files. Then reversing the Biblical injunction, sword blades would be hammered out of plowshares, with a brass guard made from a melted down candle stick and wood grip.

The quality of such merchandise was the same as the ability of the blacksmith in question—some good, some unbelievably crude, and clumsy. But meanwhile, numerous sword and blade makers had sprung up, getting contracts from the state and government, and for the interim, blacksmiths served their purpose. The cavalrymen volunteers were very efficient with their shotguns and rifles, which they had been accustomed to, off or on horseback. But this was done by one's self or in a small group, not during a cavalry charge. A muzzle-loading arm shot only once for each barrel. To reload required powder, poured from a horn or pouch into each barrel. Then, a lead ball or shot, followed by paper or cloth wadding was forced in by a wooden or iron ramrod. Then, the percussion cap (igniting unit) had to be placed on the nipple for the hammer to hit, after the hammer had been cocked. In the case of a flintlock, and there were many such used in the South, it was even harder. With these, in addition to the loading procedure, a small amount of fine grade powder had to be carefully poured into the pan, near the hammer, the covering of which was of iron so that the flint attached to the hammer would strike this iron, hopefully causing the spark which would ignite the pan powder, in turn setting off the charge in the gun causing it to discharge.

Now that we have all this, it has to be borne in mind that most of the shotguns, single or double, were four feet or more long, and the rifles were still longer. Let's face it, even to an experienced rider and shooter, the task of reloading would be more than difficult, particularly when faced by another group of men with murderous intent riding hell-for-leather towards them!

The Union troopers so quickly closing the gap between the two were armed with short rifles, slightly over three feet in length. These short rifles, called carbines, were designed specifically for cavalry and were deadly except at long range. The Southerners then went back to their blacksmiths where their present long barrels were sawed off into carbine length, thus slightly reducing their initial disadvantage.

It was some time before the Confederate cavalry was armed with carbines and never had sufficient arms, or clothing needed by its troops. This also was particularly true of revolvers. At first, most men brought to war with them a handgun of some nature, ranging from flintlock horse pistols to fine duelling pistols, with a scattering of modern revolvers of Colt, Whitney, Smith & Wesson, Remington, etc., pattern, but of several or many different calibers. Many single-shot pistols were carried by the private, and called "second shots," meaning that after their initial rifle or musket fire during a charge, in close hand-to-hand battle, they hoped to rely on their "second shot."

The invention of a revolver had been long in the evolutionary stage until Samuel Colt of Hartford, Conn., came along. His Paterson Colt Model 1836, named after the town in New Jersey where it was made, was the first of modern revolvers.

The firm operated until 1842, but lack of government support of sales caused the business to fail. Colt, however, retained copyright on his guns. The Mexican War gave impetus to all arms makers, and Colt obtained a

Federal contract for 1,000 army revolvers (Model 1847), and continued to thrive. During the Civil War, Colt supplied the Union with 386,417 of these weapons along with 7,000 revolving rifles and carbines.

Every trooper coveted a Colt revolver, Army caliber .44, or a Navy model, caliber .36, (Model 1851). At that time most soldiers believed that the Colt was the finest in the world, and they were possibly right. The North issued these Colts—the Southern soldiers secured them either before the war or by capture.

In any event, the Confederate contracts let out to aspiring revolver makers called for them to be of Colt's pattern and of .36 caliber. The larger .44 caliber was the deadlier of the two, but the .36 caliber took less lead, this metal being of great demand and short in quantity.

The improvisations made by the Confederate Ordnance were most ingenious. Remembering the shrinking means to procure metals, leather and rubber, ordnance did what Germans did in WWII, and produced "ersatz" just about everything. Some examples:

Instead of the steel, which was necessary in many munitions of war, bars of twisted iron were used, which gave greater strength to the end result, and were used for the barrels and cylinders of revolvers. The Southern made Griswold & Gunnison's, and also the Spiller & Burr revolvers, are prime examples. The barrels of the carbines, rifles, etc., produced by Cook & Bros., were also of twisted iron. When iron became hard to get the Confederates replaced it with brass, such as the frames of the Southern-made Griswold & Gunnison.

PART IV
CONFEDERATE HEROES

In the South during the middle 19th Century, the worship of God was universal. But only slightly below the Lord, the horse held second place in their worship. This animal played such a large part in their day-to-day living it became a figure of great importance. Horse and man were thrown together for hours at a time. As a result, a special relationship existed between the two. Each generation of man tried to improve upon the last and they were successful. Courage, stamina, endurance, obedience, and intelligence were highly rated. Here, breeding and bloodline in both man and beast were highly considered. There can be no question that the horses from this area were generally of the highest quality.

However, there can be no question that both men and women were good judges of horse flesh. Such a region was also bound to produce skilled horsemen, and it did. Most were "good," many were "fine" and a large number were "superb."

General J.E.B. Stuart leads a Rebel charge. (*Photo Courtesy Colonial Studio, Richmond, Virginia*)

Because of the above stated factors, there is also no question but that the Southern cavalry greatly outshone its Northern counterparts during the first half of the War Between the States. Indeed, their many victories until after the middle of 1863 is mute testimony to this fact. Starting in the latter part of 1863, the pendulum started slowly the other way, and increasingly more so as men and supplies were exhausted.

There were many reasons for this. To begin with, the Federals learned quickly and well. Each previous defeat was gone over carefully to make sure that the errors would not be repeated. Further, men and officers became more skillful. Possibly, the fact that the Northern cavalry had access to an unlimited supply of horses played the most important factor.

Nothing in the South was "unlimited," and this is certainly true of their supply of horses. The Southern government was never able to finance horses for its cavalry, and there was no exception to that rule. To join the cavalry meant that the volunteer in question also had to bring with him a horse. At this point, the government claimed title to the steed, and gave credit for his loss with a fair evaluation. It did not pay for the horse when he became disabled, worn out or jaded, even though this occurred in the line of duty, or if it were captured. The government did not replace the animal, and expected the trooper to procure another. This was patently unfair, but that is the way it was. This policy was kept through the entire war.

The unfortunate cavalryman who lost his mount, regardless of how, was given a furlough to secure another. In the meantime, he was said to have been transferred out of his unit to "Co. Q," or the dead horse company. All dismounted men belonged to this company. While horses were still available at the old plantation, it was not too hard for the Virginia trooper to obtain another. But what if the trooper came from Florida?

As the war progressed, or rather deteriorated, horses became more and more scarce. For some, it was impossible to secure a remount, and the soldier was transferred to another branch of service, which did little for his morale.

We have digressed from the subject of horsemanship, which blessed much of the Confederate cavalry. So many were considered superb, that it becomes very hard to give a sketch of only two. We could have chosen Lieutenant General Nathan Bedford Forrest, from Tennessee, or Major General "Joe" Wheeler, of Georgia, or Lieutenant General Wade Hampton of South Carolina, or even Major General "Fitz" Lee, a Virginian. All were skillful, resourceful, brave leaders of cavalry.

Instead of the above, we selected: Major General Jeb Stuart, and Brigadier General John Hunt Morgan.

MAJ. GEN'L. J. E. B. STUART

To most of the people from Virginia, "Jeb" Stuart represented the "Beau Sabreu" of the South, the perfect cavalier. From him, was expected the best, and rarely were his admirers let down.

Jeb was born on February 6, 1833, as James Ewell Brown Stuart. The issue of Archibald Stuart and his wife, Elizabeth Letcher Stuart, was born at their home called "Laurel Hill" in Patrick County, Virginia. Both parents could boast of their long Virginia lineage. They could also boast of having had 10 children, seven boys and three girls. James Ewell Brown Stuart was the youngest male of the family.

At the age of 15 he worked for a time in the county clerk's office in Wytheville, considering a legal career. The same year he entered Emory and Henry College, being taught the classical education then prevalent throughout the South. At the age of 17 he was appointed to the United States Military Academy. He reported to West Point on July 1, 1850. At the "Point" his name was changed from James, and he was better known as "Beauty" for the same reason many very thin youngsters are called "Fatty." It was said, partly in jest, that he was the only man that ever looked more comely with his face covered with hair. Jeb came after West Point.

He graduated with the standing of 13th out of 46 in the class of 1854. Brevet Lieutenant Colonel Robert E. Lee was the commandant at the time. Stuart received his commission as a second lieutenant in the Mounted Rifles, then in Texas.

In 1855, Jefferson Davis, then Secretary of War of the United States, formed two regiments of cavalry; the 1st and 2nd, to be armed with sabres, pistols or carbines. The cavalry was composed completely of horse soldiers, trained for scouting, outpost duty, and of course for mounted shock tactics. The Mounted Rifles were infantry mounted on horses and by the middle 1850's were already outmoded.

Stuart then became a second lieutenant in the 1st Cavalry, which was commanded by Colonel Edwin Sumner, and the lieutenant colonel was Joseph Eggleston Johnston. Both were to become generals in the oncoming war—but on opposite sides. Sumner for the North, and Johnston for the South.

The initial campaign of the 1st Regiment was to be against the Indians. Their base was Fort Leavenworth, Kansas Territory, to which point the regiment was ordered. In command of the 2nd Dragoons, also at Leavenworth, was Colonel Philip St. George Cooke. Here, Stuart got acquainted with Flora Cooke, a daughter of the colonel. In less than a month, they became married. The Cookes were also "old" Virginians. The following month, Stuart was promoted to the rank of first lieutenant. There followed two years of active campaigning.

By 1859, Stuart, still a first lieutenant in the 1st Cavalry, was still at Leavenworth, Kansas. However, for sometime their activities were not directed towards the redskins. They were attempting to keep the peace between the "Free Soilers" and those who had first settled there and who believed in slavery. It was here that John Brown, the abolitionist, was making his desires come true by sword point, and fell into disrepute with the authorities. The "authorities" amounted to the 1st Cavalry, so Brown was well known to Stuart.

His next encounter with this fanatic was at Harper's Ferry, Virginia (now West Virginia), acting as honorary aide-de-camp to Lieutenant Colonel Robert E. Lee. Brown had attempted to arouse the negroes to armed rebellion by arming and inflaming them with words. Being told of the situation, General Scott, commanding the U.S. Army in Washington, DC., had urgent orders

Major General James E.B. Stuart, killed in action in 1864, has been considered one of the greatest cavalry commanders of all time.

for Lee, who then was at his home at Arlington, just across the Potomac, on leave. It happened that Stuart was also in Washington, seeking to obtain a patent on a saddle device. Later he went to the War Department to pay his respects. There, Scott gave Stuart his message to deliver to Colonel Lee.

The orders to Lee were to proceed by special train to Harper's Ferry and do what was necessary to restore peace and order. Lee took Stuart with him, along with 90 U.S. Marines. This occurred on Oct. 17, 1859. Reaching Harper's Ferry, they found Brown and his few followers holed up in the village brick firehouse, using same as a fort. The morning of the 18th, Stuart led his Marine force to the only door of the firehouse and demanded surrender. This, Brown refused to do and the "fort" was successfully secured in short order.

The prisoners were taken to Charlestown, the county seat, and turned over to civil authorities. Brown, who had been wounded, was carried on a mattress to the county jail. After the law had taken due course and deliberation, which included a fair jury trial, Brown was hanged.

Lee, Stuart and Lieutenant Isreal Green, USMC., who had commanded the well disciplined Marines, were all commended with a "job well done." The whole affair had been of national importance, and the leading actors in this small action became well publicized. They were applauded or "booed" according to political views of those who approved and those who condemned! The John Brown episode probably did as much, or more, than that which occurred at the secession of South Carolina. Both opened the widening chasm between North

Colonel John Singleton Mosby, later head of Mosby's Rangers, scouted for Stuart on the historic raid of 1862. (*Photo Courtesy Bill Turner*)

and the South, and brought the Civil War closer.

The latter part of April, 1861, Stuart was promoted to the rank of captain of the 1st Regiment of Cavalry, USA. May 3rd while at St. Louis, he resigned from the army, citing "his sense of duty to his native state," as a reason. In this day and age, it seems hard to understand the intense patriotism that the citizens felt towards their own particular state, but it was there!

At the same time he wrote his letter of resignation for the U.S. Army, he also wrote to Adjutant General Samuel Cooper of the Confederate States Army requesting a captaincy in, preferably, the Cavalry of the Southern Army. Cooper, previous to going South, had for many years been Adjutant General of the United States Army. A reply was requested to be sent to Virginia's Governor Letcher, in Richmond. Stuart's mother, prior to her marriage, had been a Letcher.

Upon reaching Richmond in May, he found he had been appointed a commission as major in the infantry and ordered to Winchester, reporting to General Joseph Eggleston Johnston, CSA. On May 10th, with orders to report to General Jackson at Harper's Ferry, he was commissioned a lieutenant colonel of infantry. Shortly after this he managed to shift from infantry to cavalry, and July 16th was promoted to full colonel of the 1st Va. Cav., under Jackson. He distinguished himself at the First Battle of Manassas (Bull Run in the North), and was promoted to the rank of brigadier general September 24, 1861, and major general on July 25, 1862. May 11, 1864, he was mortally wounded after contesting the forces of Sheridan's raiders at Yellow Tavern, Virginia, only a few miles outside of Richmond. He

was sorely missed and deeply loved by the officers and men of the Confederate Army, and is still entrenched deeply in the hearts of many Virginians!

Stuart's cunning and daring leadership embodied the spirit of the southern cavalry, and until his untimely death he was a constant and painful thorn in the side of the Army of the Potomac. Of all his exploits, though, few are as legendary or exemplify his character as well as the episode now known simply as "Stuart's Raid."

At two in the morning on June 13, 1862, a rocket arose high in the air over a cavalry encampment commanded by Brigadier General James Ewell Brown Stuart, one time colonel of the 1st Virginia Cavalry until his promotion to brigadier rank in September, 1861.

At this encampment, near Kilby's Station on the R.F.&P. Railway, a little north of Richmond were some 1,200 men. They were composed of seven companies of the 9th Va. Cav., commanded by Colonel William H. F. Lee. The seven companies were roughly divided into three squadrons, each squadron equivalent to two companies. Attached were two squadrons from the 4th Va. Cav., completing a full regiment. To this were added detachments of the 1st Va. Cav., now commanded by Colonel "Fitz" Lee, nephew of Robert E. Lee, general in command of all military operations in Virginia. Still in addition was the force under Lt. Col. William Martin, with 250 of the best men from Jeff Davis Legion and the South Carolina Boykin Rangers. There was also a section of light artillery under Lieutenant James Breathed, of Pelham's Light Horse Artillery.

This very large force was not assembled haphazardly. To the contrary, a few days previous to this gathering, a very efficient scout named John Singleton Mosby was sought out to obtain certain information, extremely valuable to the Confederacy. Later Mosby would win fame at the head of Mosby's Rangers, but then he was merely a trooper in whom Stuart saw great promise.

This was shortly after the Battle of Seven Pines, only a few miles distant from Richmond, Capital of the Confederate States of America.

The Battle of Seven Pines, May 31 and June 1st, 1862, was between opposing generals George McClellan, North, and Joseph E. Johnston, South. The latter received a wound serious enough that at the end of the battle he was replaced by General R. E. Lee. The battle was indecisive, but McClellan remained stretched along the northeast side of the Chickahomny River, only a few miles from Richmond, and had shifted to the south bank of the river with the major part of his army of 100,000.

At the time, his base of supplies was at White House on the Pamunky River, about 25 miles from Richmond, as the crow flies. But McClellan was hardly a crow, and by the poor country roads, it was closer to 50. He had already started to remove his base of supplies to

Harrison's Landing on the James River, at which point the left wing of his army was already resting.

It was essential that Lee learn at least where Mc-Clellan's right wing was anchored before his expected battle with his opponent. Thus through Stuart, whom he greatly admired, the request was made to send a scout out to ascertain the state of affairs. Stuart sent the accomplished and talented John Singleton Mosby.

Mosby reported back to Stuart that McClellan's right flank was resting on air. In turn, Stuart relayed this information to Lee, who believed that a reconnoiter in strength was in order. Accordingly, Stuart picked the best men available and alerted them the day before.

The two a.m. rocket was the signal for them to start. The column headed north, which led his men and whoever else might be watching to believe they were headed towards Louisa County. North of Ashland, they altered their course to the east and camped near the settlement of Taylorsville, near the Winston Plantation.

Stuart and Rooney Lee, leaving the others, visited "Hickory Hill," home of the Wickhams. Colonel William Carter Wickham was recuperating from a wound received May 5, 1862, at Williamsburg. There was also Charlotte Wickham, the colonel's daughter, but more to the point, she was also the wife of the colonel of the 9th Va. Cav., Rooney Lee.

Early the next morning, the 9th Virginia Cavalry led the advance guard, with Will Martin, much to his disgust, commanding the rear. The column turned southeast towards Hanover Court House and Old Church, a small village some 20 miles away.

Prior to reaching this latter point, they had several brushes with Federal troops. On the outskirts of Old Church, they encountered serious resistance. Company "F" (the Essex Dragoons), led the initial encounter, losing Captain William Latane, a very promising young man. Aside from a few others suffering nondisabling sabre wounds, there were no further casualties. But the loss of young Latane filled the others with rage.

Captain Latane, who died leading with his sword, shouting, "On to them boys!" aroused the romantic fancy of all the South, who considered him the "Knight in Shining Armor!"

The Yankees were brushed aside and a guidon was taken by a member of Co. "C", 9th Va., and later presented to Governor Letcher as the first trophy of the historic trip.

Fitz Lee's 1st Va. then led the raid. The Union camp at Old Church was looted and burned and a number of prisoners were taken. Brigadier General Philip St. George Cooke, cavalry commander of the Federal cavalry, was, also the father-in-law of the Confederate, Jeb Stuart. Cooke had heard the Southern forces had several thousand cavalry, plus three to five regiments of infantry, and waited until a force of all arms could be

General Robert E. Lee, left, out-fought and out-maneuvered the Union forces until sheer weight of numbers overpowered him. His nephew, "Fitz" Lee, commanded the 1st Va. Cav. under Stuart and later rose to the rank of Major General, CSA.

gathered before starting any pursuit. The speed of this pursuit was then that of their infantry, as General Cooke did not dare risk a cavalry clash without his infantry support.

At this point, it was just as far to go back as it was forward and with local soldier guides, Stuart's column pushed on, Rooney Lee's 9th Va. in the lead.

At Garlic's Landing, on the Pamunkey River about 15 miles from Old Church, two laden schooners, along with a pack of wagons and supply train for two New York regiments, were destroyed.

Tunstall, a few miles farther, was their next stop. This village was on the station of the York River Railroad. There they found a loaded wagon train, sutlers' stores, and provision dumps. After a suitable looting, all were set afire.

Here, the young Lee was only five miles from White House Landing on the Potomac, the youthful home of his mother, then being used as McClellan's main supply base. The column rested for some three and a half hours at Talleysville, having covered some 35 miles.

Awakened at midnight they proceeded to the Chickahomny River which had to be forded, as the Confederates felt sure the "Long Bridge" would be under guard. Lieutenant Christian, one of the raiders, lived at "Sycamore Springs" below Long Bridge and knew of a ford at that point.

After reaching the supposed ford, they found it unusable, due to high water. The commander then went downstream to the Forge Bridge, but only the abutments were still standing. Boards and timber were salvaged from a nearby barn and with these, the men constructed a foot bridge across the river; the bridles of the horses being held as the troopers walked across. Fitz Lee was the last man over.

To prevent or delay pursuit, the bridge was ordered

The Morse breechloading carbine, top, was manufactured at Greenville, South Carolina, and sported a brass receiver and forestock. The Le Mat revolving carbine was imported from France and England. Like the Le Mat revolver, it had a shotgun barrel underneath the rifle barrel. (*Photo Courtesy Edward Simmons*)

to be burned, but there was no pursuit south of the Chickahomny. However, the enemy were so close that they found the embers of the bridge still smoldering when they reached it. Richmond was still 35 miles away, and it was late afternoon as they continued to Charles City Courthouse.

Reaching the Court House, Jeb and his staff were lodged at the home of Judge Christian, while his men continued to the home of a neighbor. After 36 hours in the saddle, both men and horses were in sore need of a bivouac. Stuart, with his guide, Frayser, left his troops at sunset, leaving orders with Fitz Lee to move out and follow by 11 p.m. Thirty miles later Stuart arrived at General R. E. Lee's Headquarters. Frayser was sent to notify Governor Letcher.

Stuart then rode back five miles to meet his troops, and to head their parade home. All Richmond turned out, and nothing seemed too good for these men who had tweaked the nose of the mighty General George McClellan. Accompanying were 165 prisoners and 250 horses, mules, and cattle. Only four men were listed as "missing," and the only death was that of the gallant Captain Latane.

A complimentary order from General Stuart was read to his troopers and a printed copy was given each man who participated in the affair. Some were singled out by name in the order. Stuart was presented with a sabre suitably inscribed by Governor Letcher.

The encirclement of the Union Army, which caused McClellan to move his base of supplies to Harrison Landing on the James River from White House Landing on the Pamunkey River, was a bitter pill for the Yankee commander. But that it was done by a mere 1,200 men, who lost only one killed and four missing, was the worst part of all! Naturally it was hailed with joy throughout the South. It was victory! The psychological value was incalculable, and of course it had the direct opposite effect in the North.

In addition to the prisoners, arms and livestock, a great deal of physical damage was done by the raiders. Confederate press and officials were ecstatic towards all concerned with the raid. Best, it renewed the pride of the people in the South's ability to fight and win. Such was the stuff that made the legend of J. E. B. Stuart and his rag-tag, seemingly invincible Confederate cavalry. Without a doubt, his death hastened the end for the South.

BRIG. GEN'L. JOHN HUNT MORGAN

John Hunt Morgan was born at Huntsville, Alabama, June 1, 1832. He is usually associated with the state of Kentucky, having moved to Lexington at the age of four. He was eldest of six brothers, and all but one (too young) served in the service of the Confederate States. At the time of the Mexican War, he raised a company of which he was made captain, but the war ended before he entered into active service.

Far sighted he was, and in 1857 was captain of the Lexington Rifles, which he had raised. April 4, 1862, he was promoted to the colonelcy of the 4th Kentucky Cavalry. This was the beginning of a spectacular military career which centered upon his ability as a raider.

One of his first raids began from Knoxville, Tennessee, into Kentucky, which had been taken over by the Federals, with about 1,000 men. He returned with more men than he had originally, by obtaining recruits, and lost in killed, missing, or wounded less than 100. During the course of this raid, he captured 17 towns, destroying, government property, arms etc., to the tune of over $8,000,000.

One reason for this success, and others that followed, was a portable electric battery and telegraph key. With these devices, along with a top-notch telegrapher, messages could be sent or received by hooking up to any telegraph wire. Thus, he could intercept the orders from the opposing forces before him, then cut the wire behind, so the intended receiver's wire was dead. The next thing was to wire ahead giving all kinds of information that was false and misleading, confusing his opponents beyond measure. The name of this genius on the telegraph was George A. "Lightning" Ellsworth. Morgan's next raid was to gain national and possibly even foreign recognition, a feat that had never been done before in civilized times, and never equaled again until World War II.

By this time he had exchanged his three stars of a colonel on each collar for his brigadier general's three stars encircled with a gold wreath. He also added another strand of gold braid on both sleeves.

Early the morning of July 2, 1863, Morgan crossed the Cumberland River, north of Burkesville, Kentucky, which lies close to the northern boundary of East Tennessee, and headed due north. He commanded two brigades, numbering 2,400 officers and men. The 1st Brigade was composed of four Kentucky regiments and one regiment from Tennessee, under his brother-in-law Colonel Basil Duke. The 2nd Brigade, commanded by Colonel Adam Johnson, consisted of four Kentucky regiments, and another regiment commanded by Morgan's brother, Colonel Richard C. Morgan. All these regiments were of cavalry, with tried and hardened veterans, horsed mainly with blooded stock. Along with the above was a section of artillery, under the command of Captain Edward Byrnes, and consisted of two Parrotts and two howitzers.

The command took off on a northerly course at a rapid pace. They encountered and defeated Wolford's Kentucky Union horsemen, taking, and paroling, some 500 prisoners. Many fine horses were also taken and kept to replace those that became jaded or injured.

Reaching the broad Ohio River at Brandenburg, which theoretically separates North and South, they crossed with the aid of two sizeable river boats. These had been seized by the advance guard. The passengers were permitted to go ashore. After some half of the troops had been ferried over, they were attacked by a large body of men on the Indiana shore. At this inopportune time, two small tin-clad Yankee gunboats saw fit to appear, and opened fire. It was then that the full value of including artillery with cavalry proved its full worth. Captain Byrnes' guns drove off the gunboats. Thereupon the balance of the troops were enabled to reach the Indiana shore, and the opposing force melted away quickly.

With 4,000 cavalry, Union General Edward H. Hobson was in hot pursuit behind them, separated only by the river, which he was unable to cross. Before them, many thousands of home guards and militia were gathering. Morgan's force continued north. From expe-

Brigadier General John Hunt Morgan was an innovative as well as daring raider, using a portable electric battery and telegraph key to confuse the enemy.

rience, they had learned that home guards and militia were usually poorly trained, poorly armed, and poorly disciplined. They could be annoying and time consuming, but hardly lethal.

In their path lay Corydon, where 1,200 citizens and soldiers attempted to defend the town. Their efforts were to no avail. Morgan's men took only food for the men and horses, and there was no pillaging. However, they were now in the real Yankee land, and shortly thereafter, began doing what the Union troops invading the South had done for two years—burning as he advanced.

Meanwhile, the Governor of Indiana had called on all able men to arm and form companies and hold fast until called out to active duty. He also requested troopers from the state of Illinois, believing the raiders on the way to capture the state capital, Indianapolis. The whole middle northwest states became fearful of the dread raider. They had reason to fear, as the exaggerated and garbled information reaching them led people to believe the invading force counted over 10,000 men at arms! They could not know that many of these false rumors were spread by the portable electric battery, and the genius Ellsworth.

Despite all this fuss and hullabaloo, Morgan continued his course north, turning east at Salem and still heading east until they again reached the Ohio River. The river, since their entry at Bardstown, had a northeast cant. They reached the Ohio at Buffington Island, and West Virginia was just across the river.

There, a disused fort awaited them, apparently abandoned. They attempted to move downstream to Pomeroy some 25 miles due west. Then, suddenly, they came face-to-face with the 8th Indiana, under Colonel Butler, USA and in reserve the 14th Ill. Cav. and

Henshaw's Battery, all under command of General Judah, USA. Both sides had been surprised, but the Confederates recovered faster and attempted to drive through their enemy, disabling a score and capturing twice as many, including Judah's assistant adjutant general and Henshaw's gun. But, drive through the Yankees they did not, and they retired south of the fort.

Then disaster occurred. They were attacked by Hobson's force of 3,000 and that of Judah's 5,000. To add to the Southerners' plight, the gunboat *Moose* appeared, and opened fire with 24 pounder Dahlgrens. The Rebels had already lost the two Parrotts, and the remaining two howitzers had been lost at the start of their most recent encounter. As a result, they could not return the fire of the gunboat. There was no course open except retreat. This they did in good order, mounting their horses in disciplined manner, forming columns of four and closing ranks when necessary. Several times they turned about to face the enemy and even charged, to buy time. Even so, the brave and courageous can stand only so much. The first orderly retreat turned into a rout, and two regiments were surrendered.

Morgan and only 500 of his men fought clear of their opponents and made good their escape for the moment, which lengthened into a week. Morgan's remnant held to a northeast direction up to a small stream, very close to the Ohio River, still in Ohio just short of the Pennsylvania line, and north of Pittsburgh! This was the farthest invasion north that the South had achieved, in addition to passing through hostile Kentucky and Indiana, as well as Ohio. During this lengthy journey, they had passed through 52 towns, nine in Kentucky, 14 in Indiana and 29 in Ohio. They had captured over two times the men they had started with and damaged or destroyed ten million dollars worth of Federal and public property! In addition, it kept many thousands of ac-

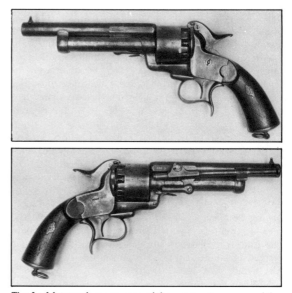

The Le Mat revolver was one of the most unique arms of the Civil War. Its nine-shot cylinder revolved around a .63 caliber shotgun barrel. (*Photo Courtesy Edward Simmons*)

tive troops chasing this elusive rebel when they were clearly needed in the most active theater of war, instead of their own backyards.

July 26, 1863, at Scraggsville Church, three miles south of New Lisbon, Ohio, Morgan surrendered to the overpowering number of opponents. There was disagreement among the Federals, but Brigadier General J. H. Shackleford claimed the victory over Morgan and his men, which at the time, was stated to have 360 prisoners and some 400 arms. His men were sent to prison camps.

Despite the fact that Morgan's activities on his raid were entirely of a military nature, and done in legitimate warfare, the Federals were outraged and refused to regard Morgan as a prisoner of war. Instead, they termed him and his officers as criminals. Morgan and 28 of his officers were sent to the Ohio State Penitentiary at Columbus. Here, they were treated as common felons, their heads being shaved and forced to wear the garb of convicts.

The 27th of November, along with six of his officers, Morgan escaped through solid stone walls. This took 22 days of digging with their only tools—case-knives. After penetrating the six-foot stone wall, they dug underground, hoping to dig beyond the outer wall. Fortunately, this was a cold wet night. The guards were cold and sleepy, and their guard dogs were safely in their kennel. They scaled the wall with a rope attached to a strong metal hook, climbed to the top and jumped down to the ground on the other side, scattering into

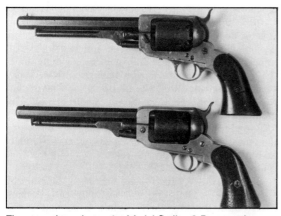

These are the only two 1st Model Spiller & Burr revolvers known in existence today. Frames were brass; barrels of twisted iron bars. (*Photo Courtesy Bruce Kusrow*)

pairs. Morgan was accompanied by Captain Thomas Henry Hines, a daredevil in his own right, and trusted friend of Morgan.

After many adventures Morgan finally made it to safety within the Confederate lines. He then went to Richmond, Capital of the Confederacy, and an ovation greeted him. However, President Davis took a dim view of the hero, believing his activities went far beyond bounds.

Nevertheless, he was given command of the Department of Southwestern Virginia. In Wytheville, Virginia, the plans of Federal General Averill came to nothing, thanks to Morgan. In June 1864, Morgan was forced into battle June 9th against 5,000 enemy with only 1,200 in his own force. The action occurred after having been surprised by General Burbridge at Mt. Sterling, Kentucky, with a divided force. The outcome was quickly settled, and Morgan's men made good their retreat. However, it was far from an orderly one, more like a rout.

Morgan was forced back to southwestern Virginia. Shortly thereafter, he determined to attack the enemy in east Tennessee. On September 3, 1864, he arrived at Greenville, Tennessee, and there chose the home of a Mrs. Williams to spend the night. Someone in the household passed the information of his presence to the Federal troops. Just before daylight on the 4th he sought to journey on, but found the enemy already near. He hid in the garden of the house, and it was there that he was shot through the heart. There were no witnesses, but the enemy claimed he was shot offering resistance to being taken prisoner. The Southerners called it a bushwack. His defiled body, caked with mud, was later taken through to the Confederate lines and buried at Abingdon, Virginia. Later the body was removed to Hollywood Cemetery in Richmond, Virginia, among countless other Confederates. He must have felt completely at home among so many other heroes.

By now attrition was telling heavily on the Confederate forces, with so many of the best and bravest leaders fallen in battle. The Union, on the other hand, had far greater manpower resources, and their generals became increasingly skilled and bold. Time was running out.

EPILOGUE

By the middle of 1864, the South was in a position only to fight defensively, as Longstreet had preached so early in the war. In May of this year, General Franz Sigel, USA, headed south in the Shenandoah Valley with an army of about 7,000 infantry, artillery and cavalry. Opposing him was only a small collection of jaded cavalry to harass and slow down the Northern forces as much as possible.

At this time in mid-May, General Lee was more than just occupied. He was attacked at Spotsylvania Court House by General Grant, who already had gobbled up the Wilderness, attempting to outflank Lee's Army. Lee was struggling to save what little remained of his forces from Grant's overwhelming masses. On the 15th of May, Lee was still fighting fiercely at the Bloody Angle.

At the same time, General John C. Breckinridge of Kentucky was heading north on his way to bring reinforcements to Lee. His force numbered under 3,500, and on this day in May, he clashed with Sigel at New Market, Virginia. The Dutchman, Sigel, who could speak only in broken English, was not only stopped, but was given the strong incentive to about face, and hastened in the other direction.

The Virginia Military Institute had supplied Breckinridge with a battalion of young boys, none of them out of their teens. They were included in the Southern Army. New Market was the first real occasion that these brave school boys had been actually called on to face enemy fire. Under fire, they behaved most gallantly, and in charging the battle-hardened troops of Sigel, their steadfastness was that of veterans. They closed ranks after each casualty, and moved always forward. Wonder of wonders, they caused the Federals to retreat!

Most certainly the South was scraping the bottom of the barrel by sacrificing their best seed corn to the God of War. The very best blood of the South had been educated at VMI. This school had furnished 1,781 former students to the Confederacy. Practically all were officers and left their marks as leaders. The loss of any of these men in particular left a great void in the South that would take generations to replace.

On June 15, 1864, the siege of Petersburg had begun. The gray lines grew thinner day by day. Then came the Battle of the Crater in front of the city on the east. This was an attempt made by the North to blow the entire Confederate line off the face of the earth. Ex-coal miners in their army had dug an enormous mine under the Confederates, packed with high explosives. When detonated, on the 30th, the North seemed more confused than the South. The attempt was beaten off with great loss to the boys in blue.

The stranglehold on that unfortunate place was being tightened, due to the loss of defenders, when Lee finally arrived, with Grant on his coattails. The siege continued until April 2, 1865.

On January 6, 1865, Lee had been pronounced Commander-in-Chief of the whole Confederate Armies. Such a move a year previous might have accomplished a miracle, but it was too late arriving. April 2, Lee evacuated Petersburg, the thin lines having finally been penetrated by the Union.

From this date until the 9th Lee retreated westerly, hoping to join Johnston's Army, 200 miles away. During the whole retreat, he was under constant harassment. He fought fiercely against overwhelming odds, but fate and the Yankee Army finally brought him to his knees at Appomattox, Va. Here, he surrendered his remaining troops—2,781 officers and 25,450 men, all that remained of his once magnificent army. The surrender did not include the cavalry of Fitz Lee, who managed to break free of the enemy in an unsuccessful attempt to reach Joe Johnston. A few others also escaped. For the surrender, Lee donned his best uniform and carried his superb sword. The surrender terms made by Grant were most generous. They permitted officers to retain their side arms, and all troops were paroled, not imprisoned. After Lee explained that unlike the Federal Army, which supplied their cavalry with horses, the Southerners had to buy and pay for their own mounts, Grant graciously acceded that such being the case, the Southerners could retain their horses.

Theoretically, the war ended on this date, but Lieutenant General Joseph E. Johnston still had the remnants of his Army of Tennessee, facing Sherman's horde, but retreating at the same time. This had been going on up through Georgia, South Carolina and North Carolina. On the 26th of April near Durham's Station, N.C., Johnston surrendered to Sherman under the same terms as that of Lee.

The 4th of May, 1865, Major General Richard Taylor, commanding the troops in the far south, (Dept. of Alabama and Mississippi), comprised mostly of the commands of Brigadier General Nathan Bedford Forrest and Major General Dabney H. Maury, surrendered to Union General Edward R. S. Canby.

The troops of Trans-Mississippi, those on the west side of the river under Major General E. Kirby Smith, also surrendered to Canby, May 26, 1865, and the war was virtually over.

However, there was still a command under Brigadier General Joseph O. Shelby which consisted mainly of men from Missouri and Arkansas. This he called his "Missouri Brigade." After the surrender of Smith, which Shelby greatly deplored, he took his brigade and headed southwest, and this without surrender, parole, or by your leave! Kirby left the surrendering troops at Corsicana, Texas, and headed for Mexico City, with some idea of joining forces with Emperor Maximilian. His brigade numbered 500 men, each of whom carried four navy revolvers and a carbine. They reached Eagle Pass, on the American side of the Rio Grande. In passing over the river, they dropped their weighted, but beloved, Battle Flag in the river, accompanied by the mournful notes from the bugler. This was on the morning of July 4, 1865, the last battle flag, lowered by an organized Southern Army. At Monterrey, Mexico, the command separated. Some joined the Liberal Chief of Corona, others went to California or Honduras. Shelby and 50 of his men went to Mexico City and settled in the Cordova Colony of Charlotta.

So, the war was finally over, the inevitable conclusion reached. However, it is still talked and written about, and far from forgotten.

This sergeant of Mounted Infantry is armed with the Spencer repeating rifle—the first successful metallic cartridge repeater, and perhaps the most celebrated arm of the Civil War. *(Photo Courtesy Herb Peck)*

CHAPTER SIX

CHRISTOPHER SPENCER'S "YANKEE LIGHTNING"

By Roy Marcot

THE CIVIL WAR marked an era of profound change for America and for the world. Historians have called the conflict "the first modern war," because it was a turning point in mobile battlefield tactics and the beginning of mass concentrations of coordinated firepower. This war also rang the death knell for the percussion, muzzle-loading rifle and heralded the birth of the modern cartridge firearm. This was a momentous time that marked the advent of the most effective breechloading, repeating rifle the world had ever seen—the Spencer repeating rifle!

When the cannon first fired on Fort Sumter at 4:30 a.m. on April 12th, 1861, the Union Army was ill-equipped to mount any prolonged offensive. Union politicians and generals mistakenly believed that it would take only a few short months and fewer than 250,000 troops to "whip those rebels back into line!" Nothing would prove further from the truth. At that moment, the northern forces had neither trained troops, nor proper firearms, to wage war. The Army Ordnance Department had on hand more than a half-million muzzle-loading longarms. Most, unfortunately, were antiquated smoothbore muskets, scarcely accurate to 100 yards, and almost useless past 300. The arms situation was grim indeed and the first engagements with the Confederates proved this to be true.

As weeks passed into months, each battle made it more evident that this would be a prolonged, difficult and bloody war. As more and more Union troops mustered into service, the demand for quality firearms increased proportionately. There were too few effective rifles in the arsenals to go around. Those fortunate troops that carried their own rifles from home were often better armed than their fellow soldiers who were issued smoothbore muzzle-loaders. The situation deteriorated quickly as the demand increased. Whole units of raw, unseasoned troops quickly became frightened and demoralized.

Out of necessity, the U.S. Ordnance Department turned to private firearms manufacturers and dealers to supply guns for the Federal troops. The Spencer Repeating Rifle Company of Boston was one such company. Their rifle was unknown, untried and unproven, but unlike dozens of other guns, was destined for glory.

The initial Army contract with the Spencer Company was signed on December 26, 1861, for 10,000 repeating rifles costing $40 each. The order called for the delivery of no less than 500 rifles in March, 1862, and 1,000 each subsequent month until the contract expired. These were reasonable terms issued by a government that was desperate for firearms for its soldiers. The Ordnance Department had not realized that the Spencer Company entered into the contract with neither machines nor workmen to build such an arm. Alas, only hand-built, tool-room models of the Spencer repeater were in existence!

Needless to say, the company was unable to meet its commitment to the Ordnance Department in March. Despite the expenditure of more than $135,000, no production repeaters would be ready for many long months. The Spencer Company was close to forfeiting its entire military contract. The workers toiled feverishly through the summer months and into the fall of 1862 as the war dragged on. The Spencer workrooms, located in the Chickering Pianoforte Building on the corner of Tremont and Camden Streets echoed with the sounds from the forging shop, the hissing of a primitive steam engine and the clattering of special machinery. What was to become the most important firearm of the Civil War was finally under production.

In the years following the war, it became traditional for veterans to gather and share their personal recollections of the conflict. Colonel Benjamin W. Crownin-shield of the First Regiment of Massachusetts Cavalry Volunteers was charged with collecting and writing his unit's "glorious" history. Like many hundreds of other regimental histories written in this period, the completed book entails slow, laborious reading. The histories are important, however, not for their literary style, but for the archival record of events that shaped our Nation's history. Most recollections are devoid of excitement, but some, like Crowninshield's, give us a glimpse of history that was all but forgotten.

In late 1862, the 1st Massachusetts Cavalry engaged rebel forces in the rolling farmlands near Smithfield, Maryland. Colonel Crowninshield remembers:

"The most important reconnaissance occurred on October 16th, when a detail of 500 men crossed the Potomac, with a considerable force of infantry and artillery under General Humphreys. The cavalry detail was in command of Major Curtis, who, with 18 men, went ahead to Smithfield. After ascertaining the situation, they retreated. They were followed by a large force of the enemy's cavalry and a pretty skirmish ensued.

Here, the first Spencer rifle, a handmade one, was used effectively in the hands of Sergeant Lombard of Company F. He had formerly been employed at the Smith & Wesson factory at Springfield and was an expert in guns. It became, afterwards, a famous weapon—the first effective repeater."

The gun which was to become the most sought after firearm of the entire war had its first use here, on the hillsides of Maryland. Just who was Sergeant Lombard? And how was it that he came to possess this Spencer repeater, months before any were delivered to the Army?

In the mid-19th Century there were dozens of firearms manufacturers and hundreds of skilled gunsmiths in New England. Some of the best-known companies included the New Haven Arms Company, the Whitney Arms Company, Smith & Wesson and N.P. Ames. It was not unusual for a skilled gunsmith to have worked for several different companies during his lifetime. Christopher M. Spencer, the inventor of the Spencer repeater, had just such an employment history.

While little is known of Francis O. Lombard prior to the war, it is quite probable that he worked with Spencer at one time or another. We know that Spencer was employed briefly by N.P. Ames and later worked at Colt's factory. Could Lombard have worked there too? It is unfortunate that nowhere in his memoirs did Spencer discuss his relationship with Lombard. The record must stand that Sergeant Lombard carried a prototype, hand-built repeater and was the first soldier to use a Spencer rifle in war. It is a bit ironic that Lom-

Those Cavalry units to be armed with Spencers were issued the shortened carbine version for combat on horseback, as depicted by this Union troop in the charge. Mounted Infantry, like Wilder's brigade, were issued the long barrelled rifle; their purpose was to use the horses as transport only and fight afoot.

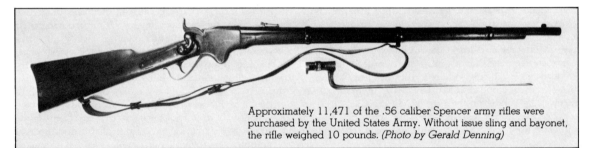

Approximately 11,471 of the .56 caliber Spencer army rifles were purchased by the United States Army. Without issue sling and bayonet, the rifle weighed 10 pounds. *(Photo by Gerald Denning)*

bard's unit, the 1st Massachusetts Cavalry, did not officially receive their Spencer repeaters from the Ordnance Department until November 1864. Evidently the unit was on a very low priority list, as thousands of Spencer rifles and carbines had been delivered to the troops by this time.

The war was not kind to Sergeant Lombard. He had mustered into the service at age 26, as his unit formed at Springfield, Massachusetts, on September 7th, 1861. As a result of continuous battlefield gallantry, Lombard was awarded a field commission as Second Lieutenant on May 30th, 1863. At New Hope Church, Virginia, on November 27th, 1863, while rescuing a badly wounded soldier, Lieutenant Lombard was killed by a single enemy rifle shot. The whereabouts of his prized, handmade Spencer rifle remains a mystery.

The question of where and when the Spencer rifle was first used by a military unit has also been a matter of speculation. Since all of 1862 was spent by the

The seven-shot Spencer was known to the Confederates as "that damn Yankee rifle that you load on Sunday and shoot all week!" *(Photo by Gerald Denning)*

Spencer Repeating Rifle Company in tooling and setup to produce the guns, the initial delivery to the Army did not come until December 31, 1862. The Navy did not receive its Spencer repeaters until even later, on February 3, 1863. Upon receipt, the Army Ordnance Department and the Navy Bureau of Ordnance and Hydrography did not rush the guns to the troops and sailors who so desperately needed them. The rifles, in unopened cases of 10 or 20 each, remained in Federal warehouses for several months.

1,003 Spencer rifles were eventually distributed to ships of the Inland Water Flotilla and were used for ship-to-shore skirmishing and for arming Marine landing parties. It can be surmised that the repeater served its Naval purpose well.

11,471 Spencer Army rifles, delivered during the Civil War, saw much more action than their Naval counterparts. Federal commanders, during the difficult days before Gettysburg, often were compelled to send their men into battle with substandard, inefficient firearms. Colonel John T. Wilder of the Army of the Cumberland had encountered just such a problem in the Spring of 1863. His infantry brigade, composed of the 17th and 72nd Indiana Infantry, and the 92nd, 98th and 123rd Illinois Infantry, changed status to "mounted infantry" in February and March, 1863. Wilder then began a search for the best available breechloading arms for his men.

His first choice was the 16-shot Henry repeating rifle, manufactured by the New Haven Arms Company. The factory was unable to deliver the 900 Henry rifles Wilder requested, so he turned next to the Spencer Repeating Rifle Company for help. Colonel Wilder had met young Christopher M. Spencer during the inventor's promotional tour of the Western battlefields in March 1863. Needless to say, he was impressed with the potential of the revolutionary seven-shot repeater and tendered an order. The 1,400 repeating rifles would be paid for not by the Federal government, but by each soldier, individually! Colonel Wilder secured the $50,000 that was needed by receiving promissory notes from each man, adding his personal endorsement and having the money forwarded to Boston by his own bank in Greenburg, Indiana. This unusual monetary transaction bespeaks the need for quality firearms that existed in those troubled times.

The Spencer Company was in a most fortunate position to fill Wilder's order; the initial Army and Navy contracts were all but complete at this time, so they could begin producing Wilder's rifles at once. The entire order was shipped to Murfreesboro, Tennessee, and received by Wilder on the 15th of May, 1863.

The brigade had less than a month and a half to familiarize itself with this altogether new and revolutionary firearm.

Prior to mounting, Wilder's men were known as the "Hatchet Brigade," this because of their chosen secondary weapon, the military hatchet. After receiving their horses in the spring of 1863, they uniformly rid themselves of the hatchets and thereby accepted a new name, "The Lightning Brigade." As mounted infantry they would be highly mobile, but would fight dismounted. In this way, soldiers would not suffer the same hardships of the "march," as would their infantry counterparts.

Wilder's first mission was to prevent Confederate General Morgan's cavalry from disrupting Federal communications behind the Union lines. As vanguard against the enemy, Wilder's Brigade would lead the

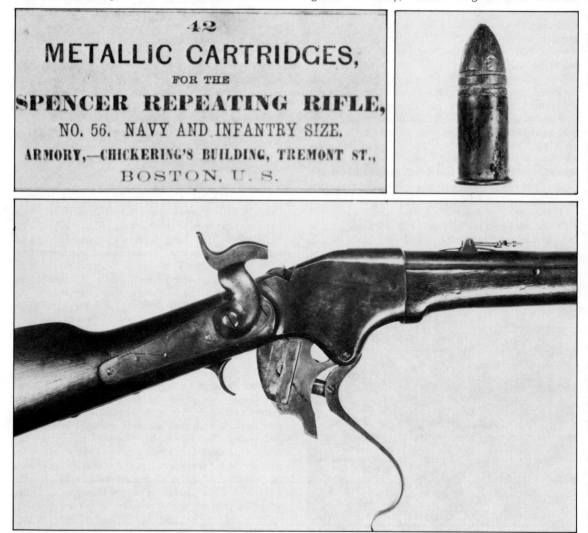

The Spencer held seven .56 caliber rimfire cartridges housed in a tubular magazine in the rifle's buttstock. The triggerguard doubled as a finger-lever; a downward and upward stroke fed a cartridge into the chamber. The external hammer was cocked by hand. *(Photos by Gerald Denning)*

main body of General Thomas' XIV Corps. The men mounted at four a.m. on the overcast morning of June 24, 1863, and proceeded south from Murfreesboro, toward Fairfield. Shortly before daybreak rain began to fall, making the dirt road a quagmire for the infantry that would follow. Indeed, the cannon attached to Wilder's Brigade found the travel both difficult and quite bothersome.

Six hours into the march, the brigade neared the northern entrance to a strategic mountain passage known as Hoover's Gap. The main body of Thomas' troops were hours behind. Unbeknownst to Wilder, the gap was defended by the same Confederate unit that his men engaged 20 days earlier, the First Kentucky Cavalry. In the downpour, the Rebel soldiers were caught completely unaware and fled in panic through the gap southward toward their main body, encamped near Fairfield. Receiving the news of the advance, Confederate General Stuart's Division of Hardee's Corps moved in haste to retake the gap and to end any further Federal movement south.

Meanwhile, Lieutenant Colonel Kirkpatric's 72nd Indiana Mounted Infantry Battalion led Wilder's Brigade through the gap, in hot pursuit of the First Kentucky Cavalry. Their offensive was so deep into enemy territory that part of their unit, Company E, was cut off. The misting rain turned into a downpour.

Realizing the strategic nature of the mountain pass, Wilder dismounted the remainder of his men into de-

Colonel John T. Wilder, commander of the "Lightning" Brigade at Hoover's Gap, proved for all time the efficiency of the repeating rifle. *(National Archives Photo)*

fensive positions at the south edge of Hoover's Gap. He placed the 17th Indiana in the center to guard the Manchester Pike Road; the 98th Illinois to their right and slightly to the rear as a reserve; the 72nd Indiana further to the right, but forward; and the 123rd Illinois along the extreme right flank. Captain Lilly's battery of mountain howitzers and Rodman guns were placed on the right flank, but well forward of the infantry.

On the opposing side, Confederate General Bate brought up the 15th and 37th Tennessee on his right flank; the 58th Alabama and the 37th Georgia Sharpshooters in the center; and deployed the 20th Tennessee on the left.

The battle commenced with a characteristically fierce rebel charge by the 20th Tennessee and the 37th Georgia Infantry. They advanced straight at Captain Lilly's battery, which was exposed, to the front of Wilder's men. By this bold manuever, General Bate hoped to strip the opposing Northern forces of their artillery support; he could not have known that Wilder's men were armed with the most devastating firearm of the war, the Spencer repeating rifle!

The Southerners charged straight into the most murderous small arms fire the world had ever known from so small a unit. The Chicago Evening Journal wrote the following account in its July 16th issue:

> *"Leaving this spur, which terminates one ridge of hills, and crossing a cornfield, Col. Jordan, with the 17th Indiana, took position in the woods crossing the second range of hills, while Col. Funkhouser, with the 98th Illinois, formed some distance to the right, on the same ridge. Soon after, the thunders of the artillery announced the opening of the battle, and the replies of the rebel gunners indicated a readiness to engage. Five regiments of rebel infantry rose from the low ground near the stream, and, cheering like men confident of easy victory, and disposed to inspire terror in their antagonists, came charging across the rolling but open field toward the 17th. The odds were heavily against us, but the boys, armed with the splendid Spencer Rifle, and true to the promptings of brave hearts that never flinched till beaten, coolly waited the auspicious moment.*
> *"The enemy approached within easy range, and received a tearing volley from the 17th, that checked but did not stay them. Supposing our guns exhausted, a cheer followed the report, and they moved on. Again the exhaustless weapons pour in their rain of bullets, and still the enemy press on. The rebels were nearing the line in largely superior force, and the Colonel looked anxiously for assistance. The bayonet might prolong the struggle, but ultimate capture seemed in-*

evitable. Not a man left the line. Comrades were falling rapidly, but threatening disaster only nerved the men to greater exertion, and they still bravely poured in their fire. Just as hope was giving way to despair, successive volleys on the right announced the arrival reinforcements, and the men took courage.

"*Col. Funkhouser, on a double quick, threw his regiment on the enemy's flank, and, with the same murderous Spencer Rifle, was mowing him at every volley, and moving forward, a perfect avalanche of destruction.*

"*The enemy faltered, staggered back, and, as if hurried to a decision by a united fire of the 9th and 17th, turned their backs and fled, leaving a large portion of their dead and wounded on the field.*

"*The importance of this victory is more clearly evinced by the remark of General Rosecrans, when he had seen the position taken. He said, after examining the formidable position, 'Wilder has saved us thousands of men.'*"

The Indianapolis Daily Journal, in describing the same fight, makes this reference to the Spencer Rifle:

"*On Wilder's right the old 17th had opened their 'horizontal shot-tower,' (as the boys call their Spencer Rifles) upon five regiments of rebels under Gen. Bates, who outflanked them and were closing on their rear, charging and yelling like the bottomless pit broke loose. Wilder immediately*

sent the 98th Illinois, Col. Funkhouser, to their relief, who outflanked the rebel left, and then you ought to have heard the rattle. The rebels stood about five minutes, or rather lay that length of time, waiting for our men to stop and load, (our Spencer Rifles shoot seven times without loading, and are reloaded in less time than an ordinary musket) finding they were fast getting their 'rights in the territories,' and that they were emigrating to the realms of the first secessionist faster than the Irish are to America, they concluded that was not just the place for the 'last ditch,' and those who could, left as fast as their legs could carry them."

Believing that they charged against a superior enemy force, General Bate halted the thrust and concentrated his firepower against the 17th Indiana, who were in position along the Manchester Pike Road at the southern entrance to Hoover's Gap. All four Confederate Regiments swung around to pour through what they thought was an unprotected opening in the Union line. The 20th Tennessee Infantry led the attack, right into the 17th Indiana's repeaters.

The 20th Tennessee Infantrymen were, by this time, seasoned troops, with numerous engagements to their credit. Their men realized that the first enemy volley would be the worst. In the 45 seconds that it would take for the enemy to reload their "muzzle-loaders," the attackers could breach their lines and in would pour hundreds of troops. For the first time in history, this was not to be!

At Hoover's Gap, Wilder's brigade used the new Spencer rifle to repulse repeated determined Confederate charges. Union losses were only 47, while the Confederates lost nearly 500.

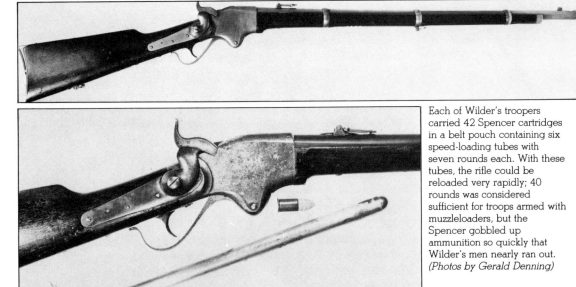

Each of Wilder's troopers carried 42 Spencer cartridges in a belt pouch containing six speed-loading tubes with seven rounds each. With these tubes, the rifle could be reloaded very rapidly; 40 rounds was considered sufficient for troops armed with muzzleloaders, but the Spencer gobbled up ammunition so quickly that Wilder's men nearly ran out. *(Photos by Gerald Denning)*

The 17th Indiana held its fire until the enemy was at the base of the hill and then opened with a devastating volley. The rebels rose to their feet and charged up the hill, fully confident of their ability to breach the hasty fortifications before the opposing side could reload. There was no such quiet. The hail of rifle fire from above did not cease—something was wrong.

Bate pitted his trailing unit, the 37th Georgia, against the 17th Indiana's right flank and they too were unable to take their objective. Ammunition was now in very short supply. Each trooper carried his loaded Spencer (seven rounds) and a leather ammunition pouch with 42 additional rounds. 100 additional rounds were carried in the saddlebags, but the horses were several hundred yards to the rear in a protective holding area. The men of the 17th were out of ammunition.

Colonel Wilder, in correct military fashion, brought up his reserves, the 98th Illinois Infantry, and they charged into the enemy's demoralized lines. The Confederates had never seen such an untiring volume of rifle power before. They had given their all, but now retreated in panic to the safety of the Confederate lines to the south.

Company E of the 72nd Indiana Mounted Infantry took this opportunity to return through the retreating Confederate forces to their own brigade in the gap.

The confidence that the Spencer rifles gave Wilder's men cannot be overstated. News of the fierce engagements now reached the Federal Headquarters, several miles north, on the other side of Hoover's Gap. Orders were sent back to Wilder to consolidate his forces and withdraw from their strategic position. Headquarters knew that Wilder was faced by General Stuart's entire division and thought that no brigade could withstand such a superior enemy force. They were wrong.

Wilder, in an unprecedented move, refused the order to withdraw. Under penalty of arrest, Wilder made ready to repulse yet another frontal attack from the south. The final attack was weak, compared to the earlier assaults that same day. Just as this last engagement was over, Generals Thomas, Rosecrans and Reynolds arrived at the scene to inquire in person why Colonel Wilder would countermand their direct order to withdraw. The reason did not have to come from Wilder's lips. Nearly 500 enemy soldiers lay dead or severely wounded in the fields in front of them, while Wilder suffered 47 dead.

General Rosecrans was ecstatic. This was the victory that the politicians in Washington and the civilians back home had hungered for. Wilder and his devastating seven-shot Spencer rifles had won the day. Rosecrans turned to Reynolds and shouted: "Wilder has done right! Promote him! Promote him!"

This was the initial battlefield trial of the Spencer repeater, which was to become the most sought-after firearm of the entire Civil War. This unique and revolutionary rifle was later to become the primary arm for the U.S. Cavalry. It retained this status until it was finally replaced with the Model 1873 Springfield "Trapdoor" carbine with its improved, centerfire cartridge. The venerable Spencer repeater, however, will always be remembered as the "lightning" in Wilder's Lightning Brigade!

Artist Frederic Remington captures the "feel" of an Indian attack, the kind Billy Dixon may have braved the day he fired his now-famous, mile-long shot that miraculously felled a mounted Indian atop a distant Texas Panhandle mesa.

CHAPTER SEVEN

BILLY DIXON AND THE MILE-LONG SHOT

By Jim Earle

IT HAS BEEN SAID that Billy Dixon fired the shot that opened the Texas Panhandle for settlement by the white man. He fired this shot from his Sharps "Big 50" buffalo rifle, dropping an Indian from his horse from a distance that measured to be almost a mile—more than 1,500 yards. The shot scattered the Indian warriors who had just finished a day-long battle with the buffalo hunters, pinned down in a small trading post known as Adobe Walls. History was made with this long shot and the reputation of the Sharps rifle would thereafter be measured by this feat.

The Battle of Adobe Walls in which Dixon fired his famous mile-long shot is often called the Second Battle of Adobe Walls, because the first battle occurred on November 25, 1864, between almost 3,000 Indians and the California Volunteers commanded by Colonel Kit Carson. That battle would have to be termed as indecisive since the Indians blocked the soldiers' pursuit and the area remained somewhat in control of the Indians for another decade until the arrival of Billy Dixon and a small band of hunters and traders.

Adobe Walls was first established around 1843 by Charles and William Bent as a trading outpost while Texas was still a republic. It was located in what later became Hutchinson County on the Canadian River. The Bents built an adobe structure from which they traded horses and mules with the Indians—Comanches, Kiowas, and Apaches. Because of the adobe structures, the post became known as Adobe Walls. The outpost was abandoned by the Bents shortly after Texas joined the Union in 1845, mostly due to raids by Indians. General John P. Hatch told Billy Dixon that the buildings were only broken walls when Hatch passed through the area in 1848 as a young lieutenant involved in the Mexican War. Dixon also claimed that area folklore included an even earlier settlement and buried treasure.

By the 1870's the great herds of buffalo in the plains states of Nebraska, Kansas, and Oklahoma were being decimated. The wholesale slaughter of the buffalo was due to enterprising hunters who earned a few cents for the buffalo hides they harvested. Meanwhile, many of the Indian tribes had been confined to reservations in Oklahoma, removed from the buffalo herds that had been such an important factor in their past lives. The expert marksmanship of the hunter and the efficiency of his Sharps rifle were bringing to an end the buffalo herds that were so important to the Indians.

In the early days of the buffalo slaughter, a popular hunting technique was to gallop a well-trained horse alongside the herd and shoot buffalo from the saddle. This dangerous tactic was considered great sport by cavalrymen and civilian hunters, but probably did little towards reducing the great herds—estimated at around 60 million as late as 1860. Shortly after the Civil War, though, the market for buffalo hides increased tremendously. With this increased demand came a different kind of buffalo hunter.

The serious hide hunter learned to spot a herd, then approach to long shooting range. By shooting slowly and methodically and making sure to drop each bison with a well-placed bullet, he could continue to shoot from one "stand" while the animals milled. Eventually, a wounded animal would panic the herd and they'd stampede off, leaving their dead behind for the skinners. Before the stampede, though, a stand would often yield more than a hundred hides.

In 1871 a new process for tanning dried hides was discovered, greatly increasing the popularity and marketability of buffalo robes. Prices increased to around

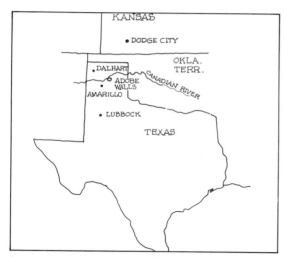

Located high in the windswept Panhandle, Adobe Walls
was established in 1843 when Texas still was a Republic.

Billy Dixon (right, seated) poses with friends after Battle of
Adobe Walls in 1874. He later won the Medal of Honor
while a scout for General Miles.

$3.50 per hide, and thousands of buffalo hunters and would-be hunters were lured to the plains. In 1870 it was thought that the Kansas and Nebraska herds were limitless; by 1873 they were nearly gone, but there were still vast herds to the south, across the Arkansas River.

The veteran buffalo hunters were a hardy breed, skilled in the ways of the plains and especially skilled in the use of their buffalo guns. The real heyday of the buffalo hunter lasted less than 15 years, from the first big Kansas season in the early 1870's to the destruction of the Montana herd in 1884. Even so, buffalo hunting was big business for that brief period, with an estimated 10,000 to 20,000 hunters in the field at one time.

In the beginning muzzle-loading rifles were used with good effect, and, with the advent of cartridge arms and the availability of military rifles, Springfield trapdoor rifles in .50-70 caliber were popular. However, the increasing numbers of buffalo hunters demanded the best rifles they could buy, and the specialized rifle known as the "buffalo gun" came into being. Such a rifle was long-barreled and heavy, often weighing 15 pounds or more. The weight aided steady shooting, and the heavy barrel enabled long shooting sessions without overheating. The buffalo hunter demanded the utmost in accuracy and power to cleanly drop a big bull bison at several hundred yards.

Remingtons, Winchesters, Spencers, and numerous other rifles saw use on the plains, but the gun that is known to this day as *the* buffalo gun was the single-shot Sharps rifle. As a breechloading rifle or carbine using conical bullets and paper or linen cartridges, the Sharps had gained fame during the Civil War and was the choice of the elite Berdan's Sharpshooters. The basic design, with a falling breechblock operated by a triggerguard/finger lever and a massive external hammer, was easily modified to self-contained brass cartridges. In the early 1870's the Sharps Rifle Company offered a number of strong, well-made cartridge rifles, some designed specifically for the buffalo trade. Calibers included .45-70, .45-100, .50-70, and .50-90. The former set of digits is the caliber designation, in hundredths of an inch; the second figure is the powder charge in grains. The hunters gradually demanded more and more power as the herds became more difficult to approach, and towards the end the massive .45-120 and .50-140 cartridges saw some use. But the legendary "Big Fifty" Sharps was the .50-90 cartridge, using a 2½-inch case, 90 grains of black powder, and hand-molded bullets weighing up to 550 grains.

Though the slaughter of the American bison is a black chapter in American history, the deadly skill of the buffalo hunter with his Sharps rifle is still the stuff legends are made of. Buffalo hunter Wright Mooar used a .50-90 Sharps to tally some 20,500 bison during his career. Frank Collinson used a 15-pound .45-120

Sharps to take 121 buffalo from a single stand! Working in pairs, one man shooting while the other let his rifle barrel cool, it's small wonder that the Kansas herds soon disappeared. Billy Dixon himself, using his favorite .50-90 Sharps, once shot 120 animals without moving his shooting sticks. Incredible though it seemed, the Kansas herds were gone by the winter of 1873, and the hide hunters had to either quit or move south.

Billy Dixon, already a seasoned hunter at 24, left Dodge City, Kansas, to scout for more buffalo in the Panhandle of Texas during the early months of 1874. He found what he was looking for: signs of great herds that could be hunted easily in the coming spring and summer. When he returned to Dodge City in March, his news was enthusiastically received by several merchants and hunters who immediately began making plans for a profitable hunt in Texas. Merchants A. C. Myers and Fred Leonard were eager to go and establish a store and supply center. James Hanrahan planned to go as a hunter and as a saloon keeper on the side. Charles Rath would join the others and open a store and trading post to supply the hunters and buy their hides.

By the end of March, 1874, Billy Dixon led about 50 men and 30 wagons into the valley of the Canadian River to build their outpost which would forever be remembered as Adobe Walls. They were in Indian Territory, but the territory had not been given exclusively to the Indians. The hunters were within their rights to be there, but so were the Indians.

The hunters and merchants built a compound that covered an area of approximately 200 by 700 feet in which several buildings were erected. These buildings were probably all made of sod with walls that were approximately two feet thick. The Myers and Leonard store was about 20 feet by 60 feet in size; the same size as Rath's store. Thomas O'Keefe built a blacksmith shop that was 15 feet square. The post took shape rapidly and was ready for business by June of 1874. Word had spread to Dodge City that the buffalo were plentiful around Adobe Walls, and the hunters began to move across the plains toward the new post.

The first buffalo of the season were spotted in early June by Billy Dixon and his party of hunters who had camped for several days a few miles from Adobe Walls. The buffalo harvest began in earnest, but it would not last long. There would be trouble.

The winter had been hard for the Plains Indians—the Comanches, Kiowas, Cheyennes and Arapahoes. They had spent it on reservations in Oklahoma and had suffered from illness and poor living conditions; they longed for freedom and for the chance to ride among their buffalo herds where food was plentiful and life was better. But it seemed only remotely possible to the dispirited Indians who had seen several of their tribes-

Two monuments—one honoring Comanche and Cheyenne chiefs and the other honoring the 29 white defenders—are now located at the site of the June 27, 1874, battle.

Indians, angered by the white man's presence in buffalo hunting grounds, turned their wrath on Adobe Walls, losing a battle that virtually ended major confrontations in Texas. The Indians were led by Quanah Parker.

men killed in uprising by the well-armed white soldiers.

Isa-tai, a Comanche medicine man, had contributed to the unrest of the Indians by convincing them that he was an invincible prophet who could provide them with protection from the Great Spirit in battle with the white man. His war paint would repel bullets and his good medicine would bring victory to the Indians. Gradually, he gained a following among the Indians who were becoming more hostile toward the whites.

Quanah Parker was the chief of Comanches. He was the son of Chief Nocona and Cynthia Ann Parker, a white woman who had been captured by the Indians as a young girl. Isa-tai goaded the Comanches into a warlike mood, convincing them that they should attack the Tonkawa Indians in revenge for their aid to the Texas Rangers, soldiers, and other whites around Fort Griffin, Texas. The Army learned of their intentions in advance and promptly called the Tonkawas into the confines of Fort Griffin for protection, foiling the raid. With increasing frustration and hostility, the Indians diverted their attention to the buffalo hunters of Adobe Walls who were in the hunting grounds of the Indians. They would attack Adobe Walls.

Billy Dixon and the hunters had been killing buffalo as long as daylight permitted. They were warned by passing hunters that many tribes of Indians were in the area and were moving toward Adobe Walls. The hunters broke camp and headed across the Canadian River toward the post. The river was out of its banks due to

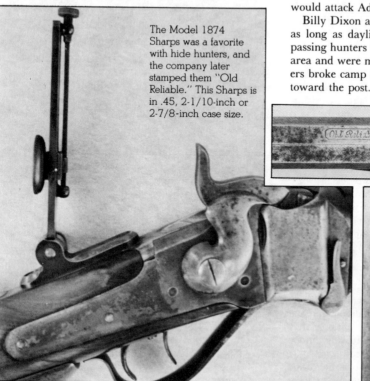

The Model 1874 Sharps was a favorite with hide hunters, and the company later stamped them "Old Reliable." This Sharps is in .45, 2-1/10-inch or 2-7/8-inch case size.

Dwindling buffalo herds and hunting grounds, shared reluctantly by Texans and Indians, served as the fuse that set off the Battle of Adobe Walls. A medicine man had promised immunity to bullets, a myth Dixon dispelled.

recent rains, and its current carried away one of the wagons along with Dixon's favorite Sharps "Big 50" buffalo rifle.

Within hours a messenger from Dodge City arrived at Adobe Walls to confirm that the Indians may attack the outpost within a few days. Feelings were mixed among those who received the warning: some disbelieved that there was pending danger, others joked about it, and several left for Dodge City and safety.

On June 26, 1874, Ike and Shorty Shadler were making their way to Adobe Walls in a wagon pulled by 28 oxen to pick up a load of hides that would be taken to Dodge City. Closely behind was Billy Tyler and a party of about five or six hunters. Several of the fleeing merchants warned them of the possibility of trouble with the Indians, but they continued onward and arrived at the Walls on the evening of June 26th. The Shadlers unhitched their oxen and bedded down in their wagon for the night.

Out of sight of the hunters, the Indians had arrived a few miles from Adobe Walls on the night of June 26th and were preparing for a raid at dawn which they hoped would be a massacre. They planned to attack the white men at daybreak and catch them by surprise. The combined force of Comanches, Cheyennes and a few Kiowas may have numbered in excess of 700, as they waited for the passage of darkness.

Unaware of the horde of battle-hungry Indians only a short distance away, the 28 men and one woman, the wife of one of the men, had gone to sleep. Luckily for them, one did not sleep that night. He was James Hanrahan, hunter and owner of the post saloon.

Perhaps by intuition, or maybe by fate, Hanrahan was compelled to awaken the occupants of the compound at about 3 a.m. by firing his pistol. The half-dressed hunters sprang to their feet to learn what the trouble was. Hanrahan yelled to them that the ridgepole had cracked and had made a sound like a shot, and urged them to evacuate the building until it could be checked. This was a believable tale to the sleepy hunters since the roof was covered with a thick layer of sod to shed the rain. The massive weight of a sod roof could easily overload the support timbers of a roof as the green timbers began to season and crack. A cracking timber could make a sound like a gunshot. Later, Hanrahan said that he purposely awakened his companions because he instinctively felt that they should be awake.

Once awakened, and having found no damage to the ridgepole, Hanrahan offered drinks to the hunters at his bar and suggested that they remain awake to get an early start for the next day. The whiskey enticed them into agreeing to this proposition.

At daybreak, Billy Dixon was walking about his wagon, loaded the night before, when he noticed the presence of Indians in the distance. In seconds they were riding at top speed directly toward the post. Stunned by the sight of hundreds of swarming Indians coming at him, Dixon found himself slow in reacting. Soon he was firing at the Indians as he felt the pounding hooves vibrating the ground on which he stood. Grasping a borrowed .44 caliber Sharps rifle, he fled for the safety of Hanrahan's saloon and its two-foot-thick walls of sod. He and 12 other hunters were now entrapped in a life-and-death situation from which there was no escape.

While Dixon was sprinting for safety, the Shadler brothers, sleeping in their wagon, were too slow in reacting to the peril that surrounded them. The stampeding Indians killed and scalped them minutes later. The wide-awake and half-dressed hunters were separated and divided among three buildings, each of which was about 100 feet apart. They frantically piled sacks of feed and furniture against the doors and windows as barricades while the encircling Indians moved closer and closer into the buildings' perimeters.

Having no humans as targets, the Indians were shooting horses and oxen. Once securely barricaded, the hunters were returning fire. It soon became apparent to the Indians that the war paint of Isa-tai could not pro-

Excavations in 1978 revealed foundation of what might have been Rath's store. On the horizon is bluff where the Indian was sitting atop his horse when Dixon spanned the distance with his borrowed gun, long-range marksmanship.

vide them with immunity to the bullets from the white man. Many were dying. The Indians changed their strategy and began a series of withdrawals followed by successive attacks. With each retreat, the Indians carried away as many of their dead as possible, making it impossible to estimate the number who were killed in the battle.

Each retreat and attack was preceded by a U.S. Cavalry bugle call. This aided the hunters by alerting them as to what to anticipate, since many of the hunters were familiar with bugle calls. It was learned that the bugler was a deserter from the 10th Cavalry stationed at Fort Sill in Oklahoma Territory who had joined the Indians. The bugler was killed later in the morning by a shot from a Sharps buffalo rifle fired by Harry Armitage while the bugler was in the process of looting one of the wagons outside the compound.

At midmorning the Indians withdrew from the field, leaving behind enough Indians to keep the hunters confined to their barricades. Quanah Parker had been wounded in the back early in the battle leaving him unable to continue the fight.

While the Indians discussed their next tactics, Dixon borrowed Hanrahan's Sharps "Big 50" buffalo rifle and was methodically picking off the Indians who remained outside of their buildings. The big rifle had

Shells, arrowheads, and horseshoes are among items found during excavation. Artifacts are on display at the Panhandle-Plains Museum, Canyon, Texas.

such power that Dixon could shoot Indians through piles of buffalo hides. By noon, the ammunition in the saloon was running low. Dixon and Hanrahan dashed from the saloon in a hail of bullets and scrambled into Rath's store unhurt and safe. Dixon was asked to stay to bolster the smaller-sized party defending Rath's store, and Hanrahan scampered back to the saloon with a supply of ammunition.

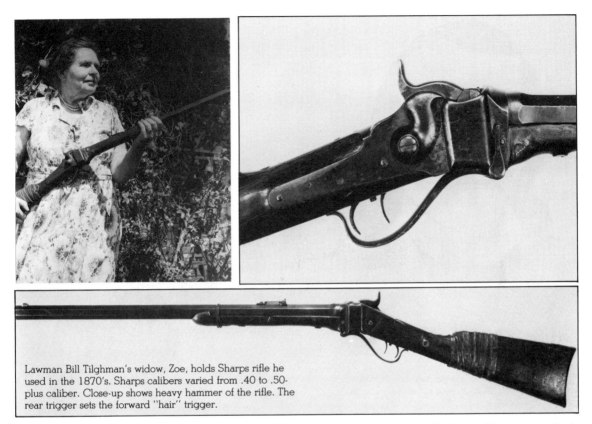

Lawman Bill Tilghman's widow, Zoe, holds Sharps rifle he used in the 1870's. Sharps calibers varied from .40 to .50-plus caliber. Close-up shows heavy hammer of the rifle. The rear trigger sets the forward "hair" trigger.

Billy Tyler and Fred Leonard had become concerned about the wounded stock and left the safety of the saloon to take positions in the corral to protect their few remaining animals. Tyler was shot through the chest before he could get behind a protective wall, and he was helped back to the saloon by Leonard. As Tyler lay dying, he was attended by his close friend, 19-year-old William Barclay Masterson, who would become famous as Bat Masterson in the years ahead. Leonard had been unhurt. So far, the battle had taken the lives of only three men, the Shadlers and Tyler, a remarkable record considering that the odds against the white men had been thirty to one.

At about two o'clock, all of the Indians withdrew, giving the white men a chance to regroup and inventory their damages. The Indians were disappointed with their lack of success. They had failed to catch the settlers by surprise as they had planned. Also, their medicine had not been strong enough to protect them from the fire of the hunters and had suffered many casualties. Adding to their discouragement was the effect of a stray bullet from a buffalo rifle at the Walls. The bullet struck and killed Isa-tai's horse which brought discredit to him as an all-knowing prophet.

By four o'clock, the Indians withdrew completely from the area, and the hunters began the grisly job of checking the aftermath of the Battle of Adobe Walls. Thirteen dead Indians had been left behind. The area was cluttered with the bodies of 56 horses and 28 oxen that had pulled the Shadler wagon to the post the night before.

A number of Indians remained in the vicinity of Adobe Walls for the next two days, but there would be no more attacks. Understandably, the white men remained alert and observant of all motions on the distant horizon.

Billy Tyler and the Shadler brothers were buried in a common grave near the adobe corral.

By the next day about 75 hunters had ridden into Adobe Walls, unaware that there had been a battle until the bodies of the dead animals became visible. One of the hunters was sent to Dodge City to bring help and fresh horses, since hardly any had survived.

The second day was spent burying and disposing of the dead animals that were creating a stench of death about the small outpost. Some were buried and others were dragged a distance away from the buildings to decay in the sun.

Billy Dixon, who became a legend at Adobe Walls, was reburied there in 1929 with full military honors. He died in 1913 at age 63.

Quanah Parker, son of Chief Nocona and a white woman, Cynthia Ann Parker, later met Dixon and shook his hand, praising his shooting ability.

The most important shot of the battle was fired by Billy Dixon on the third day, June 29, 1874, with the "Big 50." A group of about two dozen Indians had appeared on a high bluff overlooking the valley of Adobe Walls. This may have been a scouting party planning another attack.

Billy Dixon borrowed Hanrahan's Sharps rifle, aimed at the Indians a mile away, and fired. Seconds later, one of the Indians tumbled from his horse wounded. The Indians turned in their tracks and fled, carrying the wounded warrior with them.

Later the shot was measured and was found to have covered a distance of seven-eighths of a mile. It has been discussed since as the greatest shot ever made with a Sharps rifle. Although Billy Dixon considered himself a good marksman, he never felt justified in taking credit for the shot since he considered it a freak that could never be repeated. But this was the making of a legend, an impossible achievement against all odds at a time when it counted the most.

This shot ended the battle for good. The Indians had had enough war with the determined hunters, and the Sharps rifle had proven to be their master.

William Olds accidentally became the fourth casualty on July 1, 1874. While he was sitting watch on the roof of Rath's store, he spotted a party of two or three dozen Indians passing through the valley in the distance. Although the Indians appeared to be peaceable, Olds took no chances and alerted the hunters, and scrambled down the ladder from the roof to the ground below. In the process, he accidentally discharged his rifle which fatally shot him in the head. His wife, the only woman at the post, was at hand when the accident occurred. Olds was buried nearby.

What some have jokingly called the third Battle of Adobe Walls was fought over Olds' Sharps rifle that had killed him. Bat Masterson had borrowed the rifle, but Mrs. Olds was anxious to have it returned and she asked Frank Brown to retrieve it for her. Brown had words with Hanrahan about the rifle and several blows were struck by each as tempers became heated. Masterson returned the rifle to Mrs. Olds the following day and soon afterwards left for Dodge City.

Billy Dixon always had high praise for the courage of Bat Masterson during the battle. His marksmanship was surpassed only by his coolness under fire. Within

Bat Masterson was still a teenager at Adobe Walls, but went on to fame as the 21-year-old Dodge City sheriff and, later, a New York sportswriter.

three years, Masterson would be elected as the 21-year-old sheriff of Ford County, Kansas, of which Dodge City was county seat. His career would take him to Ari-zona, Colorado, and New York where he would spend most of his working life as a sportswriter with a daily column that was read by thousands of fans on a daily basis. He would also be involved with prizefighters as a manager, referee, promoter and commentator.

Within months, the small post of Adobe Walls was abandoned by the hunters and merchants, and days later it was burned to the ground by Indians. Most of the hunters returned to other pursuits and very few of them ever hunted buffalo again.

For a short while, Billy Dixon and Bat Masterson served as scouts for the Sixth Cavalry under the command of Colonel Nelson A. Miles, the noted Indian fighter. Years later, Billy Dixon met Quanah Parker and discussed the battle of Adobe Walls with him. When Dixon told Parker that he had defended the outpost against Quanah's men, Parker extended his hand to shake Dixon's in admiration of the courage shown by 28 men against 700 Indians.

Billy Dixon's roots were deep at Adobe Walls. He returned to build his home and raise his family there. He died at the age of 63, in 1913, and was buried at the small cemetery of Texline. In 1929, Billy Dixon was reburied with full military honors at Adobe Walls, the land that he had loved and defended.

Today, the battlefield of Adobe Walls is owned by the Panhandle-Plains Historical Society, but it is surrounded by private property. The history of this spot comes to life as one stands in the gusty wind of the Texas Panhandle and looks beyond the valley toward the high bluff to the east. This is where a legend was born, the legend of the mile-long shot that will always be the yardstick by which a shooter's skill with a rifle will be measured.

Major Frederick Russell Burnham, D.S.O., was photographed in London after his investiture with the Distinguished Service Order by King Edward VII. The black armband was worn in mourning for the recent death of Queen Victoria.

CHAPTER EIGHT

THE MAKING OF A HERO: BURNHAM IN THE TONTO BASIN

By Jack Lott

FREDERICK RUSSELL BURNHAM was not the average Los Angeles boy of 12 in 1873. His mother was widowed that year when her husband and Fred Burnham's father, the Reverend Edwin Otway Burnham, a Kentucky frontiersman, succumbed to the effects of chest injuries received several years previously in Minnesota. He was carrying a log from the ruins of his former log cabin in the woods near Mankato, across an icy patch, when he slipped and the log crushed his chest. He was building a barn from the timber, and due to the puncturing of his lungs by compound rib fractures, he took his family to California in 1870—a two-week trip by the new overland railway through still-visible buffalo herds. Fred's father was a Kentucky rifle-toting parson who could bark a squirrel, swing an axe or dispense the Gospel with equal fervor and efficiency.

Upon his father's death, an uncle in Clinton, Iowa, offered Mrs. Burnham and her two boys, Fred and Howard, a home, but there was no money for the return journey. Mrs. Burnham had been left destitute. Mrs. Porter, a kindly Los Angeles friend, lent Mrs. Burnham $125 for the trip, and Mrs. Burnham and Howard boarded the train, leaving young Fred, who was determined to find a job to provide his mother, brother and himself with some support, and especially to repay Mrs. Porter.

Frederick Russell Burnham was born on an Indian reservation at Tivoli, Minnesota, May 11, 1861. When Sioux Chief Little Crow and his braves attacked Mankato and New Ulm in 1862 during the Civil War, when most of the able-bodied men were in the army, hundreds of elderly folks, women, and children were tortured and slaughtered by the rampaging Sioux. Baby Fred's mother was alone in the cabin when the marauders swept through on their way to Mankato, 20 miles away, where her husband had ridden to procure more lead and powder. Late one afternoon, as she stood in the open door of the cabin brushing her hair, she froze at the flashing glimpse of war paint and war bonnets moving through the forest towards the cabin. Gathering up baby Fred, she realized she could not escape while carrying him, and taking a cue from the deer she hid little Fred in a stack of green corn shocks and escaped out the back, running fast and deceptively to evade the war party. She reached a friendly homestead six miles away in time to see the flames of her cabin above the treetops. Returning next morning with armed neighbors she found baby Fred blinking up at her and gurgling with delight. He had survived as he would always survive on the many frontiers of his great life, by keeping silent when in the presence of the enemy, and by never giving the enemy an opportunity to finish the fight on his terms! Frontier wars were an old story to the Burnham and Russell families whose combined loss of male members in Indian wars and the Civil War amounted to 22 men.

Fred Burnham, alone in Los Angeles and unemployed, tallied up his employable assets. He was strong and wiry, but short, and therefore would not tire out a horse. He was an outstanding rider and knew his way around Los Angeles and its environs. He had a fine native intelligence, cultivated by his father's home teaching, using his fine library of the best books. Western Union needed a mounted messenger—one who could ride hard and dependably throughout a 30-mile circle, from the wire ends in town to neighboring communities. He was then 13, and for the munificent sum of 20 dollars per month, furnishing his own mounts, he was hired. For night deliveries and rides outside the regular run he was paid a bonus. He was often in the saddle from 10 to 15 hours at a stretch. Soon he was able to repay the kindly Mrs. Porter the $125.

It was a violent era of Southern California's post-Civil War period, and it was the heyday of the infamous Mexican *bandido*, Tiburcio Vazquez, whose record of holdups and murders invoked stark fear at the mention of his name. Young Burnham had been trained by his father as a woodsman and an expert hunter, combining the skills of the Kentucky pioneer with Indian techniques. When Fred was eight his father decided he was trained enough to have his own rifle. By the time he was 12 Burnham was an expert with rifle or shotgun. Venison was the main table meat of the Burnham family and there were plenty of deer in the hills and canyons around Los Angeles. At 13, Fred took his brand-new Winchester Model 1873 carbine, caliber .44-40, and headed north across the eastern San Fernando Valley towards Big Tujunga Canyon. He knew all the turnings of the canyon and its dry season pools. After a leisurely ride through the outlying ranchos he entered the great cleft of Tujunga wash, a sandy disarray of driftwood and boulders surrounded by foothills covered with chaparral—good deer country then. Burnham made camp in a side arroyo and around 4 a.m. left on foot for a certain water hole to sit and wait for deer. Luck did not pay him a visit so Fred returned to camp after dawn, and to his great dismay found that his horse had been stolen. In the dust were the boot prints of somebody wearing small-heeled Mexican-style boots. The spoor indicated the theft had just occurred—there was a chance he could overtake him by running up a ridge, then across a shortcut. The tracks made a wide arc and were about five minutes ahead. If he could close the gap to 200 yards he could drop the thief with his Winchester. After a two-mile run he cut the trail again, but meanwhile the thief had brought the horse to a gallop. Beaten and stung by the shame, Burnham abandoned the chase, turning towards a Mexican woodcutter's camp. There he was informed that they had indeed seen his horse—ridden by none other than Tiburcio Vazquez. According to Burnham's book *Scouting On Two Continents* (Doubleday, Doran, 1926), "This did not lessen my indignation, and had the famous Vazquez been five minutes slower, he would have been popped off his mount as quickly as any common horse thief."

Burnham was walking with Arthur Bent along Figueroa Street on the way to a swimming hole not long after the horse theft when a wagon approached, flanked by a dust-covered posse, headed for the Spring Street Jail. The boys looked inside the wagon and saw a bearded Mexican with bloody clothes lying on a pile of straw. The boys had a hunch it was Vazquez—a hunch confirmed by Jailer Clancy. Vazquez had been hiding at Greek George's adobe house on the Rancho La Brea when a jealous woman betrayed his whereabouts to

Burnham, aged 20, was already known as a deadly marksman—in spite of his youthful "tenderfoot" visage.

Sheriff Rowland, whose posse had approached hidden in the cart's straw. When Vazquez tried to escape through a window he was brought down by the posse's rifles. Burnham was permitted to visit Vazquez in the jail where he was recovering and told him he was the owner of the pony he stole that morning in the Tujunga. Vazquez apologized with courtliness and told Burnham that if he had known whose horse it was he would never have taken it, adding with a laugh, "I will give you a better horse. Ride mine now. Some day you will be a great bandit like me—but never trust a woman." It was sweet satisfaction, if not exactly recompense, that the Sheriff allowed Burnham to ride Vazquez's pinto around town. The incident only increased Burnham's determination to even the odds the next time a thief made off with his horse or tried to rob his hard-earned wages.

At 14 Fred had repaid his mother's debt to Mrs. Porter, and when his uncle in Clinton, Iowa, offered to put him up if he came east for his first schoolhouse schooling, Fred realized it was time he had some formal education. Already a self-confident young man with frontier know-how, horsemanship and survival ability forged in Los Angeles' milieu of tough, aggressive men, Burnham was aware of his superior endurance, quick coordination and acute eyesight, hearing and sense of smell. A natural athlete, Burnham didn't drink or smoke, and his search for identity and a share of the fortunes of the southwest's treasure needed only the red

Cowboys of the 1880's were a far cry from the Hollywood image. Though Burnham didn't drink or smoke, he wielded his sixgun in the best Wild West tradition.

schoolhouse and the maturing of a quick mind that knew no fear, but which badly needed fatherly counsel. Accepting his uncle's offer, Burnham soon found himself at Clinton, Iowa, on the banks of the Mississippi amid relatives, including his mother and family friends. He submitted to the confining strictures of that settled puritan community for a year and a half, working hard at his lessons, but the restricted life had become unbearable. Recalling his recent freedom and self-reliance in

Los Angeles, he became impatient for the saddle and the reassuring presence of his Winchester at his side in its scabbard. Dreams of African adventure eased the restlessness, inspired by the accounts of the great explorers, Livingstone, Stanley, Du Chaillu and others. His free and adventurous spirit demanded to be in the wild spaces where only a man's courage and wits—or another's courage and wits—limited progress. Word of a new silver strike in Arizona made headlines in the local newspaper. Arizona with its wild Apaches, range wars and still undiscovered treasures, beckoned Burnham irresistably.

One night he loaded his clothing, gear, saddle, and his precious Winchester into a canoe and headed down the Mississippi. He crossed west to Texas and hired on as a trail driver of a herd of mustangs to Missouri which earned him a small stake. The stake was enough to get him to Santa Fe, New Mexico, but hard times had fallen on that town. Heading his pony west again he entered the badlands lying between Santa Fe and Prescott, Arizona, his objective. Along the trail his horse was stolen, a situation that for many was tantamount to a death sentence in Apache country, for they were on the warpath. Undeterred by the 500-mile foot journey to Prescott, Burnham traveled by night and slept hidden by day, surviving the Apache threat and the snows of the Mogollons. In Prescott he met an old Indian scout named Lee who hired him as a helper in a prospecting venture around Santa Maria. Lee was a scout for Gen-

U.S. Government Apache Scouts posed on a hillside in Arizona during the Geronimo campaign, around 1886. Burnham scouted for General Crook during much of this period, adding to his growing legend as a scout without equal.

eral Crook and just the sort of mentor he would listen to—a master of the plainsman's skills alloyed with an Apache's lethal wiles. Lee taught Burnham many tricks of the trade: Apache scouting techniques; what desert plants were nourishing, and tracking and hunting techniques to combine with Burnham's already formidable woodcraft repertoire.

Determined to find his fortune in the legendary trove of precious metals which nature had reputedly secreted in the Mogollons, Burnham prospected alone in the mountain and desert fastnesses until, once more broke and success proving elusive, he headed his pony downtrail from the snowy Mogollons to the sweet grass and warm air of the Tonto Basin. Though ragged, hungry and dirty, something appealing and wholesome must have shone through his disreputable exterior, motivating the hospitality of a family whose humble homestead he rode up to. Mr. and Mrs. Henry Wells, their daughters and only son, John, owned a cattle herd which had been decimated by an unusually hard winter in the Mogollons, and which was then down to a hundred or so. The son, John, was the sole range hand along with the father, and young Fred was eagerly signed on as a cowboy.

When Burnham had first arrived in Prescott he had purchased a Remington Model 1875 .44-40 revolver, serial number 11. It and his trusty Winchester shared the same 200-grain .44-40 ammo—a sometimes lifesaving advantage. All his spare cash was spent on ammunition, and his spare time on practicing with the sixshooter and carbine. He used five-gallon kerosene tins as targets, placing them in the sagebrush and mesquite to be ridden down and fired at from the saddle. He would place five cans intermittently at either side of a trail down which he would ride, until he could hit each can once while riding at a gallop. Sometimes he would ride past a can semihidden in the sage and turn and fire from the saddle. He did much the same with his Winchester. Tossing blocks of wood or clods in the air he became quite good at aerial shooting with revolver and carbine. Burnham developed a proficiency in firing the revolver or the carbine left-handed. He became skilled in firing just under a cork placed in a puddle, and then hitting the cork as it flew off at an unpredictable angle. All kinds of simulated combat and rapid and running shots were practiced, including having a companion roll a big oil drum or barrel down a hill while Burnham tried to place five shots from his revolver in it before it stopped rolling. Two-handed firing at stationary objects such as chunks of wood, eggs, and cow chips with his revolver built a consistent capability of taking game or an enemy out to 100 yards and more. It was only by shooting two-handed that the six-shooter was accurate enough for shots over 50 yards, and he made sure no deer or enemy was safe even at 200 yards when

Although the Colt was the standard Army sidearm, the Model 1875 Remington—Burnham's choice—was a secondary issue for troops such as these Nez Perce scouts.

These young cowboys of the 1880's may not be as fierce as they look, but at their age Burnham was already a man to be reckoned with.

Burnham in London, 1901, before his expedition to explore and prospect in British East Africa.

he had his Remington in his hands. His two-handed hold was a technique that was to save his life and fill his cooking pot many times.

Burnham was also adept at riding past an enemy while hanging from the saddle by one leg, Indian style, hiding his body behind his pony. The famous war correspondent Richard Harding Davis asked Burnham if he could turn in the saddle while galloping and hit a man at his rear with his revolver. Burnham replied, "Well, maybe not always to hit him, but I can come near enough to make him decide my pony's so much faster than his that it isn't worthwhile to follow me!"

Old man Wells encouraged his new-found range hand, and being an old buffalo hunter with a big double-set triggered Sharps rifle, he provided young Fred with a different kind of training than his snapshooting rapid-fire background qualified him for. The kindly and patient Wells taught Burnham how to judge range and wind—the latter by mirage and grass as it bent under the wind. How to correct for range by observing the dust of a bullet strike and trajectories. He allowed Fred to hunt deer, pronghorn and bear with the big Sharps until he could readily take standing game at 500 yards or more. Wells didn't say so, but there was other than a fatherly interest in Frederick Burnham's workmanship,

and indeed in his being part of Fred Wells' outfit.

The Tonto Basin was bursting into a flaming and merciless feud—a range war that would claim many lives. Wells had borrowed a lot of money in Globe to build back his herd. In time Burnham headed back to Globe to take care of some mining claims, returning periodically to visit the family who vainly were trying to remain neutral in the escalating feud. Unfortunately, Wells' creditors belonged to a faction in the feud, and his "neutrality" evaporated when his backers told him to join their forces in driving off the opposition's cattle or forfeit his stock. Wells refused, and when his creditors demanded immediate repayment of the loan, enforcers attached his cattle. Wells gathered his clan and cattle together and with his son, John, and Burnham riding herd, he began driving his cattle into the mountains, hotly pursued by a pair of deputies. The father covered the back trail with his Sharps, knowing the deputies were capable manhunters. It was slow going to drive the reluctant herd out of the sweet grass of the Tonto Basin and into the inhospitable mountain fastness, creating little difficulty for the deputies in overtaking them. They caught up with the girls and mother, forcing them to halt. This set off the dogs barking, which Burnham and John Wells heard. They rushed back to the girls where they found the deputies, one starting to dismount. As soon as he touched ground the deputy was bitten by a dog causing him to draw and shoot the dog while Fred and John and the two girls also drew. Suddenly the dismounted deputy pitched forward—shot dead, followed by the recognizable delayed "boom" of Wells' big Sharps. The other deputy raised his hands and was disarmed, having been beaten to the draw by Burnham and John. The captured deputy was detained long enough to give the herd a head start, then was released to return to Globe.

Trouble was only beginning for Wells, his family, and for Fred Burnham who was no longer a solid citizen, but a fugitive listed as an unnamed "gunman" and member of an "outlaw" band. Meanwhile, in Globe, a meeting was held to discuss the elimination of Wells, his son, John, and the unnamed cowboy with the icy blue eyes, five-foot-six stature and what was uncommon in Arizona—a Remington Model 1875 six-shooter on his belt. Leaders of the faction accepted a bribe of cattle to mollify the released deputy and assurances that Wells would cooperate with them in opposing their enemies, the other faction. Wells and his herd as well as Burnham had been "reprieved," but at the time it seemed the only option. Private posses for raiding the opposition demanded the services and guns of Wells, his son, John, and Burnham. Killings and counter-killings became a weekly occurrence, and wherever Fred Burnham looked, he faced the grim future of a nameless Basin grave with a rock for a headstone. He visualized his dreams of Africa as escaping through a blue .44 caliber hole between his blue eyes!

It wasn't fear of death that forced a rethink, but the sheer waste of human life in a struggle without honor, without profit—and seemingly without end. Being a hired gun wasn't exactly what he had come to Arizona for. But as was to occur many times in his life, his per-

Artist H.W. Hansen depicted a typical Apache ambush, a ploy that Burnham prepared himself for by unceasing alertness and target practice while on horseback.

sonal ambitions as a prospector or African explorer were not the reasons others sought his services. Others saw a taut-muscled, hard-riding youth with icy blue eyes, whose courage and reputation with firearms was already widespread. Fred Burnham was not slow to realize that such reputations often attract more bullets than dollars. As he put it in *Scouting*, "My best role was that of a tenderfoot from back east—a mere careless, harmless kid." Fred Burnham had many abilities, but he was not an actor in the Booth class and to disguise his capabilities in Arizona of the 1880's, where the last thing the gunslinger's victim sees is the diamond hardness of his slayer's eye, was probably beyond his ability.

It soon became apparent to Fred that he had the worst of two worlds. His faction was losing, and every new rival casualty caused by Burnham's Remington or Winchester created a new feud—a personal one—not winner take all—but winner *take on all!* Conscience, self-interest, and a respect for his family fueled a burning determination to survive and see the rest of the world beyond the Tonto's rim. He must escape the Bloody Basin's seething cauldron and do so quickly.

He decided to head for Globe and look up his friend, the editor of the *Silver Belt*, who received his mail in letters addressed to himself. Meanwhile, Burnham had adopted a variety of aliases for protection and he rode

Apache scouts or tribal police, in warpaint, before a *wickiup* in Arizona of the 1880's. The old warrior with bow and arrow and Henry rifle wears buckskin *teguas* (boots)—often worn by Burnham to avoid pursuers.

Burnham's sidearm in the Tonto Basin, the Geronimo Campaign, Rhodesia, East Africa, and Mexico was this Remington Model 1875, serial no. 11, in .44-40 caliber. Holster and Rhodesian bandolier are original; the .44-40 cartridge box bears the stamp of the Rhodesian government. Pistol grips are hippo ivory.

and walked with the coiled spring readiness of a jaguar, for he was a hunted man at just 19. Dressing in a brown shirt and trousers of an inconspicuous shade, Burnham pulled on a pair of Apache *teguas*—buckskin boots, perfect for running through the Pinals and which left the spoor of the dreaded Apache. Burnham had boots, but they were in his saddle bags—for town wear only. His blankets, ammo and carbine went on his horse with a supply of venison jerky, *pinole,* a Mexican corn flour, and *panocha,* a Mexican confection of corn and sugar for quick energy. Over his Winchester car-

bine he stretched a sheath of deer skin with the hair outside, with holes cut for the sights to protrude. This camouflage was also applied to the stock and it rendered his carbine almost invisible. A hammer and some small nails to attach pieces of raw bull hide were brought, in case his horse lost a shoe, an Apache expedient. Burnham wrapped his horse's hooves in burlap to conceal his tracks and rode into the Pinals to a secret hiding place he had discovered when rounding up cattle. It was a starlit night, and Burnham's departure was silent and left no trackable spoor.

After reaching rocky terrain in the Pinals he dismounted and led his horse to the spot, a shallow cave just below a ridge overlooking the canyon below and with nearby cover for caching his horse. After much slow going over old slides and steep grades, Burnham reached the spot around four a.m., tied his horse in the cedar thicket and made his bed under the shelter of a rock overhang just below the ridge. He threw down his poncho and blankets and enjoyed some jerky washed down with swigs from his canteen and unbuckled his gun belt. From his pocket he produced a roll of unbleached linen thread, unrolled a length long enough to extend around the approaches to his little cave, stringing it on scrub bushes and through small arrangements of stones so that any human or large animal approaching would trip the string and cause some of the stones to clatter as they fell. Small animals could move under the string, but nothing else without setting off the "alarm." Once this was completed, Burnham listened to the Pinals, but even the coyotes were strangely silent that moonless night—not necessarily a bad sign, but one which could indicate humans roving about. He laid awake for a half-hour, then dozed off, awaking at times to remove an offending rock trying to work its way into his anatomy. He was fully clothed and had left his Winchester in its scabbard on his still saddled horse in the cedar thicket. This was in case of an enforced rapid exit. At his side under the blanket by his right hand was his Remington six-shooter, removed from its holster.

Around six a.m. the seemingly innocuous clatter of small stones falling nearby awakened Burnham. No visible change of expression or position occurred—merely an imperceptible opening of eyelids to create a catlike slit and the right hand gripping the Remington and placing its muzzle so as to center any enemy, but keeping it concealed beneath the blanket. The little cave was an ideal hide since it could only be approached from above, and before any intruder could see what was in it he had to first step down and then when directly in front of the opening crouch so as to peer under the ledge. Either some large animal—a cougar or a deer—had tripped the linen string alarm, or, if it were a human, it was more than likely a hostile Apache. Burnham had not left a white man's spoor—hardly any spoor at all—only the Apache spoor of his *teguas,* and that on hard ground. In an instant a spurred boot appeared, followed by its mate, then a hesitation as the intruder must have realized he had to bend down to see what was under the ledge. The next thing Burnham saw was the outsize muzzle of a Colt .45 single-action pointing directly at his head, and the blotting out of the light by a large white man's body and a head of black stubble with a mouth of big teeth which croaked, "Git up and outta there boy, or I'll blow your head off!" Burnham had seen the man before—from afar when

watching a gang of the opposing faction's bushwackers as they scoured the Basin. He had been long in the Pinals without bathing too, as was apparent from his skunk-like scent which the breeze from below blew into Burnham's face. Burnham lost no time in answering the demand—with the blinding flash and roar of his .44 Remington. Then silence, ringing ears and the smell of burning wool.

Burnham was temporarily blinded by the flash and when his vision cleared there was no man blocking the opening—his body had tumbled down the rock slide and, as a cautious peek revealed, was lying motionless on the dusty shale below. The man was probably dead

Lord Roberts, Commander-in-Chief of the British Forces during the Boer War, sent this cable to Burnham requesting his services as Chief of Scouts.

In 1893 Fred Burnham (seated, second from right) was newly arrived in Rhodesia. As a Mounted Scout he still wears Arizona garb and carries a Winchester.

or dying, and now incapable of doing harm, but what about his companion or companions? He surely did not come alone. Burnham came out of the hiding place and cautiously raised his head above the ledge where, from behind a scrub juniper, he saw an Apache with a red headband and carrying a Springfield .45/70 holding the white man's horse and obviously in urgent need of knowing whose shot had been fired. Burnham raised both hands and his Remington to a quick two-handed rest on the ledge and let the Apache see he was covered. The sight was too much for the Indian and with a startled yell he leaped on the horse but was cut down before he could escape. The Indian moved slightly and Burn-

ham lost no time in taking careful aim at the red headband and administering the "coup de grace." He was a "friendly" Indian as the red headband indicated, and he had been tracking for the white man. This explained how he had been located, probably by the trace of *tegua* tracks on the ridge or to or from his horse. Turning the Indian over, after insuring there were no other members of the group, he recognized the still-fierce features of "Coyotero"—a White Mountain Apache brave whose skills as a tracker were unexcelled and in great demand by the Army and manhunters, legal and otherwise! His nickname "Coyotero" meant "he who hunts the coyote," a not inappropriate name for a master

On December 4, 1893, Major Allan Wilson and 33 men were overwhelmed by King Lobengula's Matabele warriors. Burnham was Wilson's personal scout and was sent for reinforcements and Maxim guns, thereby escaping the massacre. The map, right, was drawn for the Court of Inquiry; painting by Allan Stewart.

tracker. Another look down the slide at the white man showed he had not moved, but nonetheless Burnham worked his way down to his body with the gingerly caution of a cat approaching a rattler. Rolling the man over he saw that the 200-grain .44-40 slug had taken the man through the heart. Papers revealed him to be one George Dixon, a well-known rustler and hired killer. The evidence spelled "bounty hunters," but their finding his hide was probably mostly luck—at first good luck, then turned to bad luck. Burnham climbed back up the slide and found Dixon's long-barreled Colt .45 which somehow still remained cocked. He would keep the Peacemaker, but had no place to put the man's Winchester carbine. It would look suspicious if he were spotted with two carbines scabbarded to his saddle. Removing the man's supply of .44-40 ammo from his saddle bags and emptying the carbine, Burnham smashed the stock and bent the barrel over a rock then threw the remains down a deep and precipitous cut in the rocks below. It would not make some Apache happy to find it in such a condition. The Indian's Springfield met the same fate.

Burnham's horse was badly ensnared in its hiding place from a panicked effort to free itself—doubtless when it scented the hated Apache. This then, was the cause of the pair's suspicions being aroused. The horse hated Indian scent as much as it did a bear's, a fact many refuse to believe, but it is well-known that horses and dogs raised by blacks or Indians also react thusly when scenting whites. Burnham concluded the pair had coincidentally reached the spot during a search of the area and the movement and noise of his horse had attracted their attention. The little roll of unbleached linen string was the best and cheapest life insurance he had known and he tenderly rewound every inch on a whittled bobbin. Dixon's horse was urged back down the trail he had come with the help of a bit of cactus tied to his tail. He would leave the bodies where they fell—a spot well off the white man's routes. If found they would be found by Apaches.

If ever Burnham needed a better reason to escape the Bloody Basin he now had it. His only "crime" had been to stand by his friends and to earn honest wages for honest cow punching. All of his activities were defensive, he reasoned, including this latest and closest shave—but he also realized that from the enemy's view his associations and armed defense of their lives had an opposite meaning. Time had proved that neither side was all white and the other black. Both were a dull shade of grey. This was definitely not the "El Dorado" he had come to Arizona to discover. And it would never obtain him the stake he needed to secure the hand of his boyhood sweetheart, Blanche Blick of Clinton, Iowa, on the Mississippi.

If the bodies were found by Apaches they would loot

Period illustration depicts a British South African Police trooper in action against the Matabele, 1896.

anything wanted and leave them without passing the word to the white authorities. On the other hand, if whites found the remains, it would be obvious to them it had been the work of bronco (wild) Apaches. This did not bother Burnham, for he, with considerable justice, felt no guilt. Rather he thanked God for having spared him and for having endowed him with superior physical and mental qualities—and gratitude went also to the old scout Lee, and the not-so-kindly teachings picked up in many—too many—frontier gun fights. To his late father's woodsmanship he owed his start, and from the mostly hostile Indians he had encountered and from bad white men like the late George Dixon, the bounty hunter who failed.

Checking once more for signs of pursuers he led his horse down a canyon towards Globe. Once over the next two ridges he would wait for darkness and descend to the town of Globe to contact his friend, the editor of the *Silver Belt*, with his safe house.

He reached Globe around 10 p.m. and put up with his friend at the editor's house, spending several days in hiding until finding there had been no particular interest in him arising within the period of his departure

A famous painting by Frank Dadd depicts then Captain Burnham escaping from a Matabele impi after Burnham shot their high priest—one of his greatest feats.

In the aftermath of a Matabele raid on a wagon train, a Rhodesian trooper in typical "smasher" slouch hat of the 1890's gives a final salute.

from the Tonto Basin. Dressing up as a newly-arrived tenderfoot from the East he looked like anything but Fred Burnham, the gunfighter, in his new suit and bowler hat. He bumped into a Kansas chum he had met during an Apache raid, and without going into the details explained that because of the Tonto Basin troubles he would be leaving Globe and had changed his name again, this time to "Bill Montgomery." The Kansan had left a cattle outfit when they cheated him of his wages and had recently met a recruiter from Curly Bill's San Simon Valley outfit who offered him a cash market in Tombstone for any cattle with brands from north of Globe and Phoenix. He invited "Montgomery" to throw in with him, saying, "We can work it for six months, then head on back to the home states with a big stake and buy ourselves a couple of good farms." It was tempting to Fred since it offered high pay and excitement. He would be his own boss and could earn as much as he could produce, by keeping the cattle coming in to Curly Bill. He took leave of the Kansan and rode a lonely trail up into the Pinals to meditate about his options. In Burnham's own words, "Now my mind began to clarify. I saw that my sentimental siding with the

young herder's cause was all wrong; that avenging only led to more vengeance and to even greater injustice than that suffered through the often unjustly administered laws of the land. I realized that I was in the wrong and had been for a long time, without knowing it. That was why I had suffered so in the Pinal Mountains."

Burnham was given letters of introduction to responsible parties in Tombstone by his editor friend, where he went and worked in and around the silver camp. The feud was dying down as the dishonest deputies and feuding factions were reined-in by a growing assertion of law and order supported by an outraged citizenry. After a suitable interval Burnham returned to Globe and his friend introduced him to two deputy sheriffs, both named John, who informed him that they were looking for a lad with the capabilities he so amply displayed. Again quoting *Scouting*, "My past was not exploited, neither was it revealed, but I began now to see my life from another angle. Life worth living depended on property, and property on law, and these three factors were necessary to lift men from chaos and savagery. The county taxes were hard to raise, the territory vast; trailing criminals was difficult and expensive. By preliminary scouting, I could do most of their work. My youth was an asset which I gladly cashed in. I worked with such lawmen as Pete Gabriel of Florence, Paul of Tucson and Bucky O'Neil of Prescott (killed in Cuba with Teddy Roosevelt's Rough Riders). Thatcher, the famous Wells Fargo guardian of bullion shipments and treasure, taught me many simple things that everyone is supposed to know but usually doesn't. He sent me to distant points in California, mining camps, ranches and towns, and into all the underworld life. Occasionally I guarded Wells Fargo treasure out of Globe, crouching with a sawed-off shotgun in the rear boot, rather than beside the driver. The bandits shot some good men off the high seat without warning, but they quit the Dripping Springs line after they had been given a salute from the great leather boot at the rear." Burnham became a professional hunter during a drought of the

eighties in Arizona when many cattle had died. He supplied the Tip-Top and Bradshaw mines with venison, using Indians to pack out the deer.

My late friend, Roderick Dean Burnham, then the only surviving child of Major Frederick Russell Burnham, D.S.O. and Blanche Blick Burnham, told me in 1973 that his father had promised long ago to tell him the full story of Remington Model 1875 revolver No. 11, but that many of its secrets died with the Major, especially its part in the Tonto Basin feud, except of course, what I have related. From Major Burnham's writings, it is easy to understand why he didn't want this part of his early life laid out in full at the time of his writing *Scouting On Two Continents* in 1925 while there were veterans of that feud still living. Burnham did not want to open old wounds. His Kansas friend, Curly Bill's recruit, was less lucky. Inside of two years,

Major Burnham's favorite rifle was his Birmingham Small Arms (B.S.A.) .303 Lee Metford, the rifle he used to kill Mlimo, the Matabele high priest. The Lee Metford was one of the first successful bolt actions, offering high velocity and a 10-shot magazine. Burnham modified his Rhodesian bandolier to carry both .303 rifle cartridges and .44-40 cartridges for his Remington revolver. The Matabele shield and stabbing spears are from the 1896 Matabele War.

the only real estate his rustling earned was a lonely two-by-six grave on the range where he was cut down by a cowman's bullet. Burnham's uncanny fieldcraft, horsemanship and marksmanship made him in great demand during the Geronimo campaign of General Crook. Burnham served as a scout under top Government scouts, Fred Sterling, Al Sieber, Archie MacIntosh and Capt. Burbridge.

Burnham discovered some well-paying gold mines, married his sweetheart and settled her and his mother in a bungalow in an orange grove in Pasadena, California, where his first born, Roderick, arrived in 1886. Leaving the property in his mother's hands, Burnham, Blanche and Roderick sailed in 1893 to South Africa, where he outfitted and trekked from Durban to the wilds of Mashonaland—later central Rhodesia. He arrived just in time for the 1893 Matabele War and put

up in Ft. Victoria where he was recruited by Major Allan Wilson as his personal scout. Wilson was the commander of the Victoria Rangers, a mounted infantry unit. Wilson, his second-in-command, Captain Henry Borrow, and 33 men were wiped out December 4, 1893, in a mopani forest on the banks of the Shangani river by an overwhelming army of Matabele *amajaha* (warriors) of King Lobengula's Royal Regiments. Their last stand resulted in the deaths of over 500 warriors. Burnham, his future brother-in-law and fellow scout, Pete Ingram, a Montana cowboy, and Gooding, an Australian trooper, had been sent by Wilson and Borrow for reinforcements and Maxim guns from the main column of Major Patrick Forbes across the Shangani. The river was flooding and Forbes refused, resulting in the last stand and Forbes' retreat through enemy country, guided by Burnham.

Burnham in the Yaqui River Valley, Sonora, Mexico, 1912, with a strange "Mayan" stone he discovered. The hieroglyphics are similar to Mayan findings in Yucatan, representing an important archaeological discovery.

In Africa, Burnham distinguished himself with the finest scouting seen there, and his services were in great demand. When Lord Roberts took command during the second Anglo-Boer War he asked General Carrington, Burnham's commander in the second Matabele War of 1896, who he should appoint as his Chief of Scouts in the Division of Military Intelligence.

Carrington replied, "Fred Burnham. Burnham is the finest scout who ever scouted in Africa." Carrington added, "He was my Chief of Scouts in '96 in Matabeleland and he was the eyes and ears of my force." "Where is he now?", asked Roberts. "I'm told he went to the Yukon in Canada in '97, you know, the big Gold Rush." "Then we must send for him," replied Roberts.

Burnham had left the Yukon for Alaska's Klondike where he had homesteaded in Skagway. Within an hour after receiving a cable sent in Lord Roberts' behalf—which I own—he was aboard the "City of Seattle," on his way via Cape Town, all expenses paid. Burnham was invaluable in producing field intelligence of Boer movements at Pietersburg and Paardeburg. In the Orange Free State he was captured at Sanna's Post as he tried to warn General Broadwood's column they were marching into a Boer ambush by General de Wet's commandos in Korn Spruit. Burnham's efforts to warn them went unnoticed by the British column, but not by the Boers, who captured Burnham. He managed to make a daring escape and evenutally found his way to the British lines.

Later he blew up the railway line between Johannesburg and Pretoria and was ordered to blow up the line of Boer railway from Pretoria to Lourenco Marques in Mozambique. Mounted on his Basuto pony "Stembok," a gift from Roberts, he ran into a Boer ambush. Their fire killed Stembok, who fell on Burnham, crushing his abdominal wall. Coming to after periodic terrible pain and unconsciousness he dragged himself to the rails and blew them up. After the Boers repaired the damage he blew them up again. The Boers fired the grass but couldn't find him or flush him out. He had found a safe green refuge where he camouflaged himself and he was rescued when British forces took the area.

His wounds were grave, requiring several operations after being invalided to England where in 1901 he was invested (awarded) with the Distinguished Service Order D.S.O. by King Edward VII. The King also graciously confirmed Burnham's rank of major, despite his U.S. citizenship, an unprecedented honor. He was soon sent to the Gold Coast by a syndicate to explore for gold and other metals and minerals. In 1902 he was sent to East Africa in charge of a large expedition of the East African Syndicate for a similar search for metals and minerals. In both expeditions he was joined by his brother-in-law and right-hand man, John C. Blick,

Major Frederick Russell Burnham, D.S.O., in a Royal Artillery uniform. He was promoted to the regular rank of major in spite of American citizenship.

who had also distinguished himself as a scout in Rhodesia's 1896 Matabele Rebellion. The expedition employed 20 hand-picked whites and as many as 2,000 natives. Several clashes with wild tribes resulted in near disasters, but from 1902 through 1904 the expedition obtained valuable results for its sponsors. However, no rich deposits of gold or other metals were found. Burnham introduced Indian corn, coffee, and experimented with various breeds of livestock. At his Naivasha headquarters he conducted experiments with zebras to see if they could be domesticated.

Returning to England in 1904, Burnham's youngest son, Bruce, died by drowning in the Thames in a boating accident. Burnham's only daughter, Nada, had died during the privations in the Bulawayo laager in 1896. He returned to Pasadena, California, and soon was off to Sonora, Mexico, to establish an agricultural settlement on the Yaqui River delta. In the revolutionary anarchy following the 1910 overthrow of President Porfirio Diaz, Burnham and his fellow pioneers fought off bandits, Yaquis and revolutionary bands. Returning to California around 1914, he established a cattle ranch in the Sierra Nevada and became a leading conservationist and California Parks Commissioner. He recruited a battalion of frontiersmen for Teddy Roosevelt in 1917, but after President Wilson refused Roosevelt,

Burnham led the search for strategic metals such as manganese, recruiting many of the old prospectors he had known for the war effort. Around 1920, he and his geologist son, Roderick, discovered the great Dominguez oil field near Long Beach. Burnham was Lord Robert Baden-Powell's inspiration for the Boy Scout movement, and it was Burnham who introduced Baden-Powell to American Indian methods of scouting when both were scouts in the Field Intelligence during Rhodesia's 1896 Matabele Rebellion. He remained active in conservation all his life, and he was an ardent supporter of the Boy Scouts and the NRA, for Burnham was a lifelong marksman and had become a long-range match shooter in Rhodesia. He died in his mansion, "The Outspan," in Montecito, Santa Barbara, California, Sept. 1, 1947, aged 86. He lies buried near his old cattle ranch "La Cuesta" at Three Rivers at the foot of the great Sierra Nevada, beside his wife, Blanche; his son, Roderick, and other members of his family, including four brothers-in-law who served as fellow scouts in Rhodesia's 1896 Matabele Rebellion, John C. Blick, Homer Blick, Judd Blick and Pete Ingram, the Montana cowpuncher and Burnham's sidekick of the 1893 and 1896 Matabele Wars.

Seventeen miles north of the Southern California town of San Dimas in the San Gabriel range, stands Mt. Burnham in the Angeles National Forest. It is fitting that one mile east of Mt. Burnham stands Mt. Baden-Powell dedicated to Robert Baden-Powell, Burnham's friend and fellow scout who created the great Boy Scout movement. Burnham himself dedicated Mt. Baden-Powell before an audience of Boy Scouts in May, 1931. The location of both peaks is fitting, for as a boy, Burnham had ridden and climbed the San Gabriels in search of deer to feed his family. What more appropriate tribute could his fellow Americans leave to this great American than to name a mountain for the great scout who by any measure was indeed a mountain of a man?

Young Elfego Baca's calm demeanor showed little of the courage and determination that marked his entire life. This photo, taken after the siege at Frisco which marked him as a hero, shows Baca in typical dress—vested suit and bow tie. He shunned typical western garb and often wore a fedora. (*Courtesy Museum of New Mexico, Santa Fe*)

CHAPTER NINE

ELFEGO BACA: FORGOTTEN FIGHTER FOR LAW AND ORDER

By Lee A. Silva

THOUGH THE FIRST real cowboys were the sombrero-topped, riata-armed California vaqueros of the late 1770's, no western novel, history book, or western movie has ever been complete without portraying the image of the true American cowboy. That image emerged after the Civil War and lasted in reality for less than half a century, but it became the image of the American West itself—a lean, disheveled southwesterner astride his rangy cow pony, slouched beneath a battered Stetson, and with at least one Colt six-shooter strapped in a holster high on his hip or held firmly in his hand spitting out .45's in defense of his life. Those three possessions; his horse, his Stetson, and his Colt, made the difference between life and death to the American cowboy. He might not always have afforded himself the added luxury of a Winchester, but he always had a Colt stuck in his bedroll, belt, or holster.

In simplicity of design, the Colt Single-Action Army, or Model "P" Peacemaker as it was first called, was the most practical and efficient firearm ever made. With only three internal moving parts, it combined nearly 100 percent reliability with the advent of the modern self-contained cartridge, creating a repeating pistol that could be carried easily and which had deadly .45 or .44 caliber killing power. A pistol that could be dragged through rivers, coated with mud, caked with dust, soaked with rain water, or stomped by a 1,000-pound steer, and still it would usually fire its six bullets as fast as a man could thumb the hammer back and squeeze the trigger.

Introduced in 1873, the Colt single-action was an ideal gun that came along at just the right time for a unique era. In the 1850's the violent stampede for gold had filled California and Oregon with thousands of immigrants who had two things in common—shattered dreams and a muzzle-loading cap-and-ball Colt. Because it was well made and because only Colt could produce revolvers before 1857 (the year their patents expired), the cap-and-ball Colt became synonomous with the gold rush, and its efficient mechanism was, in fact, the same mechanism that was later to be incorporated without major change into the Colt Single-Action Army. By the time other companies could begin manufacturing revolvers, the percussion Colt had become a household name.

But the muzzle-loading system often fell prey to the elements of nature. Powder got wet and sometimes didn't fire. The primer caps which contained the fulminite of mercury that created the spark to ignite the charges in the cylinder sometimes fell off the nipples on the rear of the cylinder. And sometimes the holes through the nipples got clogged with dirt or mud, preventing the spark from igniting the charge. Sometimes the ignition of one chamber of the cylinder would ignite other chambers, leaving the user of the gun staring through burned eyelashes at half an exploded gun and some mangled fingers, or, at least, left with only his Bowie knife for protection. Often, poorly molded lead balls fell out of the end of the cylinder when their grease retainers dried up and hardened. And the percussion system was, at best, cumbersome and slow when it came to reloading a gun in the heat of battle.

The invention of the self-contained cartridge changed all that, although there were a few drawbacks to the early versions of the cartridge as it is known today. Some of them had a penchant for getting wet and misfiring, and before the advent of smokeless powder in the mid 1890's, the black powder cartridges had the disconcerting habit of emitting a cloud of gray smoke that obscured the vision of the shooter and also inconveniently marked his location to the enemy. But the early Colt single-actions, which were the first production-line Colts to use the self-contained cartridge (previous conversions and the Model 1872 used leftover parts from the percussion revolvers), were considered to be close-range guns anyway, and, though the screws had a tendency to work loose after a lot of shooting, the Single-Action Army, or Colt Frontier as it was sometimes called, was a welcome improvement over the old cap-and-ball revolvers.

Combined with the popularity of the gun itself, a drastic change in events made the single-action Colt the most common symbol of the West. During the rush for gold, the territories between California and the Mississippi had become nameless memories, barren lands filled with angry Indians, places to get through or to go around and then to forget as soon as possible. But the end of the Civil War brought a second look at this forgotten land. Vast herds of wild cattle, descendants of ignored herds that had pushed up from Mexico for decades, were there for the taking. Ranches were "squatted" on, bought, and homesteaded, trail drives were formed, railroads were built, and suddenly there was a way to get cattle to a hungry postwar nation that had acquired an insatiable appetite for beef. The land boom began in earnest, and with it came the discovery that all the gold and silver wasn't in California, and, with that, another discovery that, properly irrigated, the land elsewhere wasn't so barren after all.

Men being men, by the 1870's they were fighting over everything between California and the Mississippi, from women to mining claims, from cattle to water rights, from gambling tables to desolate ranches, and from sheep to Indians.

Into this picture came the Colt single-action. With Remington wallowing in post-Civil War money problems and Smith & Wesson devoting most of its production to Russian army contracts in order to survive, Colt used its past reputation to grab a toe hold on first the cowboys that were the heart of the cattle boom and then on the entire frontier, and it never looked back on its competition. Not only the cowhand, but the soldier, gambler, lawman, outlaw, miner, merchant, and the farmer was undressed without a Colt. It very seldom failed the man, but quite often the man failed it, and himself, when he wasn't quite as fast with hand or mind as he should have been.

In all walks of life, the Colt became the symbol of the American West, and, with it, names became legends, from the bad guys to the good guys, all of them with a Colt blazing away in their hands as Manifest Destiny became a reality. The Daltons, the James gang, Billy the Kid, Butch Cassidy and the Sundance Kid, Wyatt Earp, Bat Masterson, Buffalo Bill, Wild Bill Hickock, Pat Garrett, Doc Holliday, the Pinkertons; the names

Prior to turning outlaw, Henry McCarty, alias William Bonney, alias Billy the Kid, worked as a nondescript cowhand in New Mexico. Baca probably punched cattle with him, and always credited the "Kid" with teaching him his incredible skill with the Colt revolver.

Elfego Baca holed up in this adobe *jacal* in Frisco, New Mexico, and stood off 80 vengeful Texans for two days. Witnesses counted over 4,000 bullet holes in the adobe. (*Courtesy Rio Grande Press, Glorieta, N.M.*)

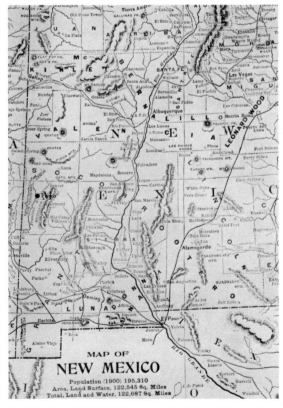

New Mexico in the 1880's was a wild and woolly country, with very little of the law and order that Elfego Baca came to stand for. The tiny hamlet of Frisco did not appear on this turn-of-the-century map, and today the town in that location is called Reserve.

were endless, and the stories are endless, and not one story was or is told, written about, or mentioned without a Colt being included—even though a Smith & Wesson or Remington may have been the arm of choice in the actual event!

Into this unique era of guns and legends stepped a fiery Mexican-American named Elfego Baca, who was ignored by the dime novelists of the time, and who is still ignored by all but a handful of history books on the American West, a man who, in 1884, shot his way into western history, if not into its books, at the siege of Frisco, the most one-sided gunfight ever recorded, one man and his two Colts against 80 trail-hardened Texas cowboys.

Eventually, like the other legends of the West, Elfego Baca (Elfego is pronounced with the accent on the first syllable) was finally discovered by Hollywood, and in the early 1960's Walt Disney produced a TV series based loosely on his life. But like Baca himself, the series is now long forgotten, and the mention of his name today anywhere else than in New Mexico is just as apt to produce the question of "what is that?" as much as "who?"

In the telling of his story, let it be said that there was never much very normal about the life of Elfego Baca. He was impulsive and hotheaded, and he attacked life as if it were a rampaging bull charging at him, yet when he was not aroused he was disarmingly mild-mannered and gentle. Things were either black or white to Elfego Baca. There were no gray areas with which to wrestle. The direct, simple way was always his way. His most important rule of life was that when trouble is looking for you, you don't wait for it—you go find it and finish it. "There is so much time wasted in this world with the little futilities that get you nowhere," he often said. "If you think that a certain gentleman has done something that warrants a sock on the jaw, the proper and only thing to do if you have regard for your own conscience is to walk up and sock the gentleman on the jaw." And when it came to a gunfight, Elfego always said that out of a gunfight came two things—a funeral and a trial, and he preferred getting tried. That, in a nutshell, was the lifelong philosophy of Elfego Baca.

Let it also be said that, as with all legends, it is difficult to separate fact from folklore. But at least in Elfego Baca's case, there were no dime novelists around to muddy up the waters. There is no question that, at times, Baca had more courage than prudent sense. But he was a righteous man who spent his life fighting for law and order, even if he was occasionally somewhat overzealous.

Fortunately, most of Baca's life is a matter of record. However, when you get past the meat and get to the bone, there never was a legend who couldn't help em-

For a quarter-century after the Civil War, long trail drives to bring cattle to market were part of life in the West. After such a gruelling drive, the cowboys would let off steam by shooting up isolated towns like Frisco.

broidering a few stories here and there. That was as much a part of the West as a Colt, a horse, and Arbuckle's coffee. Elfego had a tendency to wander some with his yarns, and although the stories were all true and never changed, sometimes his versions of them did. And there was always the "other side" that insisted that things hadn't happened that way. And over the years, newspaper and magazine writers have added to the confusion by bending Baca's words to create more romantic versions of his life. Even the noted western historian, Jack Schaefer, who wrote the classic novel *Shane,* had trouble with Baca's life story, summing it up nicely when he wrote in *Heroes Without Glory:* "The tales about him are many and they often can be picked up in pairs, both of each pair about the same happening, one for and one against."

Unfortunately, the major source of information on the life of Elfego Baca disappeared in 1972 when his entire archive was stolen from the library of the University of New Mexico. His life story, therefore, is based primarily on three sources; the 1928 book *Law and Order Limited,* written by his only official biographer, Kyle Crichto; Baca's own 1944 autobiography, *A Political Record of Elfego Baca and a Brief History of His Life*; and talks with A. B. Baca, Elfego's brother's son, who was raised by his uncle from the age of seven, and who is probably the only person still living who knew Elfego intimately.

The legend of Elfego Baca began, naturally, in an unexpected manner, in the middle of a softball field in Socorro, New Mexico Territory, on February 27, 1865. To quote Elfego, "My mother Juanita . . . was playing a game which is now called softball. When one ball was hit . . . in the direction of my mother, Juanita jumped up to stop the ball, and here comes Elfego." He was the last of six children, and though his father owned the

remnants of a Spanish land grant, New Mexico was not yet feeling the pangs of development, and the land was not worth much.

When Elfego was not quite a year old, Francisco Baca packed the family up in an ox cart and headed for Topeka, Kansas, determined to give his family a better way of life. During the journey, Elfego's first birthday came along, and, as if on cue, fate reared its head in an unusual way for Elfego Baca when a band of marauding Indians raided his camp and rode off with the one-year-old Elfego. Four days later, for some unknown reason, instead of being killed or kept as a slave, Elfego was returned to camp unharmed, cherubic as ever and none the worse for wear after his four-day pony ride with the Indians.

Years later, as his legend with a six-gun would grow, Baca's followers, and there were many, would refer to his release by the Indians as the beginning of Elfego's "charmed" existence. His enemies, however, and there were also many, insisted that the Indians had first boiled him in oil only to have him turn a healthy pink hue, and then had bashed him against the rocks only to have him bounce off, a matter that so upset the chief of the raiding party that he promptly returned Elfego to his parents. Such is the stuff of which legends are born.

Elfego and his family moved on to Topeka and settled there, but disaster overtook them when, within one month in 1872, a sister, his mother, and a brother died. Whatever disease it was that fell on half of Elfego's family, his own charmed existence had continued. Shortly afterwards, he was sent back to Socorro with his brother, Abdenago, and he became a vaquero on the little ranch that was run by his grandparents. Ironically, though he was Mexican-American, in Topeka he had used very little Spanish, and he spoke "Mexican" poorly. His English, though passable, was not much

This combination fort, bunkhouse, and stable was shared by the neighboring S.U. and W.S. ranches on the San Francisco River, near the site of Baca's siege. Some of the men in this 1880's photo may have been Baca's antagonists.

better. But he was already hardened by his austere life, and he could fight with the toughest of the kids who made fun of his fractured vocabulary.

Later, Elfego's father also returned to New Mexico and became the town marshal of Belen. Francisco Baca, however, stepped rather heavily on the toes of several members of the most politically powerful family in the area, rearranging the facial contours of one of them along the way. The resulting feud would involve Elfego in an .historic gunfight with Celestino Otero over 30 years later. For father Baca, the feud came to a head when his enemies used their influence to have him slammed in the *jusgow* for murder after he permanently stilled the guns of two cowboys who had decided to turn the town of Belen into one large sieve with the bullets from their Colts. Though he was the town marshal, Francisco Baca was "tried" in the second story courtroom of the Las Lunas jail, sentenced to a long prison term, and then put into a ground floor jail cell.

Young Elfego, however, was not about to sit still and let his father be railroaded. The night after the trial, he and a friend named Chavez snuck into the second floor courtroom and sawed a hole in its floor. Not by coincidence, the part of the floor where Elfego cut the hole also happened to be the ceiling of his father's jail cell, and, while the town slept, Elfego stuck a ladder down the hole and retrieved his father and the other two prisoners from the confines of their cell.

Rather than attempt a getaway, however, they calmly stole corn, chili, and jerked venison from the personal larder of the jailer and then strolled across the road and settled down in some tall grass not more than 75 yards from the front door of the jail. Adding watermelons that were growing in the field to their menu, they spent the next day eating and watching leisurely as posses were sent galloping in every direction of the compass in "pur-

suit" of the escapees. At the end of the day, Elfego and the others watched the pooped posses straggle back into town, empty-handed of course, and, that night the fugitives slipped out of the field to safety. Elfego's father lived in Mexico for seven years before he could return without the fear of being railroaded into jail again. Elfego would always maintain that the "picnic" that day was a valuable lesson to him when, years later as a sheriff, he captured many a criminal by looking for him within hailing distance of a crime.

Elfego always credited Billy the Kid for training him to be the fastest gun when it came to the art of outliving others with the help of the six-shooter. He met Billy the Kid at a roundup 12 miles northeast of Socorro at a place called Ojo de Perida Ranch when Billy the Kid was still just a down-and-out cowpuncher.*

*(In all his accounts of the meeting, Elfego states that he was 16 at the time and Billy the Kid was 17. In Elfego's biography, he states that he returned to Socorro from Topeka at the age of 14, which would make the year 1879, but in his autobiography he gives the year of 1872, the same year his mother, sister and brother died. It has never been proven exactly when Billy the Kid was born, but it was either late 1859 or early 1860. His real name was Henry McCarty. Later, using his stepfather's name, he was known as Henry Antrim. In 1873, his family moved to Silver City, New Mexico, where he sang and danced at Morrill's Opera House. Shortly after his mother died of natural causes, he was jailed on Sept. 21,. 1875 for a theft that he hadn't committed. He escaped from the jail and spent the rest of 1875 through part of 1877 as a saddle tramp in Arizona. It was there that he became known as Kid Antrim, then just "the kid," William Bonney, and, finally, Billy the Kid. He returned to New Mexico sometime in 1877, and he did not kill his first man and begin his short career of crime until August 17, 1877. After the Lincoln County War of July, 1878, he was a hunted fugitive until he was gunned down by Pat Garrett on July 14, 1881. If Elfego had been 16 when he met Billy the Kid, the year would have been 1881, which would have been impossible in the light of the Kid's infamy and early demise. But Elfego knew him well enough to know that Billy sang and played the piano, a fact that few people knew. If the Kid had been 17 when they met, as Elfego also says, the year would have been early 1877, the only year that Billy the Kid lived in New Mexico as an unknown cowpuncher, and the date fits. The tale deserves telling, so perhaps an old man writing his memoirs some 50 years later, slipped a few years when remembering his own age as a teenage cowboy.)

According to Elfego, one day he and Billy the Kid rode a railroad section cart to Albuquerque to see the sights. While resting under a cottonwood tree unnoticed, they witnessed a policeman gun down a man in the back and then claim that the man had drawn on him. In one account, Elfego claims that the policeman got off scot free. In another account, the policeman was hung. In either case, the injustice of the act planted a seed inside Elfego that began to ferment into a lifelong desire to see that justice was done whenever it was needed.

Elfego and Billy the Kid then proceeded to Old Town, where the saloons were located. Elfego remembers that Billy "carried a little pistol called a Bulldog Repeater, when it fired it made a strange noise perhaps louder than a .45 gun." Before going into the Martinez saloon, Billy told Elfego to leave his Colt outside, and, puzzled, he did. They went into the saloon, and in the midst of the crowded gambling hall, Billy helped ventil-

In 1913 the future looked bright for Doroteo Arango, better known as Pancho Villa. He and Elfego Baca, later bitter enemies, operated a mine in Mexico.

ate the smoke-filled room by mischievously firing three rounds into the ceiling. They were promptly searched by a bouncer who was a little more than hot under the collar because of the ruckus, but the angry bouncer could not find a gun on either one of them. A few minutes later, Billy the Kid, unnoticed, again fired three shots into the ceiling. Again they were searched, and again no gun was found, but they were rudely ejected from the place anyway. Outside, Billy showed Elfego where the gun was—on top of his head under his derby hat. He had been so quick in handling and concealing the gun that even Elfego hadn't seen where the gun had gone.

Elfego became so fascinated by the quickness of Billy the Kid's sleight-of-hand that he talked the Kid into teaching him how to handle a Colt with lightning speed, an attribute that in the future was to do a great deal towards keeping Elfego alive when others were trying to do otherwise. It is not known how long Elfego and Billy the Kid stayed together, but Elfego used to tell his nephew, A.B. Baca, that Billy the Kid was not a good gunfighter because he was always nervous and anxious to use his gun. According to Elfego, it was only because of Billy the Kid's quickness that he survived as many gunfights as he did.

Because of the conflicting dates, the Billy the Kid episode of Baca's life should probably be taken with several grains of salt. But however he learned it, Elfego Baca did become lightning fast with a Colt six-gun, and the stage was set for the famous Frisco fight, an event that would skyrocket Elfego Baca into the hearts of his fellow New Mexican Spanish-Americans for the rest of his life.

The story of the siege of Frisco began in late October in 1884. The violent passions of the Alamo and the Mexican War were not that long in the past, and there was a lot of racial unrest between the almost poverty-stricken Mexican-Americans and the anglo settlers of New Mexico. To the Anglos, the natives were "greasers," barely a form of human life. Because Texas had been predominately Confederate and New Mexico Union, the conflict of Civil War passions still lingered heavily.

About 165 miles west of the town of Socorro was a settlement on the San Francisco River, aptly known as the town of Frisco. The population of the town was mostly poor Mexican-Americans, sprinkled with some Irish settlers, ex-soldiers who had settled there in 1874.

New Mexico was an almost lawless land, a haven for cowboys who came up from Texas with cattle that they had "borrowed" from their neighbors without bothering with the technicality of paying for them. Almost as hard-bitten as the rustlers were the trail hands who drove legitimate herds up from Texas to the sprawling ranches that dotted the countryside of Socorro County.

The range-weary cowhands needed someplace to blow off steam, and, in that part of the country, it was the town of Frisco. The town was a melting pot of bars and whorehouses that existed solely from the business of hundreds of these cowhands whose one recreation was to come into Frisco on Saturday night (or any night for that matter) to drink, womanize, and shoot the town to pieces. Describing Frisco as it was in 1884, Jack Rittenhouse wrote in *Baca's Battle* "Mix in(to) one caldron these conflicts of Spanish vs. Anglo; cattlemen vs. farmer; Texan vs. New Mexican; and footloose cowboys vs. sedentary natives; spice it with one or more guns on every belt; salt it with a virtual absence of mutually recognized authority; and what happened next was only a logical consequence."

What happened next was a person by the name of Elfego Baca.

As Elfego tells it, "I was working with Jose Baca, a big merchant in Socorro . . . About the middle of October, 1884, a man by the name of Pedro Sarracino came in. He had a big deputy's badge . . . He came to talk to me frequently at that time, and he told me that he was deputy sheriff at Lower Frisco, because the cowboys at the time were raising all kinds of disturbances. He told me that if he arrested anybody his life would become thereafter in danger.

"He told me that before he left Frisco for Socorro about six or seven cowboys got hold of a Mexican called "El Burro." They laid him down on the counter; one of the boys sat on his chest and arms and the other one on his lap, and that right then and there poor Burro was altered in the presence of everybody.

"Then a man by the name of Epitacio Martinez who happened to be present objected and begged them not to do that. The result was that after they were finished with Burro the same cowboys got hold of Epitacio Martinez and measured about twenty or thirty steps from where they were and tied him. They used Epitacio as a target, and they bet drinks on who was a better shooter. Martinez was shot four different time, but still he would not die.

"I told Sarracino, the deputy sheriff, that he should be ashamed of himself, having the law on his side, to permit the cowboys to do what they did. He told me that if I wanted to, I could take his job. I told him that if he would take me back to Frisco with him I would make myself a self-made deputy."

A couple of days later, Elfego and a somewhat reluctant Sarracino hitched a buckboard to a mule and went to lower Frisco, where they stayed at Sarracino's house. Elfego went armed with an unofficial mail-order badge, plenty of ammunition, and his favorite guns, a pair of .45 caliber, 4¾-inch barreled Colts, for he did not expect any sleigh ride with the boisterous cowboys of Frisco.

The meanest outfit around Frisco was the cowboys from the John B. Slaughter ranch, numbering about 150, many of them "on the lam" from the law in Texas. The Slaughter outfit had been rawhiding the town for some time, and, for them, a drunken night on the town wasn't complete without shooting dogs, chickens, cats, or an occasional unlucky Mexican who happened to stray into their sights. On October 29, a Slaughter cowboy named McCarty went on a drunken toot at Milligan's Bar in Upper Plaza, and, as was the custom, began shooting everything in sight.

While McCarty was slinging lead all over the street in front of Milligan's Bar, Elfego asked the local justice of the peace why this sort of ungentlemanly behavior was allowed to go on, to which the justice of the peace curtly replied that he wasn't about to incarcerate one of the Slaughter outfit and allow them the pleasure of using that same justice of the peace, namely himself, for target practice while they quickly removed one of

The icy gunfighter eyes of Elfego Baca struck fear into many a lawbreaker in his later career as an attorney. In this 1906 photo, Baca was District Attorney of Socorro and Sierra Counties, New Mexico. (*Courtesy A.B. Baca*)

their compadres from the long arms of the law.

At this point, conversation came to an abrupt end when the drunken McCarty made the mistake of shooting the hat off the head of one Elfego Baca. Even more abruptly, without firing a shot, Elfego collared the cowboy, and, still fuming, towed him off to Sarracino's house just as dusk was falling, determined to leave at first dawn for the county seat at Socorro, since it was obvious that the justice of the peace was not about to hold court in Frisco against any of the Slaughter outfit, and the real deputy, Sarracino, had "mysteriously" disappeared.

The cowboys of John Slaughter's outfit, however, didn't take lightly to this brazen Mexican trying to run off with one of their own men. Liquor and the flash of Elfego's phony badge had slowed their reactions at first. But now, badge or no badge, they decided that they had not finished drinking with their pal, McCarty.

It was dark when a dozen cowboys led by Young Parham, the foreman of the Slaughter outfit, rode up to the house where Elfego was holding his prisoner. They indignantly demanded that Elfego release McCarty pronto before they found it necessary to take him back to Milligan's without the good graces of Elfego. After all, how could one lone Mexican-American dare stand up to the pride of the Texas cow trails?

Elfego dared all right, and he threw his own demands into the kettle of stew right then and there. Still inside the house with his prisoner, he invited the Texans to remove themselves to another part of the local geography that might add greatly to their life expectancy. He then informed them that he would give them to the count of three to accomplish this feat and then he would start shooting.

This unaccustomed belligerence did not set well on the cowboys, and they reached for their guns. Seeing this, Elfego, without pausing for breath, counted to three and with the sound of the last digit still rolling off his tongue emptied his two Colts through the doorway of the house in the direction of the shocked and surprised cowboys without bothering to open the door first, wounding one of them in the knee.

Very suddenly, the Texans decided to take the advice of one angry Mexican named Elfego Baca and depart post haste, but in the scurry for safer air, Parham's horse fell on him and crushed him to death.

The shock wave that was created by Elfego's unwillingness to continue his arithmetic lesson past the count of three was greater to the stunned cowboys of Frisco than that created by the death of Parham. In the confusion of the darkness of night, word passed rapidly that "the usually lazy Mexicans" had started a war against the Americans at Frisco, and riders were dispatched to the surrounding ranches for reinforcements of additional cowhands.

One of these riders reached the ranch of an English cowboy named William French. Another one stopped at the ranch of James H. Cook, who was one of the more highly respected cattlemen of the area. (In 1927, French would publish his version of the incident in *Some recollections of a Western Ranchman,* and in 1923, Cook would publish his version in *Fifty Years On The Old Frontier.*) French went on to another ranch to get more help, but, in disbelief, and being more levelheaded than the riotious cowboys in Frisco, Cook clambered aboard his fastest horse and galloped into Frisco to see if he could do anything to bring a stop to this sudden "war."

In the meantime, the "war," consisting of one Mexican named Elfego Baca, waited patiently inside the house for morning to come. For the time being, he was safer in the house than trying to find his way back to Socorro in the dark with a county full of angry cowhands stomping around itching to get a bead on him.

When Cook arrived at Frisco, he found the cowboys of the Slaughter outfit, mixed with those from other ranches, assembled some 80 strong and in no mood for anything except the blood of Elfego Baca. However, Cook, with the help of Clement Hightower and Jerome

An aging Elfego Baca holds the presentation Mauser carbine that he stole from Pancho Villa. Villa had offered a reward for Baca's death. (*Courtesy Rio Grande Press*)

Martin, all three of them known to Elfego, went to Elfego and persuaded him to bring his prisoner back to Milligan's Bar at eight o'clock the following morning, at which time the justice of the peace had reluctantly agreed to try the prisoner. Because Parham had been killed by his falling horse and not directly by Baca, Cook hoped that a peaceful settlement could still be worked out, avoiding further bloodshed.

But in the morning, just as Elfego arrived at Milligan's Bar with McCarty, the 80 cowhands swung out of an arroyo on horseback and surrounded Elfego at a corner of the building.

"Good morning, Mr. Wilson," Elfego addressed one of the cowboys that he recognized, hurriedly deciding that his only chance was to stand his ground against the overwhelming odds.

"Good morning, you dirty Mexican _____._____," answered Wilson hotly, and at that moment, a shot rang out from the rear of the tightly packed knot of cowboys. The shot missed Elfego, but it convinced him that his own skin was worth considerably more to him than that of McCarty's. Elfego's two Colts appeared in his hands so fast that the cowboys in the front rows didn't even

have a chance to draw on him, and, covering them, Elfego quickly backed down an alley beside Milligan's Bar and a *jacal* that stood by itself.

McCarty was "tried" on the spot, fined a few dollars, and set free, presumedly to join the 80 cowhands who now were in no mood to let the matter rest until Elfego Baca, the upstart, was fed his just desserts.

In the meantime, William French had arrived and was convinced by the other cowboys that Elfego should be captured and also "tried." With more bravado than brains, he and two others, led by a fourth cowboy named Bert Herne, rushed the *jacal* where Elfego had barricaded himself, and Herne started trying to pound the door down. Elfego, knowing that he would probably never get out of the *jacal* alive anyway, promptly gave the Texans another lesson in arithmetic, putting two .45 caliber slugs through the middle of Herne and ending forever Herne's concerns about tomorrow. Elfego could have killed French and the other two cowboys as they dragged Herne away, but he peppered the air around them instead, missing them on purpose. At this point, two dead men were enough. But the cowboys now knew that Elfego would defend his life dearly.

This .45 Colt Single-Action, 4 ¾-inch barrel, serial number 272440, is one of a pair that Baca carried throughout most of his career, and this is the pistol he used in his gunfight with Celestino Otero in 1915. The gold badge, with three rubies and a diamond, was given to Baca by the New Mexico Cattle Grower's Association. (*Courtesy A.B. Baca*)

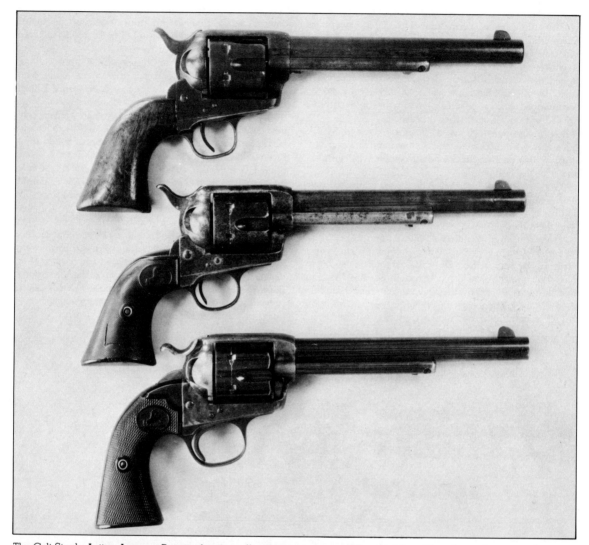

The Colt Single-Action Army, or Peacemaker, was offered in numerous variations and barrel lengths, and was without question the most famed gun of the Old West. Top, the original Army model featured walnut grips with a 7 ½-inch barrel. Center, hard rubber grips later became standard, along with better steel (in 1896) to ensure safety with smokeless powder. Bottom, the Bisley Colt had target style grips, trigger, and hammer. (*Courtesy George Metivier*)

With Herne dead, there was now no turning back for the Texans, for as he had lay dying, they had promised him that they would get Baca. Elfego had to be captured or killed, and the cowboys would just as soon it be the latter. But Elfego had used Herne as an example of his deadly accuracy with a six-gun, and none of the Texans cared to test that accuracy across the long distance of the open clearing to the *jacal* where Elfego waited.

There was a futile effort to get Elfego to surrender, but he was having none of that at this point, for he knew that if he surrendered he would keep breathing just long enough to get to the nearest tree.

A *jacal* (pronounced hack-awl) is a small building that is constructed by hammering long stakes into the ground about two inches apart and then covering them with adobe mud inside and out to make walls. The walls are more mud than wood, and they made a flimsy fortress that Elfego found himself trapped in.

Knowing the basic construction of the *jacal*, the Texans decided to "fog" the building from all sides in an attempt to mow it down with lead by firing fusillades

Brigadier General Jose Salazar was arrested for violating U.S. neutrality when he retreated from Mexico into the U.S. Elfego Baca was hired as his attorney, and when Salazar escaped Baca was arrested, tried for conspiracy in masterminding the escape, and acquitted.

and volleys rather than by firing sporadic shots here and there.

The siege at Frisco had begun.

Volley after volley slammed through the *jacal* while Elfego popped shots off in return, keeping the Texans mystified by his seemingly miraculous ability to avoid their onslaught of bullets. What they didn't know was that the dirt floor inside the *jacal* had been shoveled out to more than a foot lower than the surrounding ground, and that Elfego, resigned to his fate, lay safely in the depression, like a modern soldier in a foxhole, coolly taking potshots at any careless Texas head that he could spot from his earthen haven.

Inside the *jacal*, Elfego had found a plaster of paris statue of the saint "Mi Senora Santa Ana," and when the volleys lessened in fury, he pleasured himself with the game of depositing his hat on the head of the statue and taking carefully placed shots at the Texans while they fired at the statue.

The deadly standoff continued, and the day dragged

New Mexican rancher James H. Cook epitomized the Westerner in this 1886 photo. Cook was present at the siege at Frisco, and he arbitrated with the cowboys for Elfego Baca's surrender "with his sixguns," no doubt saving Baca's neck—and the lives of several Texans!

on. By six o'clock in the evening, the *jacal* was so riddled with bullets that suddenly, another barrage of shots finally cut one wall in two, and the entire wall and a section of the roof collapsed in a cloud of dust, pinning Elfego beneath it. But Elfego had done such a good job of splattering dirt and pieces of adobe walls into the faces of the hidden cowboys that, somewhat snakebitten by now, they continued their barrage instead of rushing the *jacal*. For the next two hours, Elfego lay trapped under the safety of the debris as bullets whistled through it from all directions.

Finally, when darkness came, Elfego pulled himself gingerly from under the debris and retreated to a corner of the *jacal* that was still standing. In the corner was a still-hot stove that had been left somewhat hurriedly by the owner of the *jacal* when Elfego had suddenly arrived unannounced. Being a practical man, Elfego decided that he needed to eat, so, while bullets continued to whistle through the *jacal* in the night, he cooked himself a supper of coffee, beans, and tortillas. At least he would die with a full belly.

Finally, the cowboys decided to stop shooting until daybreak, and they stationed sentries around the edge of the clearing so that Elfego could not sneak away in the night.

Along about midnight, Elfego watched through the holes in the side of the *jacal* as a light bounced along the ground towards him. He did not fire at it because he thought that it was just a burning cigarette drifting in the wind. What he did not know was that one of the cowboys had been sent to the nearby Cooney mining camp for dynamite, and that what he was watching was actually a lit fuse in the hand of a cowboy that was crawling towards him. The light kept coming, and Elfego kept watching, and, suddenly, the world exploded around him.

Half of the *jacal* collapsed in ruins, but when the debris from the explosion had settled, Elfego found himself standing in the only corner of the building that was still intact—the corner where the stove and the plaster saint stood.

The Texans had had their fill of this charmed Mex-

The shootouts on the streets of the Old West are largely myth, as is the fast draw—few people practiced it, and most Westerners, whether lawmen or outlaws, did their shooting from ambush. Baca was an exception—he had no fear of facing an armed man in the street, and many of his contemporaries called him the fastest gun that ever lived.

ican. Surely the dynamite must have finished him off. Just to be sure, they decided to wait until dawn to close in on the ruins of the *jacal*. But when dawn came, instead of a dead Elfego, the Texans were greeted by the sight of smoke curling from the chimney in the one corner of the *jacal* that still stood.

Elfego Baca was nonchalantly preparing himself some breakfast!

Furious, the cowboys once again began to pump fresh volleys into the remains of the *jacal*, but Elfego and the statue of the saint miraculously remained untouched by the bullets. Inside the *jacal*, everything else was hit by the rain of bullets, including knives, forks, and the stove.

About 10 o'clock, with both Elfego and the incredulous Texans wondering why he was still alive, Elfego was astonished to see a piece of the front of a cast-iron stove moving towards him in the clearing. There was, he surmised, one of the braver of the cowboys crawling behind it, using it for a shield. The cowboy behind the stove front made it halfway to the *jacal*, and, finding to his surprise that he still didn't have any bullet holes in him, his curiosity got the best of him and he ventured a peak around the side of his iron protection.

Elfego obliged the curious cowboy by installing a bullet hole through the top of his scalp. The cowhand wasn't killed, but Elfego had already dispatched two more of his compadres into eternity since he had killed Herne, and the armored attack on Elfego's corner of the world ended abruptly with a hasty retreat on the part of the cowboy.

The frustrated cowboys next tried throwing burning sticks into the *jacal*, but the debris wouldn't ignite, and as the afternoon wore on, the siege at Frisco was still a deadly standoff.

By now, the cowboys were getting tired of the game and were demoralized by the fact that Elfego had managed to remain amongst the living against everything they had thrown at him. Still thinking that Elfego was a real deputy sheriff and thus had only been trying to carry out his duties, Cook took advantage of the mood to hold a conference with the cowhands. They were cowboys, not gunfighters, Cook told them, and they had become nothing more than an unruly mob. He reasoned with them where it would hurt the most. If they killed Baca now, it could mean an all out civil war with the Mexican-Americans, a war that could make many of the cowboys very dead or at least busy dodging bullets instead of herding cows, cutting down drastically on their future playing time in the saloons of Frisco. He finally convinced the cowboys that Baca should be allowed to surrender if Cook could guarantee to Elfego that he would be taken to Socorro for a fair trial instead of being allowed to decorate the nearest tree on the short end of a rope.

Reluctantly, the cowboys agreed, and a cease-fire was called. The only problem now was: who was going to get close enough to Elfego to tell *him*?

About that time, a real deputy sheriff named Ross arrived from Socorro, and he agreed to take Elfego back to Socorro as long as Cook, speaking for the cowhands, guaranteed that they would get safe passage back without any surprise necktie parties. But he had already heard about Elfego's lesson of one, two, three, *bang*, and he was not about to stick his neck into the clearing to get the ball rolling.

In desperation, Cook now went to the Mexican population of Frisco, most of whom had adapted the Mexican attitude of *"asi es la vida"* (such is life) towards the one-sided siege and had ringed the surrounding hillsides to watch, since few of them had guns to use in any attempted rescue of Elfego anyway. Cook found a Mexican named Francisquito Naranjo who knew Elfego well, and Naranjo agreed to risk his own neck to try to get close enough to Elfego to convince him to surrender.

Unarmed, Cook, Ross, and Naranjo got as close as they dared, and Elfego, recognizing Naranjo's voice, quickly realized that he was being offered the only chance he had of finding out what he would look like as an older man. Elfego jumped through a window from the debris of the *jacal* into the fading daylight, a cocked Colt in each hand. No bullets came whistling at him. There was a tense moment as the Mexicans on the hillsides yelled for Elfego to make a run for it, while around the clearing the Texans were having second thoughts about their agreement after laying eyes on their quarry for the first time in two days. Cook assured Elfego that he had staked his own life on the surrender, for if Elfego was killed now, the Mexicans would surely retaliate by killing Cook sooner or later, and the cowboys could not break their word for that would be breaking the Code of the West, the only thing that they respected.

So there, in the deadly stillness of the evening, surrounded by some 80 exasperated cowhands who would not have been greatly disappointed if Elfego Baca was no longer breathing, Elfego Baca agreed to surrender, but *only on his terms*.

What happened next proves without a doubt that if Elfego Baca never played poker in his life he should have, for with a hidden ace showing up the sleeve of every Texan, Elfego drew to his own four aces and won the pot.

No, he would not surrender his Colts! He would just as soon jump into a mine shaft filled with rattlesnakes at the bottom. He would keep his Colts and be taken to Socorro on the back of a buckboard. The cowhands could come along to make sure that he was jailed at Socorro, all 80 of them if they were inclined to, but they would have to ride at least 30 feet ahead of the buck-

The Colt Single-Action Army revolver was the standard military sidearm from 1873 to the turn of the century. In this rare photo, taken in 1898, the 12th Company, Signal Corps, posed for a unit photo. The front rank proudly displays their Artillery Model Colt single-actions in .45 caliber. (*Courtesy Will West Collection*)

board while he kept one Colt trained on them and the other one on Ross. And he made it very clear that he would kill Ross if the cowboys tried to shorten the trip. Otherwise, Elfego would just as soon jump back into the *jacal* and start from scratch!

Perhaps the sheer audacity of it pulled it off. For whatever reason, the surrender was agreed to, astoundingly, entirely on Elfego's terms, and Baca kept his Colts as he walked away from the *jacal*.

The siege at Frisco was finally over.

For the next day and a half, Elfego sat on the rear of a buckboard driven by Ross for the entire 165 miles to Socorro, one Colt in Ross's back and the other Colt trained unerringly on six humiliated cowboys who rode ahead of him, never closer than 30 feet to the buckboard.

Elfego was jailed in the brand new, as yet unfinished jail at Socorro, which ironically was being built on the very softball field where he had been born. Though there was no roof yet, Elfego never attempted what would have been an easy escape. He was the first prisoner of the jail, where he remained locked up for four months, the first person brought to trial in it.

He was tried for murder and acquitted, and then tried again on a change of venue in Albuquerque and acquitted again. And during the trials, the sensational statistics of the siege at Frisco became a matter of record, for according to testimony:

The siege had lasted 33 hours, during which time, one man, Elfego Baca, stood off 80 Texas cowhands entirely by himself. (In comparison, the most famous of all

gunfights, the O.K. Corral shootout, pitted four men against five, and lasted less than a minute.)

When the siege was over, Baca had killed four of the Texans (counting Parham) and wounded eight. Elfego was uninjured. Witnesses at the trials had counted over 4,000 bullet holes in the walls of the *jacal*. There were another 367 bullet holes in the wooden door of the *jacal*, which was brought into court as evidence. Even a broom handle that had been inside the *jacal* had eight bullet holes in it.

That the cowboys were indeed snakebitten by Elfego's miraculous survival also came out in court when one of them testified at the trials that he was convinced that if he took a .45 Colt pistol, aimed it directly at Baca's chest from a distance of a foot away and fired, somehow there would be absolutely no effect.

And so, the legend was born, along with the legend of Elfego's charmed existence. Elfego Baca had become a hero, especially to the Mexican-Americans of New Mexico.

There is one more story to add to the saga of the siege at Frisco. When Kyle Crichton was writing Baca's biography he received a letter from Alfred Hardcastle of England, who had had a cattle ranch near Frisco in 1884, and who, it turned out, had been at Frisco on the first day of the battle. Because of the deaths of Herne and Parham there had been, Hardcastle wrote, a kangaroo court held on the behalf of Elfego Baca at Milligan's saloon during the first hours that Elfego had been holed up in the *jacal*. Mr. Milligan, the owner of the saloon, had the honor of being "coronor," and Mr.

Hardcastle, somewhat astounded, had the unique distinction of having been elected foreman of the "jury" and also appearing as a principal witness, since he had seen Elfego shoot Herne. Elfego was found "guilty" and sentenced to death, a decree that Elfego objected to quite vehemently.

Mr. Hardcastle then added the very tardy news that, unknown to Elfego and against the word of honor given to Cook, some of the cowhands from the Spur and Jons outfits had decided to try to lynch Elfego anyway while he was getting his buckboard ride back to Socorro. The only reason the attempt wasn't made, Hardcastle wrote, was because each outfit thought that the other was going to attempt the lynching, and neither one showed up at the chosen spot.

When Crichton informed Elfego of the letter which had come almost 40 years after the battle, Elfego was very indignant about the news and insisted that he had known about the lynching plot all the time and that it had been thwarted because of a bad case of a yellow streak on the part of the cowboys when they had thought of facing Elfego's guns once again. More than likely, the "attempted" lynching had been just a matter of post-battle bravado bunkhouse talk at the time, but it served to fuel the fire of the legend of Elfego Baca almost four decades later, and it kept Elfego snorting around his office for days afterwards.

The other survivor from inside the *jacal*, the plaster saint, had become a good luck charm to Elfego, and he tried in vain to buy it from the family who lived in the *jacal*, even offering them ten cows for it. But it had become their good luck charm too and they steadfastly refused all his offers to buy it. The good luck statue still exists today, occupying a prominent place in the Catholic church in Magdalena, New Mexico.

Referring to the Frisco fight, Elfego wrote in his autobiography: "From then on I made up my mind, I wanted the outlaws to hear my steps a block away from me. I always had been for law and order and I will be 'til I die. Since that time I wanted to be an 'A Number One' peace officer; likewise a criminal lawyer."

There were some lighter sides to Elfego's escapades after the Frisco fight.

Shortly after the siege at Frisco, Elfego was called to the rescue of a cousin named Conrado Baca. It seems that Conrado and Frank Shaw owned a combination saloon and store in the little mining town of Kelly, and the local cowboys, somewhat overexuberant on Saturday nights as most were wont to be, had been using their six-guns to convert the Baca-Shaw store into a shooting gallery. When the cowboys started shooting the buttons off the vests of *Señors* Baca and Shaw instead of merely drilling holes in their inventory, the partners went scrambling to Elfego for help. According to the legend, the final straw had been when two vest

buttons, his hat, and his belt buckle had all been plucked by bullets from the person of Conrado Baca all at one time. Conrado and Shaw had hightailed it to the safety of Socorro and Elfego, and, moreover they refused to leave Socorro until Elfego could redeem their store for them.

Elfego, as always, was eager to help. He galloped the five miles to Kelly and found the saloon and store filled with rambunctious cowboys and miners, helping themselves to whatever they wanted, which at the moment was the liquor supply. Once again undaunted by the uneven odds, Elfego walked boldly into the midst of the crowd with his Colts still in their holsters and loudly and profanely told the freeloaders to depart. Not in the mood to be ramrodded by a "Mexican," several of the cowboys went for their guns, only to find themselves suddenly staring down the barrels of Elfego's .45's, which had just as suddenly appeared in his hands. When the dumbfounded cowboys asked who he was, it only took the name of Elfego Baca to jog their memories back to the stories of the recent Frisco fight, and the cowboys prudently decided that they would be happy to turn the saloon and store over to their friend Elfego.

Now, however, showing a side of himself that was to create many political enemies during his life, Elfego decided that his cousin and his partner had been too cowardly to deserve the continued proprietorship of the store. So Elfego sent word to the Mexicans of the surrounding *jacals* to come to the store at nine the next morning, whereupon he proceeded to give away the entire $3,500 stock of food and hard goods to the people who, in Elfego's eyes, were much more in need of them than the cowardly partners. To top it off, he also gave all the liquor away to the mule skinners of the giant ore wagons that came rumbling out of the mines on the way to the smelters, and legend has it that the hauling of ore came to be an unexpected holiday thanks to the generosity of one Elfrego Baca and the liberated liquor of Conrado and Shaw.

When Conrado and Shaw heard the news, they were, not surprisingly, in hysterics at the manner in which Elfego had "helped" them. But in Elfego's mind, the partners had no right to property they couldn't protect. Besides, he told them, if they had had a store to return to, they would have allowed themselves to be harrassed by the cowboys again anyway. Elfego was not concerned with the possibility that the partners could have sold their stock instead of giving it away. He had simply taught them a lesson and that was the end of that, which it was. He never admitted that, at the time, he was beginning to itch with political.ambitions and that his becoming a local Robin Hood as well as the local hero certainly wouldn't hurt him in future elections.

Conrado Baca was not the only relative to fall prey to Elfego's one-sided way of thinking. Elfego had gotten married in 1885 and found himself sadly lacking in funds. Since his new-found reputation as a hero and Robin Hood could not buy him one dollar of security for a loan with either Prince Brothers, the local bankers, or his uncle, Esteban Baca, who was a well-to-do store owner, Elfego proceeded to secure his loan in the Elfego manner. Knowing that Eddie Price, the head of the bank, was almost stone deaf, Elfego went to his uncle and, face sadly grieving for the reputation of his uncle, "innocently" informed Esteban that the less-than-honorable Mr. Price had insulted one Esteban Baca by refusing to honor him as a cosigner on a $500 loan for Elfego, omitting the fact that Mr. Price hadn't even considered a cosigner.

His Spanish honor at stake and his Spanish temper past the boiling point, Esteban Baca stormed into the Price Brothers bank with Elfego following innocently and indignantly shoved a check for $500 through the teller's window at Price. Though Price could not hear the words, he could see by his angry gestures that the elder Baca was more than distraught. Price quickly cashed the check, whereupon, without taking his glowering eyes from the face of Price, the "insulted" elder Baca handed the $500 over to Elfego. Throwing a dirty look at Price for effect, Elfego hurriedly ushered his still enraged uncle out of the bank before Price could communicate with his astounded employees. It is not known whom Elfego eventually paid back the money to, but he had gotten his "loan."

Keeping his vow to himself to be an "A Number One Peace Officer," Elfego was a Deputy Sheriff of Bernalillo County in 1885, 1886, and 1887, and it was during this time that he once again jumped into the spotlight with the capture of Jose Garcia, one of New Mexico's more notorious bad guys. Garcia, it seems, had followed up a spree of crime by killing a man in Belen because it was the most expedient way of ending the man's marriage to a woman with whom Garcia had become passionately enamored. Garcia and the woman rode off together into the hills and the next time the woman was seen she had been drawn and quartered like a side of beef and was found hanging from the limb of a tree in four separate parts.

The heinous crime shocked even the most hard-core residents of New Mexico, and Elfego wasted no time in taking off in hot pursuit, determined to exact retribution from the despicable Garcia. After three months of trailing Garcia through some of the roughest country of New Mexico, Elfego ended up in Bernalillo, where he hired as a guide a young boy named Alfredo Montoya, who, according to his reputation, knew the surrounding country better than the back of his hand. When they were a safe distance from town, Elfego proceeded to blacken his entire body with burnt cork and they continued their search with Montoya leading the way and

his "negro" servant following. After six days of tracking, they finally found Garcia in a camp with three sheepherders. Elfego's disguise caught Garcia off guard, and when Garcia took his eyes off the "negro" for a moment, it was his last mistake. He turned back to find himself staring down the yawning barrels of Elfego's .45's and gave up without a whimper.

When Elfego and Montoya reached the town of Thorton with their prisoner, word immediately spread that Garcia had been caught, and an enraged lynch mob formed so quickly that they chased the trio into the tiny Santa Fe railroad train depot.

"When's the next train for Albuquerque?" Elfego asked the station agent while the mob outside yelled for Garcia's neck.

"Four hours," the agent replied, eyeing the mob apprehensively.

"When's the next train anywhere?" Elfego countered.

"Fifteen minutes going the other way," the agent quavered.

That was good enough for Elfego. He was now wishing that Garcia had had enough courage to face him down so that he could have killed him on the spot, but it was his duty now to protect the coward from the mob. When the mob learned that the by now mottled "negro" was actually the famous Elfego Baca, it gave in to him long enough for Elfego to push his way sternly through the crowd, his Colts waving menacingly, and get his prisoner onto the train bound for anywhere. It was probably one of the few times in Western history that a train was on time, but it was a welcome sight for Elfego, and one more story was added to the legend, for Elfego had captured the notorious Garcia and gotten him to jail without having fired a shot.

There is no record of what happened to Garcia, but, given the temper of the population, presumedly he was hanged. Montoya went on to become a famous sheriff himself.

As for Elfego Baca, his life was just churning into second gear.

In the winter of 1887, Elfego was appointed U.S. Deputy Marshal for the Territory of New Mexico, a post which he served in his usual Baca manner. Ambitious, and with his sights set on a life in politics, in 1890 he began studying law in the office of Judge H.B. Hamilton of Socorro. He was appointed County Clerk of Socorro County in 1893 and was elected to the same post in 1894, and served as clerk until 1896. He was admitted to the bar of the State of New Mexico in December of 1894, and in February of 1895, the law firm of Freeman and Baca was established. Judge Freeman, Elfego's new law partner, had just stepped down as Associate Justice of the Supreme Court of New Mexico, and his distinguished reputation did much to add the word "prestige" to Elfego's own reputation along with "hero" and "Robin Hood."

Elfego dabbled in mining ventures on the side, and in 1896 the now distinguished Elfego Baca became City Mayor of Socorro and served as such through 1898. Never idle, he was School Superintendant of Socorro County in 1900 and 1901, and in 1905 and 1906 he served as District Attorney of Socorro and Sierra counties, New Mexico.

Never one to rest on his laurels, in 1906 Elfego retired from his post as District Attorney four months early in order to accept the more lucrative post ($500 a month) as both investigator and special prosecutor for the Cattle Association of Sierra County, and in 1912 Elfego Baca became the most distinguished when he was admitted to practice law in the Supreme Court of the United States.

In his younger days, Elfego always carried two Colts, and many gunfights didn't happen because when a man reached for his gun he found himself staring down the wrong end of Elfego's Colts before he could clear his holster. Even throughout the terms of his many political and legal positions, Elfego was never out of arm's length from at least one of his Colts just in case someone needed stronger persuasion than the mere letter of the law. There was always a loaded Colt in the desk drawer of every office he ever had, and he scared the wits out of many a visitor when he would pull a well-oiled six-shooter out of a drawer and wave it in emphasis to a story about the "good old days."

But the good old days were far from over for Elfego Baca.

Once he was invited to attend the convention of the New Mexico Cattle Growers' Association in Magadalena. At a dance afterwards, a liquored-up cowpoke drew on Elfego, but Elfego was so fast he knocked the cowboy out with his fist without bothering to reach for his Colt. Shortly afterwards, a man named Saunders tried the same thing, only to find one of Elfego's Colts sticking in his ribs before he could so much as thumb the hammer back on his own Colt. Realizing that he had been set up by enemies who had used the convention to call him out, Elfego went to his room, got his second Colt, and waited in the street for someone to challenge him. No one did.

In 1906, Elfego had gotten heavily involved in mining ventures in the town of Parral, Mexico, a sideline that did not seem to interfere with his many public offices. One day, when he was inspecting a mine by himself a ladder broke, plunging him 40 feet to the bottom of the mine shaft. He lay at the bottom of the mine unconscious for most of the day before he finally came to and was able to climb back out of the mine, and all his life he was to say that that incident had been his closest brush with death. Perhaps the fall had dimmed his

memories of his precarious predicament at Frisco over 20 years before.

It was also in 1906 that Elfego spent months chasing a cattle rustler named Gillette who had a large price tag on his head. Gillette's trail ended in Parral, Mexico, where he had bribed another American to go to Kansas City, where the reward had been posted, and swear that Gillette had been killed. In Parral, Elfego had made friends with a local bandit named Pancho Jaime who had been riding around with a bounty on his head for 12 years. In Mexico, Elfego could not have legally arrested Gillette, so he had arranged to pay Pancho Jaime $1,000 to take Gillette to the border after Elfego had "found" him.

The reward on Gillette, however, had been canceled because he had been declared dead. But in the meantime, Elfego had formed a warm friendship with the irascible Pancho Jaime, real name Doroteo Arango, alias Francisco Villa, who later would be known as Pancho Villa. Eventually, they started a mining operation together. They would ride to the mine in the morning in one of Henry Ford's first Model T's, emptying beer bottles along the way, and then use the beer bottles for target practice on the way back to town in the evenings. The mine didn't produce much, but both Elfego and Pancho Villa managed to hone their shooting eyes in direction proportion to their consumption of beer, which was ample.

In 1910, the series of revolutions in Mexico began that ended three decades of dictatorship by its president, Porfirio Diaz, and as the names of successive generals and presidents began to pop out of Mexico like popcorn, the name of Elfego Baca, naturally, began to pop up also. By 1911, the revolution was in full swing, and when the revolutionary forces of Francisco Madero, led by General Orozco, surrounded the Federalist-held town of Juarez, Elfego just happened to be in El Paso. Hearing a familiar name, he went across the border to the Orozco encampment and was on hand to read the promotion to colonel to the man who illegibly scrawled "Francisco Villa" at the bottom of the commission. Elfego became Colonel Pancho Villa's American agent for purchasing arms and supplies.

Later, Villa and Orozco, against Madero's orders, started the bloody three-day Battle of Juarez by launching their initial attack across the international bridge from El Paso, violating U.S. neutrality laws in the process. At a victory meeting in Juarez, Elfego was again on hand when the battle-scarred and rag-tag Pancho Villa, enraged because Madero had grabbed all the glory for the victory and left Villa standing on the sidelines, got into an argument with Madero and tried to strangle him.

By the time Elfego got back to El Paso that night, it had been reported that Villa had been executed. But later, a messenger from Villa came to Elfego's room. Mexico being Mexico, Villa had managed to bribe his way to freedom and wanted to meet with Elfego. Elfego and Villa met secretly in El Paso, and it was arranged for Elfego to come to Juarez the following day to get jewels and money from Villa to take back across the border. But because of the previous violation of the neutrality act by Villa and Orozco, American troops finally sealed off the border, and Elfego never got to Juarez at the appointed hour.

Elfego and Villa never met again. The next thing that Elfego heard, Villa had set a $30,000 price tag on Elfego's head, a seemingly exorbitant amount just for not showing up for an appointment. According to A.B. Baca, however, the reason for the huge reward was that Villa had sent a large sum of money to Elfego to purchase guns with, but Villa's courier stole the money and claimed that he had delivered it to Elfego. Villa chose to believe his courier instead of his ex-friend, Elfego, and

thus the reward. Later, in defiance of the reward, Elfego somehow arranged to steal one of four special presentation engraved Mauser carbines that Pancho Villa had had custom made for himself, and the two remained bitter enemies from that time on. Elfego even hatched a plan to have himself delivered to Villa in an exchange for $30,000 in gold, at which point some sharpshooters hired by Elfego would relieve both Elfego and the gold from the clutches of Villa, but by that time Villa was off fighting the revolution again and the confrontation never took place.

Later, in 1914, when Elfego was asked to testify before a U.S. congressional committee that was investigating the actions of the Mexican revolutionary leaders along the border, Chairman Flood, in questioning Elfego about his ex-friend Villa, asked him: "So Villa was a cattleman who bought and sold cattle, did he?"

"No," replied the always candid Elfego, straight-faced, "He didn't buy them. He just sold them."

Elfego Baca, far left, poses menacingly with some friends from Roswell, New Mexico. This undated photo is probably from sometime near the turn of the century. (*Courtesy Rio Grande Press*)

Despite his falling out with Pancho Villa, however, Elfego Baca wasn't done with the Mexican revolution. In 1913, Diaz's ex-general of the army, Victorio Huerta, had overthrown and killed Madero and become President of Mexico. As the revolution raged on, against Herta now, the four leading revolutionary leaders were Obregon, Carranza, Zapata, and one Pancho Villa. Changing horses in midstream, Elfego naturally became one of Huerta's American agents for procuring American business concessions in Mexico, and once again Elfego Baca was thrust into the limelight, this time at a national level.

In January, 1914, Huerta's leading commander along the border, Brigadier General Jose Ynez Salazar, was badly defeated by Villa and Obregon in the battle of Ojinaga, and he retreated with the remnants of his command across the border into the U.S. The Salazar soldiers were arrested by American troops for violation of the neutrality act, and Salazar himself was arrested on the same charges at Sanderson, Texas, on January 17, and put in prison at Fort Bliss in El Paso. Elfego was subsequently hired by Huerta to be Salazar's attorney, and Elfego was sent to Washington, D.C., to collect his retainer from a Huerta representative at the Riggs National Bank. When asked how much his fee was, Elfego, with Pancho Villa's reward still in mind, came up with the figure of $30,000, and, to his surprise and delight, the amount was immediately accepted and paid. He could only gulp and stammer when, as he was leaving, the official mentioned how delighted *he* was with Elfego's fee for he had been authorized to pay Elfego $100,000 if necessary!

It was, however, more money than Elfego had ever been paid in his life, and he pursued the defense of Salazar with his usual tenacity—with too much of the wrong tenacity, the U.S. government was soon to insist.

Salazar's case dragged on for months, and on Oct. 9, 1914, a grand jury in Santa Fe indicted him for perjury

Though the Colt Peacemaker was the most popular handgun in the West, it wasn't the only sixgun. The Colt, top, was given fairly stiff competition by the Remington Model 1875 single-action, center, and the Smith & Wesson Schofield top-break. (*Courtesy George Metivier*)

because of his contradictory testimony in court, and he was taken to the Bernalillo County jail at Albuquerque on Nov. 16 to stand trial. At exactly 9:30 p.m. on the night of November 20, two masked men overpowered the jailer and left with Senor Salazar without the usual formalities of getting the consent of either U.S. or Albuquerque officials. The sensational escape made headlines all over the U.S., but Salazar made it safely back to Mexico.

Soon afterwards, Elfego also made the headlines when he was arrested, along with the District Attorney of Bernalillo County, for having been the ringleader of the daring and perfectly executed escape. Elfego and a dozen others were tried for conspiracy against the Government of the United States because Salazar had been a prisoner of the U.S. Government itself. All were acquitted, Elfego because he "conveniently" just happened to have been standing at the bar in the Graham Saloon in Albuquerque with some local dignitaries at exactly 9:30 when the breakout had occurred, and who, "coincidentally" just happened to ask the correct time when he set his watch at exactly 9:30.

Elfego always insisted that he had nothing to do with the breakout and that it was pulled off by a contingent of some of Huerta's best officers who had snuck into the U.S. posing as farm workers. The truth may lie in both versions, for Elfego Baca was not a man to collect $30,000 without earning it. Whatever had really happened, the hero, Robin Hood, and distinguished attorney, had become a mysterious good-guy, bad-guy to the nation, and another chapter was added to the legend of Elfego Baca.

Elfego didn't stay out of the headlines for long. Shortly after the conspiracy trial he was in El Paso and while he was sitting in a car at a railroad crossing with a friend another old acquaintance, Celestino Otero, approached the car with several friends after having attempted to set up Elfego in ominous meetings in out of the way places all day. Sensing what was coming, Elfego jumped from the car, but before he could reach for his Colt, a shot from Otero tore into Elfego's groin. It was the last thing that Otero ever did, for Elfego calmly returned the favor by putting two bullets through Otero's heart a quarter of an inch apart, killing him instantly.

Once again the legend of Elfego Baca spilled forth across the New Mexico countryside, for, it turned out, Otero had also been one of the defendants in the Salazar conspiracy trial. Elfego was tried for murder and quickly acquitted. But during the trial the defense opened an old can of worms by contending that Otero had been paid $8,000 to kill Elfego by the same prominent family that had been feuding with the Bacas ever since they had gotten Elfego's father railroaded into jail in Las Lunas the time that Elfego had helped him escape. More recently, the same family had blamed Elfego for the "mysterious" death of one of their members. The local rumor, however, was that Salazar had hidden out on Otero's ranch during his escape and that Elfego had set up Otero because Otero had gotten greedy and wanted more money for the part he played in the escape.

A.B. Baca has still another explanation, straight from Elfego's mouth. It was Otero, he says, who was the courier who stole the shipment of money from Pancho Villa to Elfego and accused Elfego of taking it, causing the break between the two friends, and the shootout had been fermenting ever since because of it. Take your pick. Otero was no match for Elfego's quick gun and one more story was added to the legend.

Elfego next turned up as a combination bouncer and head of security for the Tivoli, a huge gambling hall in Juarez. In fact, it was the only gambling hall in Juarez thanks to a *mordida* of $84,000 a month paid out by the owners to the federal government for the privilege of being a singular monopoly. Elfego was paid the whopping salary of $750 a month, free room and board, and got a chauffeur-driven car in which to escort American patrons safely back and forth to the border. For that kind of money he probably would have stood off another 80 Texas cowboys every day of the week and twice on Sundays, but his main function was to keep the casino from being robbed, an occurrence that had happened altogether too frequently before his arrival as its protector.

One gang in particular, headed by a bandit named Numero Ocho, had long considered the Tivoli to be its own private oyster bed and had previously relieved the casino of far too much of its money without the benefit of first placing bets. Supposedly the gang had operated with the blessings of the Juarez police, which had no compassions one way or the other about the federal government sanctioned casino, and Numero Ocho wasted no time in calling Elfego's cards and telling him to beat it while he was still in one piece.

This, of course, was not the right thing to say to Elfego Baca, especially when the message was not even delivered eye to eye, and especially by a crook who, in Elfego's eyes, couldn't even dignify himself with a name. Words like that cut Elfego's fuse short, and he went looking for Numero Ocho by himself, without the aid of the 14 guards he had working for him at the Tivoli. Elfego stunned the entire Juarez underworld when he walked alone into the supposedly secret cellar headquarters of the Numero Ocho gang, slapped Numero Ocho all over the walls, covered the rest of the gang with his Colts, and then told them in typical Elfego manner to never get near the Tivoli again. The story, like others, might be taken with a grain of salt, but the Tivoli was never robbed while Elfego Baca held

William S. Hart, the most famous cowboy actor of the silent film era, used two short-barrelled Colt single-lactions in true Elfego Baca style.

the reins as the guardian of its vast intake of money.

The job ended only when Elfego, showing no discrimination whatever, threw one last rowdy patron of the Tivoli into the local *jusgado*. The patron, however, happened to be the son of the Juarez chief of police, ending the lack of compassion on the part of the Juarez police towards the Tivoli, Mexican politics, as always, being on a day-to-day basis.

Elfego was elected sheriff of Socorro County in 1919 and was sheriff through 1920. And in the Elfego Baca manner, he found a unique method for arresting wanted people without the rigors of time-consuming chases on the part of Elfego Baca. He simply called in the chief clerk and dictated a letter which said:

"Dear sir. I have a warrant here for your arrest. Please come in by . . . and give yourself up. If you don't I'll know that you intend to resist arrest, and I will feel justified in shooting you on sight when I come after you.

Yours truly, Elfego Baca, Sheriff."

Filling in the appropriate dates, Elfego sent the letter to everyone he had a warrant or indictment for, and the parade of volunteer arrests at the office of Sheriff Elfego Baca went on for the entire two years he was in office.

Once, however, one man chose to defy him. One day Elfego received a note that read: "Ef yu want me, you ____ _ ____ Mexicun, cum and git me. i will be under the big cottonwood by the river at noon wednesday."

It was signed just as illegibly as it was written by one Art Ford. Elfego heartily accepted the invitation, but no Art Ford showed up under the cottonwood tree, and when Elfego gave up and returned to his office, there was Art Ford, his courage ebbed by sobriety, sitting meekly in Elfego's office, his guns on Elfego's desk.

Even as sheriff Elfego made his own rules, regardless of what the law actually said. Once he returned from a trip to find his jail filled with 11 residents who had been imprisoned under a new state debtors' law that sentenced them to jail for 60 days for owing as little as $11. Without hesitating, Elfego immediately released them all, and when the stunned district attorney called him for an explanation, Elfego replied succintly, "They ate too much." According to the rules of Elfego Baca, justice had been served, and that was the end of that. The debtors' law was repealed shortly afterwards.

Another time, one of two young cowboys who were awaiting trial on a minor offense got himself promoted to cook while Elfego was again away on business. The cowboy used the opportunity to depart to places unknown, leaving his friend fuming in his cell because they were supposed to have escaped together. It was the only escape from Elfego's jail while he was sheriff, and the young whippersnapper had to be taught that he wasn't supposed to do things like that to Elfego Baca. But Elfego was afraid that if he chased the escapee down he might have to shoot him if he resisted arrest and the charges he had been jailed on were not severe enough to merit such a final ending. So Elfego threw the rule book away again. He took the errant prisoner's cellmate out to a huge dinner of steak and potatoes, pinned a deputy's badge on him, gave him handcuffs, a gun, and $75, and told him to go bring his derelict friend back. Elfego made the boy two promises; if he brought his friend in, the act would get him a lighter sentence. Second was that Elfego would chase the two of them around the world if they didn't come back. A week went by, and the locals were dying to see egg on the face of Elfego Baca, besides the fact that his job was now on the line as well. Finally, a telegram arrived from the prisoner-turned-deputy, but, to Elfego's chagrin he had to pay $8.75 for the exuberantly worded message which told in every detail of the successful capture of the recalcitrant escapee and ended with the words, "What shall I do with him?" Elfego sat down and carefully wrote out a reply, using exactly the ten maximum words allowed for the minimum telegraph rate. "Kiss him twice and bring him in you damn fool," the telegram said, and Elfego's lost pigeons returned to their roost.

Elfego had a heavy hand in the political rise of Albert Fall from the time Fall was a New Mexico cowpuncher, to attorney, State Attorney General, State Senator, and finally U.S. Secretary of the Interior before Fall took his own terrible fall in the Teapot Dome Scandal in 1923. When Fall took office as Secretary of the Interior in 1920 he inherited "the Indian problem" with it. The biggest problem at the time was a band of Piaute Indians in southern Utah, who, for several years had been relieving local ranchers from the responsibility of owning livestock and then running off all the Federal officers who had tried in vain to teach them that all horses and cattle weren't theirs for the taking. Fall, however, had a solution—an old friend named Elfego Baca. While Fall's staff admonished him for sending such a nice, portly old man to certain doom, Elfego quietly pinned his old Deputy U.S. Marshal's badge on his left suspender, packed his pair of Colts for Utah, and soon was on page one of the Salt Lake City newspapers for single-handedly ending the Indian raids.

Elfego attacked the legal profession the same way that he did a gunfight. During a half century in court, he was a Jekyll and Hyde, intimidating juries with his most baleful stare and cajoling others with grandfatherly innocence. In the usual Elfego Baca manner, he fractured court etiquette so badly that he often had opposing prosecutors and attorneys screaming demands for contempt charges that never came, for Elfego's sincere homespun shenanigans were welcome entertainment to judges who were constantly put to sleep by the droll legal jargon of the other attorneys. Even judges were not safe in their own courtrooms with Elfego around, and he shot back at them verbally with the same marksmanship that he had with a gun, even succeeding in getting one judge disbarred.

Once, a fellow attorney advised Elfego that he could not pursue a case any further without violating legal ethics as an attorney, but that the matter in question could be properly pursued by a private detective. Thus satisfied, Elfego produced a business card with the words "Elfego Baca, Attorney at Law" printed on one side. On the other side was printed "Elfego Baca, Private Detective," and Elfego went on to "ethically" finish his case.

Another time, Elfego and a local citizen were at opposing ends as to whether or not Elfego owed the gentleman $500. One day, the man stopped Elfego on the street and asked him what to do about a man who owed him money and wouldn't pay it. "I'd sue the son of a gun," Elfego shot back without hesitating. Several days later, Elfego was sued by the man for the alleged $500 debt, whereupon Elfego sent the man a bill for $500 for legal advice rendered and taken, neatly canceling out the lawsuit.

Even in the early days of prohibition, Elfego's stern sense of what he felt was right and wrong did not waver. For some time in the '20s, Elfego published a local newspaper named *La Tuerca,* the subscription rate of which was $2.00 a year to good citizens, $5.00 a year to bootleggers, and $5.00 a *month* to prohibition agents." Editor Baca also added that "he was in favor of light wines and beers and 110 proof whiskey!"

In Albuquerque in the mid '20's, Elfego one night came to the rescue of a local drunk who was being arrested by several policemen of New Albuquerque. For some time, the local night judge had been abusing his powers by sending his policemen into the streets to arrest citizens on trumped-up charges to line his own pockets with the "fine," which was always one dollar less than whatever money the unlucky arrestee had on him at the time. Elfego wouldn't think of using his guns against a policeman who was "doing his duty," but in his fervor to help the drunk, he bopped one of the policemen over the head with a huge silver pocket watch, knocking him out, and Elfego, instead of the drunk, was hauled before the judge. Elfego was sentenced to 30 days in jail because he refused to pay his "fine." Unknown to the judge, however, Elfego had just taken over as Albuquerque jailer, and as such was entitled to be paid 75¢ a day to feed his prisoner, namely one Elfego Baca. At the jail, he signed himself into the log and "served" his 30 day sentence while acting as jailer for himself, pocketing $22.50 from the city of Albuquerque for his troubles.

There were further escapades. Elfego was stabbed with a dagger once and with an icepick another time, and he was shot at so many times he couldn't remember them all.

Even the new-fangled inventions almost got him a couple of times. He made the "adjustment" from horses to cars in the same manner that he did everything else, and for some years the mere sight of Elfego's car storming down the street was enough to send other drivers scurrying for safety in every direction. Once, on a trip to Santa Fe, his car went out of control and rolled over three times and came to rest upside down. When onlookers rushed to pull his body from the wreckage, they were stopped in their tracks as Elfego crawled out of the dust, kicked the car once, shook his fist at it in disgust for letting him down, and walked away. Another time, he was run over by a fire engine on a street in Albuquerque and injured so badly that he was not expected to live. But he survived, and, years later, he was still cantankerous enough to climb into the ring after a local prizefight ended with an unpopular decision and punch the referee in the nose in return for his bad judgement.

Even his appearance was always important, and all his life he shunned the standard western frontier garb in favor of vested suits and bow ties, belying his short-fused temper. And short-fused or lighthearted, his homespun candor never left him at a loss for words, whether it be a matter of seriousness or fun. Presiding over a legal hanging in 1913, he walked to the dangling corpse, felt for the pulse that was no longer there, and said to the 20 witnesses, "This is one of the nicest hangings I ever saw. Everything went off very smoothly." When he was working at the Tivoli in Juarez, the Chicago Grand Opera Company played in El Paso and Mary Garden, the *prima donna* of the American opera visited the Tivoli. They established an immediate rapport, two legends from two different worlds, and she gave him tickets to see Carmen in which she was appearing. When asked afterwards what he thought of the opera, he replied unabashedly, "I didn't like it. You know, all that hollering around. I like the Mexican string bands better."

Elfego's political ambitions faltered in his later years after the Teapot Dome Scandal, partly because of the lingering onus of his friendship with Albert Fall, and partly because he had moved to Albuquerque, where his voter following wasn't as loyal and he was considered by most newcomers to be too old and too old-fashioned. He ran for governor of New Mexico and lost and ran for judge and lost.

But he never stopped fighting for law and order, whether it be with a gun, in court, or in the legislature.

A.B. Baca tells of how his uncle used to bait Texans by kidding them about making themselves easy targets by wearing their Stetsons during a gunfight. It was easy, Elfego said, to look for a hat and aim ten inches below it. The first thing he ever did in a gunfight, he said, was to throw his hat to the ground so that he wouldn't be as big a target. For the same reasons, he always wore a fedora instead of a large Stetson.

Elfego never stopped practicing with his six-guns. His nephew used to watch him load his Colts and then roll over and over on the ground in a mock gunfight, emptying his guns into the surrounding fence posts and never missing one of them. Other times, he would gallop a horse down a roadway at full speed, Colts blazing in each hand at the fence posts that whisked by him on each side.

Some experts claim that Elfego Baca was the fastest man ever with a six-gun. Perhaps he was. But whatever he was, the most important thing to him was that he had become a champion of his race, an idol of the Spanish-American population of New Mexico, and protector of his people whether it be with a Colt or a law book.

He became a legend, but he never slowed down.

He appeared on Ripley's "Believe It Or Not" radio show on May 24, 1940, at the age of 75, and at the age of 79 he ran unsuccessfully for district attorney.

From the historic siege at Frisco to his capture of Jose Chavez Chavez, one of New Mexico's most infamous desperados, Elfego Baca, the legend with the "charmed" life, always got the job done. In the process, by his own admission he had killed eight men in gunfights, some of which were "unofficial and didn't count," and he was tried for conspiracy by the U.S. government and acquitted and was tried for murder three times and was acquitted.

But his most important battles were the ones he won in court for other people.

Elfego Baca was a true native son who epitomized the real spirit of America and the West and helped tame its frontiers in its most lawless years. He brought law and order to a large part of New Mexico at a time when it was needed the most. Lawman, attorney, politician, he is a unique symbol of what made America great.

The Colt single-action was manufactured in a multitude of calibers without major change from 1873 to 1941. Production was begun again in 1956 and will end for good at the end of 1981. It created legends in the West and became a legend of its own.

Part legend, part folklore, part human being, Elfego Baca never stopped fighting for law and order until he took his last breath. Old age finally did what bullets couldn't do to the "charmed" life of Elfego Baca, and even the prestigious Time magazine remembered him long enough to give him a glowing obituary when the legend of New Mexico died on August 28, 1945—at the age of 80, in bed, with his boots off.

As a young scout and buffalo hunter in the late 1860's and early 1870's, William F. Cody already possessed the sense of showmanship that marked him for greatness. In later years, as in the 1895 photo, right, Cody's poise and fringed costumes came to epitomize the American West. *(Photos Courtesy Buffalo Bill Historical Center)*

CHAPTER TEN

BUFFALO BILL AND THE GRAND DUKE

By James Bellah

LUCRETIA BORGIA WAS a breechloading, .50 caliber Springfield rifle. The day 26-year-old Will Cody loaned her and his horse, Buckskin Joe, to the Grand Duke Alexis of Russia, he could have had no idea of the long-term ramifications.

Cody was, at the time, something of a minor celebrity. He was America's undisputed champion buffalo hunter, having proven his exclusive right to the sobriquet, "Buffalo Bill," a few years earlier in an eight-hour hunting duel with another army scout, Billy Comstock. His name had also appeared in the New York *Ledger* and *Weekly* in exciting but absolutely preposterous "penny dreadful" stories written by promoter-author-swindler, Ned Buntline. Still, he was not yet the single, undisputed embodiment of the American plainsman he was later to become.

The loan of rifle and horse would be instrumental in creating a legend, but the story involved much more . . .

It began in May of 1870 when the prototype of a new pistol was submitted to the Small Arms Board of the United States Army. That pistol was the first large caliber handgun produced by Smith & Wesson. The revolver, chambered for the .44-100 Henry cartridge, was known at the time simply as Model No. 3.

The army looked the pistol over, tested it, liked it and, on December 28th, ordered 1,000 of the new, centerfire, six-shot revolvers. That order was delivered in March of the following year.

Two months later, the Russian government contracted with Smith & Wesson for 20,000 more. This was the first Smith & Wesson pistol to use a break-open design hinged at the bottom to allow simultaneous cartridge ejection by means of an extractor lodged within the barrel and cylinder.

Then, in September of '71, the popular war hero and dashing bachelor, General Phil Sheridan, returned from Europe where he had been a military observer of the Franco-Prussian War. One of the first things Sheridan did when he again took over command of the Department of the Missouri was to make arrangements for a long-postponed buffalo hunt.

Years before, at President Grant's summer home in Long Branch, New Jersey, the General had met Commodore James Gordon Bennett II, soon to inherit the New York *Herald*. He had regaled Bennett with stories of Indian fighting and buffalo hunting to the point where the wealthy New Yorker wanted nothing more than to travel west to experience personally the wonders of the Great Plains.

Unfortunately, Sheridan's orders sending him to Europe interrupted the trip. Now, however, he was back home and lost no time in making good his promise to Bennett.

There was never any question in the general's mind as to who would lead the hunt. He insisted upon his friend Bill Cody who was, at the time, Chief of Scouts for the 5th Cavalry.

The cream of society left New York on the Hudson River Railroad. They traveled to Chicago, transferred to the Northwestern then, at Omaha, to the Union Pacific. They left their sleeping cars at North Platte Station, Kansas, to establish a "rough and tumble" camp near Fort McPherson.

There tents were all equipped with floors and carpeting. Each man had a regular bed with a comfortable mattress. Their guns and personal luggage were carried in three four-horse ambulances and two more wagons were set aside exclusively for ice and wine. The party enjoyed full-course dinners cooked by a French chef, served on imported porcelain by waiters in full-dress livery and eaten in style with fine silver utensils.

They also enjoyed meeting a very remarkable young frontiersman.

If any one of them had expected Buffalo Bill Cody to be the desperado described by Ned Buntline in New York's *Ledger* and *Weekly* he was pleasantly disappointed. The brown-eyed, fair-complected Cody was mild-mannered and agreeable. He was strikingly handsome, dynamic, amusing and confident. In fact, young Cody *was* the West—expansive, gregarious, dressed in beaded buckskin and, incidentally, armed with one of the new Smith & Wesson revolvers soon to become known as the *American.* Undoubtedly, the pistol had been issued to him by the Army for use if needed in his capacity as a scout.

During the next several days of wining, dining and hunting, the New Yorkers introduced Cody to champagne for which he developed an instant and life-long taste. He, in turn, introduced them not merely to the Great West, but to one of its most fascinating and colorful personalities—himself. So impressed were the Easterners by the young man's charm and abilities that, once they returned home, they literally bombarded all their friends with stories of the dashing buffalo hunter.

It's hardly a coincidence that, when Russia's Grand Duke Alexis came to the United States, he, too, would hear of Buffalo Bill Cody. What is coincidental is the fact that, in the Grand Duke's luggage was one of the 20,000 Smith & Wesson Model No. 3 revolvers ordered by his Imperial Army the previous May. The Russian nobleman and the American plainsman were armed with identical handguns!

Light-haired and blue-eyed Alexis was the somewhat

Brevet General George Custer, left, Grand Duke Alexis, and W. F. Cody had the center stage for their great buffalo hunt, held in January, 1872, in Colorado. *(Photo Courtesy Buffalo Bill Historical Center)*

troublesome third son of Tzar Alexander II. Despite the fact that the young man seemed to care for little other than wine, women and cards, his father had seen fit to send him on a good will tour of the United States in order to pay Russia's official respects. Relations with Imperial Russia had been good during the Civil War when Alexander had openly supported the Union and, as a result, probably prevented English military aid to the Confederacy. With the purchase of Alaska in 1867, however, the United States and Russia twined into an association that was almost a marriage. When Grand Duke Alexis arrived in New York late in the autumn of

Though not as famous as the Colt Peacemaker, the top-break Smith & Wesson revolver preceded it by a few years and was favored by many on the frontier. Cody was issued a .44-caliber Smith & Wesson as a scout, and the government of Russia also purchased large quantities as a military sidearm. Thus it was that Cody and the Grand Duke carried nearly identical revolvers. "Buffalo Bill's" skill at shooting bison from horseback with such a revolver was to make a lasting impression on the Grand Duke—and the entire world.

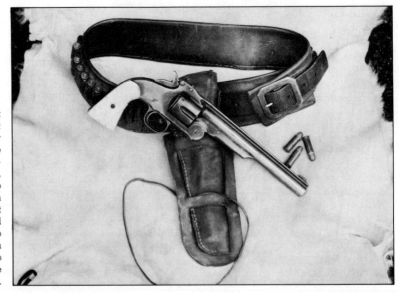

Through superior marksmanship and horsemanship, Cody made "buffalo running" look easy. In actuality, the practice was quite dangerous to horse and man, and relatively few attempted it.

1871, he immediately became not merely the toast of the town, but of the entire nation as well.

Soon after his arrival, Alexis went to the nation's capital. There, at a dinner party, he was introduced to General Phil Sheridan who, as was his wont, infatuated the Russian with story after story of his recent buffalo hunt with Cody and the cream of New York's society.

Alexis, himself an excellent equestrian and marksman, was understandably eager to go on a hunt of his own—a hunt, incidentally, which was destined to confer immortality on one William Frederick Cody.

The hunt might have been organized immediately had not General Sheridan been sent to Chicago there to establish order after the disastrous fire early in October. As it was, it could not be scheduled until January of 1872. Then, despite the fact that the Great Plains were suffering the worst winter anyone could remember, anyone who could possibly dream of getting there wanted a piece of the action.

In organizing the hunt, Phil Sheridan outdid himself. He ordered his staff to spare no expense in terms of food or other supplies. He personally requested Buffalo Bill to act as head scout and, in addition to a large number of other notables, invited Lieutenant Colonel George Armstrong Custer to the party. Custer, a one time Major General by brevet and courtesy, but never by paycheque, had a special political reason for being asked. At that time, he was in command of the 7th United States Cavalry which regiment had already earned for itself the title, "Cossacks of the Western World."

Apparently not yet satisfied, Sheridan added one more touch. He arranged for the famous Sioux warriors, Spotted Tail and Whistler, to accompany the hunters and asked the Indians to bring along a hundred or so of their braves. In the unlikely event that one of these young men might take the opportunity to shoot in the wrong direction once hunting started, the general made sure that, at all times, there would be sufficient numbers of armed American cavalrymen accompanying the royal party to make any attempt at hostilities on the Indians' part instantly suicidal.

As the hunting party boarded sleeping cars in the East, Sheridan and Bill Cody made their final arrangements. It was on Cody's suggestion that orders were issued to all Sheridan's scouts to notify the general immediately if any sizable herd of buffalo was spotted. All arrangements made, Sheridan and Cody rode to North Platte Station there personally to meet the royal party.

Amid more pomp, circumstance and ceremony than the West had probably ever seen, Sheridan and Cody met the visitors, paraded with them and rode with them to Denver where a grand ball was scheduled. As their train stood by, the visitors changed from traveling clothes into formal evening wear and the dance began.

Everything proceeded perfectly until exactly midnight. The theatrics could not have been handled more perfectly if rehearsed. The ball was at its zenith when, at the stroke of 12:00, General Sheridan was handed a telegram. He read it, smiled faintly, then announced that a large herd of buffalo had been spotted in Colorado's Kit Carson County.

Near pandemonium broke loose. The grand ball disintegrated. Still in full dress, the would-be hunters dashed to their train which sped them toward the herd.

Nearing the area where the animals had been spotted, the royal party detrained and, on horseback, began tracking the herd. The weather was unseasonably warm and pleasant for January and the spirits of the men were high. Occasionally, along their route, they spotted isolated buffalo or small groups of old bulls congregating like old men in city clubs.

With these groups, Bill Cody gave the visitors a few spectacular samples of how he had won his undisputed championship as a buffalo hunter. Astride Buckskin Joe, possibly the greatest long-distance horse of his day, Cody would gallop up to a buffalo until he and Joe were alongside the animal. Then, giving Joe free rein at a full gallop, Cody would lift Lucretia Borgia to his shoulder and kill his buffalo with one shot to the base of the skull.

The Grand Duke and all his party were thoroughly impressed, not merely with Cody's kills, but with the dramatic flair with which they were made. Horse, man and rifle all appeared to be one. The shooting of the buffalo was skillful to the point of being poetic.

At about 4 p.m. on January 13th, with the Colorado sun streaking the sky a crimson only seen in the West, the large party reached the site of their evening's camp. There, in a bend of Red Willow Creek christened Camp Alexis, they stopped for the night. A 10th Cavalry band played, "Hail to the Chief" and as tents were being pitched, the Indians gave a spectacular show of their own.

Even though General Sheridan had asked Spotted Tail and Whistler to bring along a hundred or so braves, the Sioux could not resist a party or a chance at the twenty-five wagonloads of food and trade goods which would be theirs. Over 1,000 Indians, feathered and beaded, wrapped in their best blankets, showed up. Led by Spotted Tail, they treated the visitors to sensational displays of archery and trick riding amid the popping of many corks.

An elaborate camp was established. The distinguished guests and officers had wall tents, there were hospital tents for the messes and long rows of A tents for the troops and servants. Naturally, the quarters of officers and nobility were floored and carpeted as well as heated by box or silby stoves.

The first evening's meal might have been far more elaborate had not General Sheridan put an end to festivities. The main herd had been spotted. The hunt, he announced, would begin the following day.

The great hunt began on Sunday, January 14. That morning—perhaps because it was the Grand Duke's 22nd birthday, perhaps only because he was a naturally generous person—William F. Cody loaned the Russian Buckskin Joe. Joe had once belonged to a Pawnee scout, but was much bigger than most Indian ponies. Although an excellent hunter, Joe's strong point was his ability to gallop long and hard over seemingly impossible distances. The main consequence of the loan

In 1894, 22 years after the fact, artist Louis Maurer immortalized on canvas the "Great Royal Buffalo Hunt." *(Courtesy Buffalo Bill Historical Center)*

was not that the Grand Duke would ride an excellent horse so much as it was that Cody himself would now be forced to ride another mount. He chose a horse named Brigham.

Brigham had also once been owned by an Indian who had named him for the Mormon leader, Brigham Young. Cody liked the name and continued it. The horse was reputed to know as much about buffalo as any man and was perhaps the undisputed best bison hunting horse in the world. It was Birgham Cody had ridden in his famous duel with Billy Comstock and it was Brigham who, in his own way, had taught his master much of what he knew about buffalo hunting.

So—with scouts and guides, soldiers, heroes of Indian wars and some of the Indians they had fought—the royal party left camp. Dressed in buckskin, his long hair shining in the morning sunlight, William Cody, a magnificent picture of western manhood, led them to the hunt.

Astride Buckskin Joe, the Grand Duke Alexis was, he undoubtedly thought, ready for anything. Not only did he have a rifle, but at his side, he wore the .44 Smith & Wesson revolver he had brought with him from Russia. He probably had no doubts whatsoever about his abilities as a soon-to-be-killer of buffalos. He was an excellent rider as well as a good marksman. He was not, however, an experienced running shot and he had had no practice whatsoever in this kind of hunting. The only thing Alexis knew about the business involved what Cody had shown him the previous day.

The herd was spotted and, because it was his royal perogative, Alexis was given the chance for first kill. He did not hesitate. Pressing his heels to Buckskin Joe's flanks, he galloped toward the herd.

Then, the Grand Duke Alexis did a very peculiar thing.

By 1900 Cody the great scout had become Cody the great showman, with a tremendous following the world over. *(Photo Courtesy Buffalo Bill Historical Center)*

The reason will probably never be known, but the fact is that he did not pull his rifle from its boot. Instead, he galloped near one buffalo and drew his revolver. When he was close to the beast, he fired one shot with the Smith & Wesson.

Whether he missed the animal entirely or simply did not wound it sufficiently to cause an obvious reaction is not known. The fact is that the buffalo did not go down.

At this point, William Cody, American scout and plainsman, loaned the Grand Duke Alexis, third son of the Tzar of all the Russias, his rifle. Cody then flicked Buckskin Joe and the horse again galloped toward the herd. Cody shouted to the Grand Duke to shoot, the Russian did and, this time, a buffalo fell to the ground.

Alexis reined to a halt, made a whoop worthy of any attacking Indian or Confederate cavalryman and waved his hat in an enthusiastic show of victory. It was the signal for his servants to open a large basket filled with bottles of champagne.

Obligingly, everyone—including, of course, Bill Cody—celebrated before resuming the hunt again.

At this point, conjecture must be relied upon, for what historian can honestly know the hidden motivations of long dead actors on life's stage? Was it the champagne or merely enthusiasm for the hunt—was it an innate, inborn sense of showmanship or the fact that there was no other choice which made Bill Cody do what he did?

The real reason will never be known. What we do know is that when Cody loaned Buckskin Joe, he himself elected to ride a horse who, although smaller and not such a great distance runner was, in fact, a far better buffalo hunter. We also know that when Cody loaned Alexis his Springfield rifle he left himself unarmed except for a new, centerfire large caliber pistol.

When the hunt continued, the other riders pursued and shot their buffalo in the conventional manner while Cody treated the party to a spectacle which was not only dramatic in the extreme, but according to many, almost impossible. Astride Brigham, allowing the nimble pony absolutely free rein, Cody would ride abreast of a buffalo until his right knee in some cases was actually touching the animal. Then, with his revolver mere inches from the base of the animal's skull, he would, at a full gallop, kill it with a single shot.

After each kill Grand Duke Alexis insisted upon the ritualistic consumption of a seemingly inexhaustible supply of champagne. This imbibing lasted so long that, despite the size of the herd, it took the Russian three days to kill eight buffalo.

There were other aspects to the hunt, of course. An Indian named Two Lance shot an arrow entirely through the body of a bull and Cody showed the royal party his skill as a stage driver using an old fashioned Irish dog cart pulled by four cavalry horses. A woman, one Mrs. Raymond, was discovered in the hunting party and the visitors were treated to war dances and other pageants.

The main result of the hunt, however, came as a direct result of the loan of a horse and a rifle. Cody had made an indelible impression on Grand Duke Alexis.

After the hunt was over, the Russian invited Cody into his railroad car at North Platte. There, he offered the plainsman a huge sum of money which Bill refused and a fur coat which he accepted. Alexis also had especially made for Bill a pair of cufflinks and a diamond stick pin.

But the main point is that the Grand Duke Alexis *endorsed* Buffalo Bill Cody.

Cody himself went to New York later that year and, as a direct result of the Grand Duke's endorsement, became first, the toast of the town, and then a performer. He began, in 1872, a career which ultimately would see him become one of the greatest showmen the United States has ever seen.

One cannot but pause to wonder what would have happened had not Bill loaned his horse and rifle to Alexis. If, on that January day, he had killed his buffalo in the usual way, astride Buckskin Joe using Lucretia Borgia, would he have impressed the Russian as completely as he did? Would he have been invited into the Grand Duke's railroad car and then to Chicago and on to New York where, because of the favor of the Grand Duke and many other men of prominence, he ultimately became a living legend of Americana?

One must also pause to wonder what might have happened if, on that long ago day in Colorado, Bill Cody had not possessed a Smith & Wesson Model No. 3, an extraordinary new high caliber handgun capable of creating a legend . . .

An *American* legend.

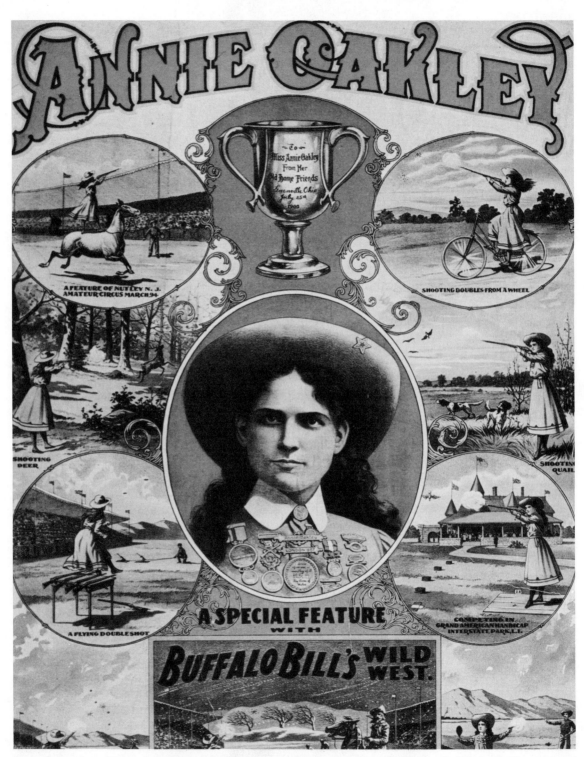

Annie Oakley, born Phoebe Anne Moses, grew up hunting with a Kentucky longrifle. Amazingly skilled with rifle, pistol, and shotgun, she remains one of the best-known marks-persons of all time.

CHAPTER ELEVEN

ANNIE OAKLEY— SHOOTING STAR

By Angela Hynes

YOUNG PRINCE WILHELM of Germany stood on the turf at the Charlottenberg Race Track near Berlin. His back was straight, he held his crippled left arm by his side, and with his right hand brought a cigarette to his lips.

The American slowly raised a rifle to shoulder level. With cheek pressed against the smooth, wooden stock the marksman held the Prince's blond head in the sights, adjusted slightly to the right, and squeezed the trigger. A shot cracked and, in a puff of ash, the end was neatly clipped off the Prince's cigarette.

"Wunderbar!" *"Wunderbar!"* Applause rang out from the grandstands. Wilhelm's face broke into a grin, and Miss Annie Oakley lowered the gun and took a curtsy.

If Annie's aim had been a little off that day it might have changed the course of history. Twenty-seven years later when the First World War broke out in 1914, Wilhelm II was Kaiser of Germany. Many a soldier of the allied forces must have dreamed for the opportunity Annie Oakley had at that shooting exhibition in 1887.

It was unlikely that "Little Sure Shot" would have been off target, renowned as she was for phenomenal accuracy. Not even performing before the crowned heads of Europe could unsteady her hand, and this was the second time within a few months that Annie had held the fate of Royalty in that hand, quite a feat for a little girl from the backwoods of Ohio.

Pheobe Anne Moses was born in Darke County, Ohio, in 1860. She was the fifth of seven children of a Pennsylvania Quaker couple who moved west after their inn burned down. Annie—as she was called by her family—lost her father when she was six years old. Her mother remarried only to be widowed a second time with yet another daughter added to the family.

For the next five years little Annie's life was one of poverty and hardship, including two years spent working as an unpaid drudge on a farm. Life became bearable after her mother married for a third time.

Annie was now the oldest child at home since her sisters were married. With her father's old .40 caliber cap-and-ball Kentucky rifle Annie roamed the woods and fields around Greenville perfecting that skill which was to make her the most famous markswoman in American history. Annie and that rifle—which was almost bigger than she—fed the family and paid off the mortgage on her stepfather's farm.

By the time she was 14 her game was being sent to the best hotels in Cincinnati, 80 miles away. Annie's quail and grouse, always shot cleanly through the head, were in great demand. The ladies and gentlemen eating in Cincinnati's finest establishments never had to bite the bullet when dining on one of her birds!

She went to Cincinnati to stay with her married sister, Lyda, when Jack Frost, owner of the Bevis Hotel, could hardly believe that this quiet little country girl was the shot who had given his table such a good reputation. It was more temptation than he could resist to pit Annie against one of his guests—a jaunty showman named Frank Butler.

Butler was an adventurer. Born in Ireland he, like Annie, came from a poor family. When he was eight years old his parents left him with an aunt while they emigrated to America. But Frank ran away and came to the United States by working his passage as a cabin boy. He never did reunite with his family and took care of himself by doing a variety of jobs—selling newspapers, driving a milk cart, cleaning stables, and as a sailor on a fishing boat. But Frank's whole life changed the day he bought an old Spencer rifle from a Civil War veteran.

Before long he had it working like new and within

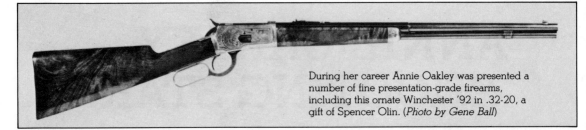

During her career Annie Oakley was presented a number of fine presentation-grade firearms, including this ornate Winchester '92 in .32-20, a gift of Spencer Olin. (*Photo by Gene Ball*)

five years Frank Butler was widely regarded as the best shot in the country. He formed a partnership with Billy Graham and toured the eastern states giving demonstrations of sharpshooting in theaters, and taking on all comers in competition. "Butler and Graham" were appearing with a stock show in Cincinnati when Jack Frost proposed a match against the crack shot up from the country.

It was an unlikely couple Frank Butler and Annie Oakley made when they met on Thanksgiving day, 1875, on a hill high above Cincinnati. But the 15-year-old girl, barely five feet tall, in a pink gingham dress and with chestnut hair falling about her shoulders, did not seem intimidated by the tall, handsome Irishman 10 years her senior.

Using her old muzzle-loader, Annie won the match hitting 25 out of 25 targets to Frank's 24. In years to come he often teased that he let her win the contest. That's not impossible since the generous-spirited Butler later gave up his own career to manage Annie's. However, it's more likely that she won fair and square. Frank's last target quartered sharply to the right, and although he touched it, it didn't break so was not counted as a hit.

Annie's was a double victory that day. Not only did she win the match but she also captured the heart of Frank Butler and they were married barely a year later. Billy Graham dropped out of the act to be replaced by Annie. The Butlers called themselves "Butler and Oakley"—Oakley being a name pulled out of the blue because they liked the sound of it. For five years they played vaudeville and stock companies, and then joined "Sells Brothers Circus." By now Butler had recognized the audience appeal of a dainty woman who could outshoot any man and he no longer took billing but just acted as Annie's assistant.

In the winter of 1884 the circus headed for New Orleans and the World's Fair. It was a wet and dismal season and the bleachers remained empty. "Sells Brothers" was in trouble but did not fare so badly as a rival outfit appearing across town at the Metarie Race Track—"Buffalo Bill's Rocky Mountain and Prairie Exhibition."

The great showman, Col. William F. "Buffalo Bill" Cody—$60,000 in debt from his previous season—had

This 1892 photograph, taken in London, shows Annie Oakley in typical "show" costume, including medals and hat. (*Courtesy Circus World Museum, Baraboo, WI*)

lost all his stock and props when the riverboat carrying them to New Orleans sank in the Mississippi. With funds wired by his partner, Cody assembled a new outfit and now the show which boasted "heaven's azure canopy our canvas" was washed out by rain.

Despite all this, the Butlers were intrigued by the idea of the show and felt their act was more suited to it than to the circus. They were signed up and told to report to the show at the start of the new season when it was changing its name to "Buffalo Bill's Wild West." There was a superstition among the show folk that Annie Oakley brought them good luck. Others felt it was the change of name that did the trick, but whether it was either or neither, the luck did change and "Buffalo Bill's Wild West" and its new shooting star, Annie Oakley, were on the way to becoming household names the world over.

Distinguished Visitors to Buffalo Bill's Wild West. London.1887

Distinguished Visitors to Buffalo Bill's Wild West. London.1887

1887 was perhaps the most glittering and best-remembered season throughout the long history of Buffalo Bill's Wild West. In a rare public appearance, Queen Victoria attended the show at Earl's Court, London, and commanded a second performance at Windsor Castle. Guests included the Queen and five European kings.

The show had a series of triumphant seasons—Boston, Chicago, Canada, Staten Island, Madison Square Gardens. Then in March 1887, the whole company boarded the S.S. State of Nebraska and set sail from New York bound for England and what was to be remembered as the most glittering season of all.

It was the year of Queen Victoria's Jubilee and the show was a featured attraction at an American Exhibition at Earl's Court, London. The city was in a festive mood when the boat load of buffalo, broncs, braves and buckskinned cowboys landed. The British press and London high society quickly took this strange American contingent to their hearts.

Prince Edward and his family paid a surprise visit to the showgrounds during rehearsals and Cody staged an impromptu show for the royal guests. Edward was so impressed by this taste of the wild-and-wooly West that he waxed enthusiastic to his mother the Queen. Two days after opening night, Queen Victoria, who had attended few social engagements since the death of her consort 25 years earlier, came to Earl's Court for a command performance. She, too, was delighted with the show and especially Annie Oakley, to whom she said

when presented, "You are a very clever little girl."

The Queen commanded a second performance to be part of her official Jubilee celebrations in June. This time the show came to the Queen and set up an arena in the grounds of Windsor Castle. Among the Jubilee guests were five kings, three crown princes, and other assorted titled personages.

As this distinguished audience took its seats the cowboy band struck up a rousing medley of American tunes. Then a mounted cowboy proudly bore the Stars and Stripes around the arena. In front of the royal box he stopped, and for the first time in history, an English monarch saluted the American flag.

Col. Cody, dressed as always in white buckskins and riding a magnificent white horse, introduced the grand entry. With a wild whoopin' and hollerin' the arena was filled with galloping horsemen carrying flags. They exited and it was time for Annie. She always opened the show, as Cody reasoned that a woman shootist would break the audience in gently to the sound of gunshot.

Annie rode into the arena on the back of a perfectly groomed calico pony. She wore an elaborately beaded and fringed kneelength costume of broadcloth with matching leggings buttoned down the side. On her head was a felt hat, upturned on the left side and with a silver star near the brim. After the noise and confusion of the grand entry it was a dramatic entrance that the petite, lone rider made. She encircled the arena waving and blowing kisses to the crowd.

Frank galloped in and the two rode around the arena at a fast run—he throwing glass balls into the air, and Annie, using a lever action Winchester, breaking one, two and often more at a time. At the first shots there were squeals of alarm from the ladies in the audience, but soon they were so captivated by the charm and skill of Annie that the cries of fear quickly changed to cries of admiration.

On a second go-round of the arena, Annie and Frank repeated the trick, but this time with Annie standing on the horse's back. Then they dismounted and their horses left the arena alone. Annie was a consumate showwoman and never walked in the arena. Now she skipped and danced to a table on which a number of guns were laid out. Frank picked up some 2×5-inch playing cards and from 50 feet, using a Stevens sporting rifle, Annie shot through the ace of hearts on the cards. Frank tossed some of these into the audience for souveniers, others he held edge-on and using a Smith and Wesson .44 caliber pistol Annie sliced them in half.

Clay pigeon shooting was next on the bill. Cowboys set up traps in the arena and using a Parker double-barrel 12 gauge shotgun Annie broke the red clay pigeons as they soared high in the air four at a time.

Now came the hard part! Frank twirled a glass ball on a string around his head and Annie, lying backward over a chair, her gun upside-down, broke the ball. Frank then whirled another ball about his head and Annie used a gleaming bowie knife for a mirror and broke the ball by firing her pistol over her shoulder.

By now the royal crowd was completely enthralled by the little bundle of energy darting about the arena, and there was more to come. The intrepid Frank held a cigarette between his lips while Annie shot the end from it with a rifle—the part of the act which obviously impressed Prince Wilhelm of Germany seated beside his grandmother, Queen Victoria.

For a finale, Annie threw three glass balls into the air, jumped over the gun table, picked up a Spencer pump action shotgun and with shots as rapid as machine gun fire shattered all the balls before they hit the ground. While the audience were still dazzled she ran to the arena exit, turned and executed a little dance and kick before leaving to thunderous applause.

There were other trick shooting acts in the show but none captured the imagination of the audience—not only at this royal performance but also at Earl's Court—as did Annie Oakley. With royal patronage adding to the glamor of the show, the crowds poured

Annie Oakley was a champion live bird and clay pigeon shooter; she was the first woman inducted into the Trapshooting Hall of Fame. (*Courtesy Herb Peck Jr.*)

into Earl's Court, between 20,000 and 40,000 a day. Buffalo Bill and Annie Oakley continued to be the darlings of the English press and appeared on the front pages almost daily. Annie received many honors and awards for her shooting prowess and was especially honored to be the first woman allowed to shoot at the prestigious London Gun Club.

Behind the scenes the mundane chores of the show went on. Frank Butler, content as always to let his wife take the limelight, personally took care of Annie's guns. After every performance he cleaned the guns 'til the barrels gleamed and the stocks shone. Then he wrapped them in cotton blankets and packed them in trunks ready for the next performance. The guns and the ammunition were kept in the ammunition wagon where the shells for the trick shooting acts were loaded by hand. The ammo wagon was a hive of industry as even the glass balls used in the various acts were made there daily by hand.

One summer day a messenger brought a note for Colonel Cody. It read, "Dear Sir, would the little girl that shoots so cleverly in your show, shoot a match with the Grand Duke Michael of Russia?" It was signed by Prince Edward. Duke Michael had remained in London after the Jubilee celebrations to court Princess Victoria but the prospective marriage was an unpopular one in England.

Shooting exhibitions were extremely popular in Annie Oakley's day. "Doc" Carver, who once worked with Cody, had his own show and was Buffalo Bill's main competitor.

Cody was uneasy about the match knowing that Annie would probably defeat and embarrass the Duke. But Annie refused to back down from the contest. On the appointed day a number of royal spectators arrived with the Duke who was splendid in full uniform and bedecked with medals. All the medals in the world couldn't make up for lack of skill. Using her Parker double-barrel shotgun Annie resoundingly beat the Duke taking 47 clay pigeon targets out of 50 while he only managed 36.

As Prince Edward congratulated Annie he could hardly keep the smile of triumph from his face—it was clear that he had been hoping that Annie would win. Within a couple of days Duke Michael was on his way back to Russia having been rejected by Princess Victoria. The newspapers were jubilant and proclaimed that his defeat at the hands of Annie Oakley and her seemingly infallible gun was so humiliating that the Princess had been swayed against him, making the American markswoman a deciding factor in a royal marriage.

Toward the end of the season in London, Annie received an invitation to go to Germany to shoot for the court. Cody, who had displayed some resentment at the amount of attention Annie had received from the British press and high society, was further upset that this royal invitation did not include him. The two decided to go their separate ways. Annie would rejoin the show a year later, but for now "Buffalo Bill's Wild West" went on tour of the North of England without its premier shooting star. Annie and Frank Butler left for the trip to Germany and that historic day when Annie held the head of the future Kaiser in her sights. All told, in that summer of 1887, Annie Oakley and her guns made quite an impression on the royalty of Europe.

Through all of her 50-year shooting career, Annie showed an impartiality for any one type of gun. She used pistols, rifles, and shotguns from every manufacturer in her act and was always ready to try new models and innovations. Many times she had guns made to her own specifications for different parts of her act. Also, because of her stature in the shooting world, she was often presented with special models by various gun manufacturers.

But regardless of which gun she used, from the old Kentucky rifle she learned on to the gold-plated, pearl-handled specials she shot as a star, Annie Oakley's guns all had one common denominator—in her hands they were unfailingly accurate. A German Prince, a Russian Duke and an English Queen could all bear witness.

Rancher, adventurer, war hero, President Theodore Roosevelt was for millions of Americans the embodiment of the American spirit. The strong, self-assured countenance of this 1903 photo belies a sickly childhood and the chronic asthma that plagued him all his life; rather, it bespeaks the resolution and drive that so characterized "TR."

CHAPTER TWELVE

TEDDY ROOSEVELT'S QUEST FOR THE FRONTIER

By Rick Hacker

GIVEN THE INCALCULABLE possibilities of human traits that can combine to form the personality of a single individual, the odds of blending courage, resourcefulness, humor, determination and a personal magnetism into the mold of one man is highly remote. Yet at least one such person lived and, during his time, captured the imagination and following not only of personal acquaintances, but of the entire world; his name was Theodore Roosevelt.

Born on October 27, 1858, in a brownstone which still stands at 28 East 20th St. in New York, "Teedie," as he was called by the family, did not come from a humble background. His Dutch ancestors were an integral part of our nation's early history, and one such relative sat in with the Continental Congress. Indeed, his father, also named Theodore (although no "Jr." was ever affixed to young "Ted's" name) was a highly successful glass merchant as well as being a respected citizen who was active in all matters of civic affairs. Newspaper accounts in the *New York Times* during the War Between the States often mention both monetary and material contributions the elder Roosevelt made to the Union cause, including supplying the entire New York militia with turkeys during the grim holiday season of 1863.

By contrast, young Roosevelt's mother, Martha Bulloch, came from a proud and aristocratic line of Southerners, who traced their lineage back to Scotch ancestry. This combination of North and South, blending the industrial and rural societies of our nation in one man, was to prove a major asset to Roosevelt in his political career, for both sides of the country could lay claim to him as their own.

However, the immortal qualities that were to make him a notable politician, respected rancher, rugged outdoorsman and hunter, widely read author and even-

tually 26th President of the United States did not come easily to Theodore. They were earned, the hard way.

With this infallible combination of background and wealth, it would seem that Theodore Roosevelt's path through the world would be a clear and easy one, yet such was not the case, for from birth he was plagued by the one thing that neither money nor heredity could free him from: a weak and frail body. When born, he was not expected to live and if so, he was not expected to live long. But he did, through a fierce inner determination not just to survive, but to better himself, a driving force that continued to motivate Roosevelt throughout his entire life.

Although he was continuously haunted by asthma, through a series of self-imposed exercises Roosevelt increased his anemic frame to a point where he could ride and hunt for days in the rarified atmosphere of the Rockies by the time he was in his twenties. Still, his occasional gasping for breath, especially when excited or hyperventilated over a political issue, was the real impetus behind the famous "TR smile," his massive set of teeth clenched together and lips stretched wide as he struggled for air. By dedicating his physique to what he later would call "the strenuous life," he was able to transform his body from a frail frame in boyhood to a massive 200-pound bulk as an adult, a countenance which cartoonists of the day often compared to the mighty grizzlies TR loved to hunt. In fact, so closely allied was he to this mightiest of North American beasts, that they often became the very symbol of his politics during his Presidency. The bond between TR and the bears became inseparable when, during one of his hunts, he refused to shoot a cub because it was too small and helpless. The story quickly made the rounds of newspapers and a toy merchant that Christmas labeled all his stuffed bears "Teddy's bear." The mer-

chant sold out in record time, thereby establishing a
motivation for other toy makers to quickly follow his
lead. The Teddy Bear was born for all time.

Unfortunately, there was nothing Theodore could do
about his poor vision and in later years, his nearsighted-
ness would cause him great concern over the types of
sights he would special order on his hunting rifles, as
scopes of the day were not only far from being per-
fected, but were looked upon as unsportsmanslike.

As emphatic as Roosevelt was about perfecting his
physical frame, so was he driven to equip his mind with
as much knowledge as it could hold. As a youth, unable
to indulge in the roughhouse games that other, healthier
children enjoyed, he sought escape in books, reading everything from dime novel adventure stories to the clas-
sics, such as Dickens and Robinson Crusoe. He also
took up taxidermy, bird study and botany, a portent of
a Roosevelt-to-be: naturalist and hunter.

Scholarly writings also caught TR's interest and he
developed a fascination with world history, geography
and nature, topics which would serve him well in later
years, as a politician, author and conservationist. In
fact, so extensive and varied was his knowledge that he
often left his contemporaries far behind in terms of
speech and perception. Once, after a talk he gave in
Chicago in 1912 in which he used the phrase, "We
stand at Armageddon . . ." reporters went scurrying out
to find just where Armageddon was. They found it in
the Bible.

TR was born during a unique time in our nation's
history, for his public career straddled both sides of the
20th Century. His exuberant personality enabled him
to accept politicians and cowpunchers with equal enthusiasm and his acquaintances included such diverse
individuals as Buffalo Bill Cody and the German Kaiser. Roosevelt was the first President to have his voice
recorded (surprisingly, his high-pitched, staccato sound
belies his bullish figure). His childhood photographs
were taken in tintypes, his inauguration exists as a ste-
reoptic set, and his terms as president are voluminously
recorded on film, the first U.S. President to have his
actions preserved in this fashion. He was also the youngest man to hold the nation's highest office, being only
43 when McKinley was assassinated, moving Roosevelt
up from a Vice Presidency he did not want to a position
that he would hold from 1901 through a second term to
1909. When born, muzzle-loaders and black powder
arms were the norm; he hunted with the best of cartridge arms (Springfields, Winchesters and Colts above
all others) and lived to see the advent of machine guns
and aerial warfare.

Young Roosevelt's father was not a hunter in the full-
est sense of the word, but he did enjoy going after Long
Island ducks. TR's first gun (not counting an air rifle)
was a 12 gauge Lefaucheux pinfire shotgun, given to

In 1880, a young TR posed with his brother, Elliot, holding
his first gun, a Lefaucheux pinfire shotgun given to him in
1871. *(Courtesy Harvard College Library)*

him when he was 13 years old by an uncle. Although
Teddy (the nickname he acquired while attending Harvard and which stuck with him all through the remainder of his life) did not have to work for a living,
due to the inheritance he had received from his father's
death in 1878, he also inherited a deep sense of civic
duty and personal pride from both sides of his family.
He was a great admirer of Abraham Lincoln, and perhaps it was a combination of these elements that led
him into the world of politics in 1880, shortly after
graduating college. That same year he married Alice
Hathaway Lee and two years later became the youngest
member ever elected to the New York State Legislature.
It was during a break in the legislative session of 1883
that Theodore decided to "succumb to my impulses,"
and satisfy a romantic curiosity of the West that had
haunted him from boyhood, spawned in part, no doubt,
by the many novels he had read. He decided it was time
to see the frontier while it was still there.

In outfitting himself for that grand adventure, Teddy
special ordered two Winchesters, going through a New
York gun dealer at the time (in later years, as President,

For the frontispiece of his book, *Hunting Trips of a Ranchman*, Roosevelt posed with his favorite Winchester Model '76 and a silver-plated Bowie knife.

On a cold day in the Dakotas, Roosevelt paused from a hunting trip to pose with two friends and a Marlin-Ballard rifle. *(North Dakota State Historical Society)*

he would keep both his personal secretary and the Vice President of Winchester busy with volumes of correspondence concerning additional rifles he would be ordering direct from the famous gunmaking firm). The first of these now-famous repeaters was a Model 1876 in caliber .45-75 and a matching Model 1873 in .32-20. Both rifles featured deluxe wood, shotgun buttplates, half-round, half-octagon barrels and fancy engraving by famed craftsman John Ulrich. As a finishing touch that would foretell their use, TR had the buttstock of the '76 inletted with a gold oval engraved with a bear, while the '73 featured a similar inletted gold oval, only this time depicting a rabbit. The '76 would eventually take over 100 head of game and in TR's lifetime would be sent back to the factory four times for overhauling. It was one of his favorite guns and was the firearm he chose to hold when he posed for the frontispiece of his first book on the West, *Hunting Tales of A Ranchman*.

The "four-eyed dude," as he was sometimes called by waddies who had not yet had a run-in with Roosevelt, also knew that sidearms played an important part in a frontiersman's life. Therefore, to serve this purpose for

his inaugural trip out West, he ordered two Colt Single-Action Revolvers, with 7½-inch barrels and in caliber .44-40. Both guns were engraved by Colt's renowned L.D. Nimschke and featured gold and silver plating. Gun No. 92248 had ivory grips with a buffalo head on the left side and the initials TR on the right; Single-Action Army No. 92267 featured mother-of-pearl grips. Roosevelt is shown wearing one or the other of these two magnificent Colts in practically every photograph ever taken of him in Dakota.

Properly armed and with buffalo hunting as his goal, TR set out by train in September, 1883, and many days later, disembarked at the small town of Medora, North Dakota, where the West was still very much untamed.

Roosevelt's love affair with the American West was instantaneous and no small part of its beauty was lost on him, as he wrote ten years later in his book, *The Wilderness Hunter*:

"In after years there shall come forever to … mind the memory of endless prairies shimmering in the bright sun; of vast, snow-clad wastes, lying desolate under gray skies; of melancholy marshes; of the rush of mighty rivers; of the breath of the evergreen forest in summer; of the crooning of ice-armored pines at the touch of the winds of winter; of cataracts roaring between hoary mountain passes; of all the innumerable sights and sounds of the wilderness and of the silence that broods in its still depths."

Yet always with a bit of the realist in his otherwise romantic soul, TR was not immune to the hardships that his new-found frontier held. In 1884, while still in the Dakotas, he wrote to his friend Bill Sewell, a gruff but well-educated guide in Maine who had befriended TR:

> *"Now a little plain talk, though I think it unnecessary, for I know you too well. If you are afraid of hard work and privation, don't come out west. If you expect to make a fortune in a year or two, don't come out west. If you will give up under temporary discouragements, don't come out west. If, on the other hand, you are willing to work hard, especially the first year; if you realize that for a couple of years you cannot expect to make much more than you are now making; if you know that at the end of that time you will be in receipt of about a thousand dollars for the third year, with an unlimited world ahead of you and a future as bright as you yourself choose to make it, then come."*

Later in the year, Sewell and Roosevelt would go into the cattle business together, largely as a result of that letter. Before he left North Dakota in the winter of '84 to return to civilization, Theodore Roosevelt put $10,000 down on a $40,000 ranch, called the Maltese Cross, located at Chimney Butte, just eight miles outside of Medora.

His return East held the portent of misery and defeat for the young legislator from New York. In February of that year, his mother passed away; two days later his wife died while giving birth to their daughter, Alice. TR's personal life was crushed and that November, his political life also collapsed, for the Republican Party was defeated at the polls. In 10 months' time the 25-year-old Roosevelt had undergone the same amount of emotional pain that most men experience in a lifetime. Needing to find himself, to restructure his life, he did what thousands of pioneers had done before him—he sought refuge in the West.

Returning to his newly-purchased ranch on the banks of the Little Missouri, he saddled his horse, Manitou, packed his Winchester '76, a book and blanket along with some tea, salt and biscuits, a slicker and a metal cup, and rode off into the prairie to be by himself for the first time in his life. He rode for 10 days, living the life of the hunter, shooting what game he needed to eat and contemplating his recent sorrows and finding solace within himself, with only his horse and his rifle as companions. In this respect, TR was cementing the bond that would forever unite him with sportsmen around the world, both in his time and beyond.

Roosevelt's Chimney Butte ranch was too close to town to afford him the self-imposed exile he sought. He needed seclusion to write, privacy to hunt. Besides, local townsfolk were always dropping in to chat about politics, a fascinating topic for them but a tired one for

Teddy. All he wanted was to immerse himself in the lore of the West; the only news he cared to hear was of the latest cattle market prices and where the best big game hunting could be found. He needed a quieter place to pursue his new-found lifestyle of loneliness.

At last he discovered it, many miles distant from Medora, on a site that bordered the famed Bad Lands. Finding the skulls of two bull elk whose antlers had interlocked during a battle that had resulted in their dual deaths, Roosevelt the romanticist was moved; he immediately christened his yet unbuilt ranch the Elkhorn and promptly purchased the site for $400.

He jumped into the task of setting himself up as a rancher with all the enthusiasm of a small boy. It was characteristic of him. In a letter to his sister in New York he wrote:

"I now look like a regular cowboy dandy, with all my equipment finished in the most expensive style." To his friend, Henry Cabot Lodge, he described his accoutrements in greater detail, " . . . You would be amused to see me in my broad sombrero hat, fringed and beaded buckskin shirt, horsehide chaparajos . . . and cowhide boots, with braided bridle and silver spurs."

Roosevelt's tastes were obviously not that of the common drover and as a result, his appearance created much commotion whenever he came to town. Indeed, his buckskin tunic, fancy guns and thick spectacles caused many to misjudge him. He may have looked like a dude, but his inner fire and spirit would not permit him to be one. In his autobiography he freely admits:

> *"There were all kinds of things I was afraid of at first, ranging from grizzly bears to 'mean' horses and gun-fighters; but by acting as if I was not afraid, I gradually ceased to be afraid."*

During his two-year stay in the West, tales of Theodore Roosevelt's dramatic experiences became as oft-told as any frontier legend, and did much towards elevating him to a hero's status in the country's eyes, even before his famed charge up San Juan Hill. One such verified incident involved the Marquis de Morés, a flamboyant European aristocrat who operated a ranch near the Maltese Cross. The two men were destined to tangle by the very nature of their mutually exuberant personalities. Their first meeting was cordial, largely due to Roosevelt's polished diplomatic courtesy, a technique he had learned in the political frontiers of New York. However, the Marquis, like many self-impressed men who are insensitive to their surroundings, mistakenly interpreted Roosevelt's courtesy as a sign of weakness. Therefore, he sent a team of local gunmen to the Chimney Butte spread to inform TR's cowhands that the Marquis owned the land they were on and that it could be bought for money or blood. The choice was

In the spring of 1886, Roosevelt, second from left, was a dude no longer. In place of the fancy buckskins are the clothes of a working cowboy, with his Colt single-action handy. *(Photo Courtesy Herb Peck)*

up to Roosevelt. Upon learning of the incident, TR immediately buckled on one of his engraved Colts and rode over to the gang leader's cabin. He knocked on the door and it opened.

"I understand you want to kill me on sight," he said to the surprised pistolero. "I have come over to see when you want to begin the killing." The adversary, notably flustered, backed down and apologized, assuring Roosevelt that there must have been a misunderstanding. So ended the Marquis' attempted takeover of the Roosevelt ranch.

Another documented occurrence, one that took place in the Nolan Hotel, 35 miles west of Medora, is best told in TR's own words:

"I was out after lost horses . . . It was late in the evening when I reached the place. I heard one or two shots in the bar-room as I came up, and I disliked going in. But there was nowhere else to go and it was a cold night. Inside the room were several men, who, including the bartender, were wearing the kind of smile worn by men who are making believe to like what they don't like. A shabby individual in a broad hat with a cocked gun in each hand was walking up and down the floor talking with strident profanity. He had evi-

dently been shooting at the clock, which now had two or three holes in its face. As soon as he saw me, he nailed me as 'Four Eyes,' in reference to my spectacles, and said, 'Four Eyes is going to treat.' I joined in the laugh and . . . sat down, thinking to escape notice. He followed me, however, and though I tried to pass it off as a jest this merely made him more offensive, and he stood leaning over me, a gun in each hand, using very foul language. In response to his reiterated command that I should set up the drinks, I said, 'Well, if I've got to, I've got to.' and rose, looking past him. As I rose, I struck quick and hard with my right just to one side of the point of his jaw, hitting with my left as I straightened out, and then again with my right. He fired the guns, but I do not know whether this was merely a convulsive action of his hands, or whether he was trying to shoot me. When he went down he struck the corner of the bar with his head . . . he was senseless. I took away his guns, and the other people in the room, who were now loud in their denunciation of him, hustled him out and put him in the shed."

During his entire two-year stay in the Dakotas, there is no incident of TR using his guns to kill another man, although he did use his rifle to bring three cattle thieves back to town after trailing them for two days. The locals, rather than being impressed, were disappointed with the dude rancher from New York; they could not understand why he did not hang them on the spot, as was the custom of the land.

For almost all of his hunting and shooting activities, Roosevelt preferred the rifle; he had practically no use for shotgunning, as he stated in *Hunting Tales Of A Ranchman*:

> *"To my mind, there is no comparison between sport with a rifle and sport with a shotgun. The rifle is the freeman's weapon. The man who uses it well in the chase shows that he can at need use it also in war with human foes. I would no more compare the feat of one who bags his score of ducks or quail with that of him who fairly hunts down and slays a buck or bear than I would compare the skill necessary to drive a horse and buggy with that required to ride a horse across country . . .*

> *"I am far from decrying the shotgun. It is always pleasant as a change from the rifle and in the Eastern States it is almost the only firearm which we now have a chance to use. But out in cattle country it is the rifle that is always carried by the ranchman who cares for sport."*

With his remarkably poor eyesight, one might think it odd that the "four-eyed dude" would prefer the exactness of the rifle over the scattergun. Yet, his very preference for the more exacting mode of firepower is an insight to his personality, a trait in which he demanded the utmost not only of himself, but of others around

him. Years later, a family member, Nicolas Roosevelt, recounted target practice at the 200-yard range Roosevelt had built at Sagamore Hill, his famed Long Island estate:

> *". . . He had a small rifle range in a safe hollow and not only kept up his own skills at marksmanship, which was considerable, but also taught us youngsters how to shoot . . . He gave us detailed instructions about the care and handling of guns, the sighting and aiming, and above all, the manners of the rifle range. He warned us against ever pointing a gun, whether loaded or not, at anyone, anywhere, any time. Among the few recollections I have of his showing sharpness toward any of us youngsters was if someone was careless with a weapon."*

Considering his vision and frail beginnings, TR's expertise with the rifled shoulder gun was nothing short of admirable. Recollections of close friends, such as Sewell and Wilmot Dow, tell of his shooting the heads off of grouse (most probably with his '73 Winchester) so that none of the meat be wasted. There is also the tale of TR, during his first year in the Bad Lands, dropping two blacktail bucks with one shot from his '76, the 350-grain bullet breaking both their backs.

Although not a handloader (he much preferred "store-bought" ammunition throughout his hunting career), Teddy did experiment with a 330-grain hollow-point slug and 85 grains of Orange Lightning smokeless powder. He wrote high praises of his discovery to Winchester, but there is no evidence the company ever followed his suggestions for a commercially available loading of this type.

His coolness and calmness in the face of danger, a

Roosevelt always demanded the finest in sporting arms. This little-known three barrelled set of Sharps rifles was customized throughout by famed gunsmith F. W. Freund. The set consists of .45-70 and .45-90 rifles, and a shotgun barrel, all engraved and embellished. *(Photo Courtesy U.S. Interior Dept.)*

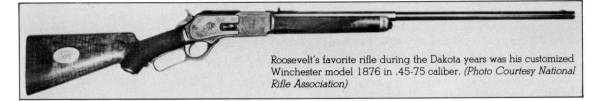

Roosevelt's favorite rifle during the Dakota years was his customized Winchester model 1876 in .45-75 caliber. *(Photo Courtesy National Rifle Association)*

trait that would carry him into the public spotlight after San Juan Hill and later, during many political confrontations, also manifested itself in the hunting fields. On one such occasion, while hunting in the Big Horn Mountains, a grizzly surprised Roosevelt by rearing up less than 15 feet from where the future President stood:

"Doubtless my face was pretty white, but the blue barrel was as steady as a rock as I glanced along it until I could see the top of the bead fairly between his two sinister-looking eyes; as I pulled the trigger I jumped aside out of the smoke, to be ready if he charged; but it was needless . . . the bullet hole in his skull was as exactly between his eyes as if I had measured the distance with a carpenter's rule."

After two years in the West, during which time he shot all manner of big game (preferring it to small game and bird shooting) he returned to the East, where he promptly began writing about his exploits. The result of those efforts were six volumes of Western travel and history, including his now immortal four-volume set, *Winning of the West*. The first book to be published, however, was his *Hunting Tales Of A Ranchman*, the subject nearest to his heart. The now-familiar photo of TR used for the frontispiece, in which he wore his buckskins and fur cap, with a silver Bowie in his belt and his beloved Winchester '76 stoically carried "at the ready," made many people on both sides of the Mississippi River chuckle. But the book was immediately acclaimed not only as a well-written adventure, but one of the most thoroughly scientific observations of wild game and their habits. It became a respected chronicle of Western big game hunting. It was a far cry from his first published work, a rather dry treatise on *The Naval War of 1812*, published in 1882, shortly after his graduation from Harvard. During the vibrant course of his lifetime, Theodore Roosevelt wrote over 35 books, the last of which was *The Great Adventure*, published the month before his death. Many of his books dealt with hunting and the great outdoors, a subject that was always a close part of him. Volumes such as *Ranch Life and the Hunting Trail* (1888), *American Big Game Hunting* (1893), *The Wilderness Hunter* (1893) and *African Game Trails* (1910) detail the sporting life and Roosevelt's own observations with as much fascination

Roosevelt would later abandon the cross-draw holster, but not the Colt. *(North Dakota State Hist. Soc.)*

and adventure today as they did for readers of a different generation many years ago.

TR's return to the East also signaled his return to politics. Although he was defeated in his run for mayor of New York (he would later turn down the governorship of that state twice), he became U.S. Civil Service Commissioner from 1889 until 1895, when he took over as President of the New York Police Commission. From 1897 until 1898 he served as Assistant Secretary of the Navy, resigning to organize the First U.S. Volunteer Cavalry, more popularly known as Roosevelt's Rough Riders, to fight in Cuba. The troops were largely made up of men who had known him in the West and were flattered by the opportunity to "ride with Teddy."

In truth, TR saw little action in that war, but he received worldwide acclaim for his celebrated charge up San Juan Hill. By 1899 lithographed posters were on display in thousands of American homes, depicting the gallant Colonel Roosevelt, on horseback, leading his mounted troops towards victory. In actuality, Teddy was the only one on horseback and he had to use his sword and no doubt some equally sharp words to motivate his men to make the charge. But in the thick of battle these things do not matter; it is the victory that counts and Theodore Roosevelt emerged from that skirmish victorious.

His overwhelming popularity upon his return home carried him into the vice presidency as the running

mate of William McKinley. Six months after taking office, McKinley was assassinated and Roosevelt found
himself the President of the United States. He ran for a
second term and was once again elected by an enthusiastic populace.

Although criticized by many as a "warmonger," TR
successfully negotiated an end to the Russo-Japanese
war in 1905 and was awarded the Nobel Peace Prize.
He helped secure the protection of the United States by
completing the Panama Canal. He reinstated America's
military determination by sailing The Great White
Fleet around the world. But his hunter-conservationist
links were not overlooked either, much to the confusion
of some, even then, who were uneducated as to the
closeness the outdoor sportsman has to nature. During
his presidency, TR established the National Forest Service, implemented the rebuilding of America's bison
herds, created the National Conservation and Inland
Waterways Commissions, set aside 51 of our country's
first bird sanctuaries and formed the National Monuments system to preserve our country's scenic wonders.
TR the sportsman was well and alive in the White
House, and created a legacy that has been handed down
to us today.

As a hunter, Roosevelt was well aware of the national
need for this pastime:

> "... The encouragement of a proper hunting
> spirit, a proper love of sport, instead of being in-
> compatible with a love of nature and wild things,
> offers the best guarantee for the preservation of
> wild things ... we can preserve deer, for example,
> only thru the efforts of sportsmen. If they were
> never shot at all they would increase so that the
> farmers would kill them completely out. They
> have to be kept down somehow, and it is best that
> they be kept down through legitimate hunting."

In his lifetime, Theodore Roosevelt shot practically
every style of gun that was available to sportsmen of his
era. He personally owned more than 50 firearms, including at least a dozen of which were his much-favored
Winchesters, ranging in models '73 all the way up to
the '95, which he helped make famous, just as he did
the '76 and to a lesser extent (because he was not pic-
tured with it as often) the '86. He also owned rifles
made by Marlin, Ballard, Webly, Flobert and Stevens,
to name a few. His handguns included Colts, Smith &
Wessons and Lugers. While he was President, he joined
the National Rifle Association as a life member and
was responsible for prompting Congress to support civilian marksmanship training.

Because of his poor vision, throughout his hunting
career Roosevelt was always meticulous about the design of his rifles, especially the sights. On many of the

As President, Roosevelt occasionally took time to pursue his
favorite sport, hunting. On this 1905 bear hunt he carried a
new 1903 Springfield sporter.

firearms he hunted with in the West, he had famed
gunsmiths F.W. and George Fruend fix his big game
guns with custom sights. He preferred the openleaf,
folding models; he did not care for peep sights. He once
wrote:

> "At long range, I am sorry to say, I never was
> really good for anything ... the rear sight I like
> very open, but with a little U that takes the bead
> of the front sight."

It was not until years later, in 1917, that a New York
Times reporter learned Roosevelt had been doing all of
his hunting since 1905 with only one eye; his left eye
had been blinded during a boxing accident while he was
working out in the White House. Luckily, it was not
his "sighting" eye.

True to his sportsman's instincts, immediately upon
leaving the Presidency (he refused to run for a third
consecutive term) TR and one of his four sons, Kermit,
left for a long-awaited African safari. Here was his new
frontier, for the West of his youth was now settled and
had, in reality, lost much of its lure. But for Roosevelt,
Africa held the thrill of the unknown.

"I speak of Africa and golden joys," TR wrote in the
foreword to his subsequent book, African Game Trails,
published in 1910.

> "The joy of wandering through lonely lands; the
> joy of hunting the mighty and terrible lords of the
> wilderness, the cunning, the wary, and the grim."

Here was a new adventure, unlike anything he had
encountered in the West.

"Camping in the Rockies or in the North Woods can,

The child's game of "Teddy Bear," marketed during TR's presidency, illustrates not only his popularity but his identification with the outdoors.

with advantage, be combined with 'roughing it,' " he wrote, "and the early pioneers of the West . . . always roughed it . . . if Indians and accidents permitted. But in tropic Africa a lamentable portion of the early explorers paid in health or life for the hardships they endured; and throughout most of the country, no man can long rough it, in the Western and Northern sense."

For his expedition into the Dark Continent, in which he was to bring back new and undiscovered species of fauna and flora for the Smithsonian Institution, TR eventually settled on the following guns: a sporterized Army .30 Springfield, a Holland & Holland double rifle .500-.450, which friends had presented to him while he was in the White House, a Fox double-barreled 12 gauge shotgun and of course his beloved Winchesters, this time two identical Model 95's in .405 ("I don't want to run any chances," he wrote Winchester). Just to be sure, he also packed along another 95, but this was in .30 caliber.

Needless to say, Roosevelt's admiration of the Winchester product was long-lived and sincere. Earlier in his hunting career he had written:

"The Winchester . . . is by all odds the best weapon I have ever had and I now use it almost exclusively, having killed every kind of game with it, from a grizzly bear to a big horn. It is handy to carry, whether on foot or horseback and comes up to the shoulder as readily as a shotgun; . . . it is deadly, accurate, and handy as any, stands very rough usage, and is unapproachable for the rapidity of its fire and the facility with which it is loaded."

For his African safari, Roosevelt also wanted to take along a favorite rifle of his, the Winchester '86 in .45-70 (the newer gun and cartridge having surpassed the older ballistics and design of the Model '76), but the Winchester company advised against it, stating that the .45-70 " . . . is amply powerful if the bullet is placed in exactly the right spot, but not as powerful as arms generally used in that country (Africa)."

Evidently TR was convinced that three Model 95's were better than one Model 86. Thus armed, along with *four tons* of salt for curing the hides of game that was to be taken, vast quantities of canned food and a case of judiciously selected books for him to read at night (which included everything from *Alice in Wonderland* to *The History of Rome*), the widely celebrated safari sailed for Africa on March 23, 1909, just 19 days after Theodore Roosevelt left the Presidency. They would be hunting through the heart of East Africa to the Sudan.

Roosevelt's party was guided by the celebrated big game hunter of his day, R.J. Cunningham, who tells this tale of TR's encounter with a bull elephant, which gives a clear insight into the ex-President's character:

"The Colonel (as he was called after San Juan Hill) was determined to get an elephant, and a tusker at that. I told him what it meant, and how much risk there was, but he said he was willing to face it. That was the Colonel all over. Tell him the risks and . . . if he decided they were worthwhile, that was all there was to it.

"Well, we found an elephant in a forest on Genia Mountain. We had been hunting for three days, and it was really hard work for a man of the Colonel's bulk in that heat and at that altitude, 11,000 feet. At last I caught sight of (an) elephant . . . about thirty-five feet away . . . it was a fine specimen. I pointed it out to the Colonel and he fired with complete coolness and got the elephant in the ear and dropped him . . .

"As the shot went off the forest all around roared with trumpetings. We were in the midst of a herd . . . and one of the (bulls) thrust his head through the bushes right over the Colonel's head. I . . . fired at once and it bowled over. Then I rushed to the Colonel and said, 'Are you all right, sir?' But I could see that he was . . . he hadn't turned a hair. He went right up to the old chap he had killed and gave it the coup-de-grace and then let himself loose. I never saw a man so boyishly jubilant."

By the time the safari was over, TR's expedition had claimed 4,897 mammals, over 4,000 birds, 2,000 reptiles and 500 fish for the Smithsonian. Roosevelt had gained renewed respect from the world; he was hailed

Artist Philip R. Goodwin did a series of sketches depicting Roosevelt's 1909 African safari to illustrate TR's book, *African Game Trails*. The nine-month safari essentially opened Africa to sport hunting, and was much publicized. Here TR's son, Kermit, drops a leopard with a Winchester Model '95.

as "Bwana M'Kubwa"—Big Chief, as the Africans had christened him.

So strong was Theodore Roosevelt's popularity upon his jubilant return from safari and subsequent two-month tour of Europe that he was once again proposed for the Presidency. This time he accepted, feeling that the country's military preparedness had waned under the Taft administration, a particularly bitter realization for TR, who had endorsed his successor four years before. Failing to get the Republican nomination, his enthusiastic multitude of supporters retaliated by splitting from their party and forming the Progressive Wing. Taking a line from one of his speeches, in which he claimed, "I feel as fit as a bull moose," the party lay claim to that nickname. However, not everyone was in favor with Roosevelt's "might-is-right" philosophy.

During one of his campaign speeches he was shot by an assassin. Although blood soaked the front of his shirt (he kept his coat buttoned to shield his audience from the sight), he insisted on continuing with his talk and would not leave the platform. Only when he had finished did he permit friends to take him to the hospital. Many in the audience did not know Roosevelt had even been shot until they read about the incident the next day in the newspapers. TR survived; fortunately, the wound was not deep. The bullet had been partly deflected in the folded up papers the Colonel kept in his breast pocket.

The Bull Moose party went down in political history, but it also went down in defeat. Woodrow Wilson won the election that November. Theodore Roosevelt's views were now outmoded, claimed some of the observers of

The North Room of Sagamore Hill aptly reflects Roosevelt's varied and fascinating life. The room was built onto the house during TR's presidency, and was used to entertain dignitaries. The elk and buffalo once hung in the White House. *(Photo Courtesy Harvard College Library)*

the day. But rather than Roosevelt losing pace with the times, the times were losing pace with Roosevelt. A world war was brewing, and he sensed it, but amidst his cries for preparedness, the country demanded peace. Later, after his death, the German Kaiser admitted that Roosevelt was the only American he had truly feared.

The years after the election were frustrating ones for TR. In a letter to a constituent, just before the outbreak of World War I, he wrote that he was "really saddened" by the way in which some of his countrymen "have been completely misled on this peace-at-any-price issue. There are plenty the other way, thank heavens, who place righteousness first."

After the outbreak of war, Roosevelt applied to President Wilson for permission to raise troops and lead the fight in Europe. He was refused. But his four sons

went, the youngest of whom was killed in France, two others wounded. All were cited for gallantry in action. "I am proud of my boys," said TR, in a rare moment of understatement.

Although Roosevelt lost the election in 1912, he went on to other adventures. He traveled to Brazil and discovered The River of Doubt. He returned home and his speeches, editorials, books and columns were even more prolific than before, for the spirit of the man had not dimmed with age, but rather, grew more vibrant. And America, although not always understanding what he was saying, listened. Many of his pet phrases had already become a part of the national language; words like "bully!" and "dee-lighted," and "the strenuous life," which later became a popular song. Some of TR's words survive to this day: "Speak softly, but carry a big stick" (first uttered by him during a speech in Chicago on September 3, 1903), "My hat is in the ring (used to announce his candidacy for the president). Other phrases are less well known today, but no less applicable to our times:

"I am for the square deal," (a phrase that lent enthusiasm to an entire country)

"Damn the law! Build the canal!" (shouted when his advisors began informing President

Roosevelt of the legal obstacles against the Panama Canal)

"Never strike soft—if you must hit a man, put him to sleep," (spoken in one of his later speeches, which shows that Roosevelt had never lost his vitality)

During his lifetime, his popularity was exemplified by the fact that his well-known image adorned everything from pipe tobacco to baking powder, from sewing

Roosevelt's insatiable thirst for adventure led him first to the Dakotas, a dapper dandy whose inner toughness was soon respected. In 1909, fresh out of the White House, the call for adventure took him to Africa, where his coolness astounded veteran hunters. *(Photo at left Courtesy N.D. Hist. Soc.)*

needles to poker chips. Even today, the force of his personality survives, not only in his many volumes of writing, but in the very name of the man himself. But although his spirit may be ageless, the body is, after all, only mortal and must eventually rest. Thus it was on January 6, 1919, in his beloved Sagamore Hill, that Theodore Roosevelt, 61 years of age, died in his sleep. His last words were, "Please turn out the light . . . I am in for a bit of sleep."

Fortunately for America and the world that knew him, the memory of Theodore Roosevelt has never slept. As long as there are men who can still find beauty in the golden glow of sunset, as long as there is game to hunt and wilderness in which to roam, and as long as sportsmanship and freedom remain a part of our national pride, the memory of Theodore Roosevelt shall continue to live.

In some of the early fighting, sailors from the battleship *Oregon* and gunboats *Callao* and *Samar* storm ashore to take Vigan on the northwestern coast of Luzon. The Spanish War ended quickly, but guerrilla warfare in the Philippines was to drag on for 14 long years. These sailors carry 6mm Lee Navy rifles and Colt .38 revolvers.

CHAPTER THIRTEEN

A JUNGLE WAR CASUALTY

By Lee A. Rutledge

MAY 30, 1902. Memorial Day. None of the seven men standing in the cool Philippine dawn could foresee how tragically ironic this holiday was going to be. As they faced the officers' quarters, they were probably thinking about the sultry heat that would soon be in the air and the trick they were about to play on Lieutenant George Rodney, their troop commander.

The rainy season was due any time now, but there were no signs of it this morning. Over their shoulders, beyond tall palm trees, the yellow ball of sun was slowly picking its way through an early morning mist hanging over the nearby rice swamps. There was no doubt about it—this was going to be another hot day in Tanay, a small town of several thousand souls which huddles between tall ridges and sprawls down to the shore of Lake Laguna de Bay.

On a contemporary American military map, Tanay is in the Department of Northern Luzon. It shows up on the lakefront as an insignificant speck just a few miles southeast of Manila. In the spring of 1902, Tanay was the main station of the 5th U.S. Cavalry.

Most of the men's thoughts probably turned briefly to Corporal Lie who had recently died of cholera. They buried him at Binangonan, a former 5th Cavalry sub-post also on the lake but about 20 miles to the east. Because of the cholera, the detachment was quickly pulled back to Tanay. Corporal Lie was popular in "C" Troop. Just yesterday, Sergeant Stewart had asked permission for the group to ride over and decorate Lie's grave. Lieutenant Rodney had consented.

They were jarred back to the present as Rodney and Second Lieutenant Sommerville clumped out of the officers' quarters—a native Nipa house of bamboo, balanced on eight-foot-high poles. Rodney's practiced eye took them in at a glance.

All seven troopers—Sgts. Stewart and Spree, Cpls. Black and Finnegan, Trumpeter Davis, and Pvts. Crane and Carr—stood at easy attention, grasping their mounts' bridles with their right hands: they looked like what they were—regulars. Each wore the regulation drab campaign hat, characteristically battered and bent to his own satisfaction. Brass crossed-sabre insignia, surmounted by a small numeral "5" over the letter "C," glinted on the left sides of their hats.

Around the waists of their khaki-colored trousers were blue Mills belts studded with 100 rounds of brass .30 caliber carbine ammunition; dark leather holsters with Colt service revolvers, caliber .38, hugging their right hips. The butts of seven Krag carbines protruded from saddle scabbards secured along the right sides of their McClellan saddles.

Out of habit, the officers strode up and down checking the men in detail: every button on their dark blue pullover shirts, the laces in their brown canvas leggings, and the brass spurs on their heels. In moments, Lt. Rodney gave his blessing to the detachment. He reminded Sgt. Stewart to return before nightfall. On July 4, 1901, nearly a year before, the islands' newly-appointed civil governor, William Howard Taft, declared that the Philippine Insurrection was officially over. But island-based Army, Navy and Marine Corps servicemen knew better.

Lts. Rodney and Sommerville stood watching for a moment as Sgt. Stewart gave the familiar commands and mounted his little group. They swung their horses into line and clopped off down the road, leather creaking, brass spurs clinking, and disappeared into the mists along the lakeshore road. Only two would come back alive.

Even though it had been relatively quiet, everyone in

the 5th Cavalry was well aware of the standing regimental order—troopers were not permitted to leave the
barracks area alone and any who did go forth had to
arm themselves with at least a revolver and a belt of
ammunition. Variations of this same order were in effect throughout the islands. The bloodcurdling massacre
of the 9th U.S. Infantry detachment at Balangiga, Island of Samar, just eight months before, was still fresh
in everyone's mind. At home, 8,000 miles away, the
massacre had shocked the anti-war protesters back into
action after a period of quiet, and had made every Filipino—however docile appearing—a dangerous suspect.
And no one needed reminding about the dreaded *juramentados* in the south.

On May 29th, Lt. Rodney had instructed Sgt. Stewart that every man must be armed with his carbine as
well as his revolver for the trip to Binangonan. Most
5th Cavalry officers on Luzon would have agreed with
Lt. Rodney that seven fully armed troopers traveling together were safe anywhere in their sector.

But Sgt. Stewart decided to take a chance. After leaving the officers, who had immediately turned their attention to the day's holiday activities, Stewart's party
turned down a side street and trotted to the rear door of
their barracks. The barracks were about 200 yards
from the officers' quarters but on another street and out
of sight. There the troopers relieved themselves of the
carbines and carbine ammunition—extra weight in the
coming heat.

When they trotted off again, they were armed only
with their Colt revolvers and about 21 rounds of revolver ammunition per man.

A few hours later, they were ambling along an old
Spanish road near Binangonan when some mounted
Filipinos materialized ahead of them in the road, all
armed with rifles. After a moment, half the Filipinos
dashed into a fringe of jungle nearby. The other half
stood their ground and fired through the dust.

What happened next was right out of the Old West.
Unfortunately, Sgt. Stewart did not recognize a favorite
trick used by American Indian warriors. So he roared at
his tiny command to raise revolvers and charge. With a
shout, the seven blue-shirted troopers plunged straight
into their antagonists, scattering them right and left.
Without command, the triumphant soldiers reined in
their horses then stared in disbelief—through the slowly
shifting dust they could make out a second group of
horsemen, 200 it turned out, straddling the road a quar-
ter-mile ahead, silent and ominous.

Stewart reacted immediately. "Face about an' charge
back!" he bawled. While executing this movement, they
were caught in a murderous crossfire. In the swirling
dust and din, Pvt. Crane's horse was killed outright.
Crane pitched head over heels, losing his revolver, and
landed clear of the road. The 200 Filipinos closed in

quickly. Crane watched helplessly from his vantage
point in the tall grass as his comrades dismounted to
face the onslaught. His last view of the melee was a
swirling dust cloud punctuated by roaring Colts and
flashing bolo knives.

Looking about frantically, Crane noted a small boat
beached by the nearby lake. He struck out for it. The
only other escapee was Sgt. Spree, who broke clear and
hurried on to Binangonan. Crane paddled back to
Tanay, arriving at sunset. In 10 minutes, Lt. Rodney's
relief party was in the saddle. The rainy season began
that night, but the column sloshed on. At the skirmish
site, all they found were two dead horses, so they continued following the soggy trail.

The trail led to a village where Rodney interrogated
several natives, most of whom were apparently in sym-
pathy with (or in fear of) the bandits. After some coax-
ing, they discovered that the five missing cavalrymen
had killed 19 of their attackers before being overwhelmed. For this staggering feat, the bandits exacted a
final, gruesome price. A few days later the relief column
found the detachment's remains—hacked to pieces.
Somewhat later, some of the killers were rounded up
and they in turn met their punishment.[1]

To modern day American arms students, the forego-
ing may come as something of a mild shock. For many
years, it has been fashionable among military arms
writers to depict the .38 Long Colt cartridge as an utter
failure in the Philippine War. But quite often it did not
fail, as shown by the performance of the 5th Cavalry
detachment. Though outnumbered and under heavy
pressure, the men and the .38 (used by itself) accounted
for a remarkable number of opponents. There were
times when the .38 revolver cartridge held its own with
the best of them.

But the .38 Long Colt was inconsistent; a soldier
could never really be sure that it would do its job, and
that was unforgivable. More damaging was the fact that
the older .45 revolver cartridge was still being used
alongside the .38. And the .45 left no room for doubt or
for argument. So the .38 Long Colt became one of the
"one-war" cartridges; discarded after its first baptism.
In a different war against a different foe, it may have
survived.

So this is a story about the military .38 revolver and
cartridge; about some of the men who used it, and about
its downfall. This is also about a peculiar war fought a
long time ago by Americans long forgotten. Who remembers the Philippine Insurrection?

Three quarters of a century ago, American fighting
men were engaged in the almost-forgotten, intensely
controversial jungle war known as the Philippine In-

[1]Rodney, George B., *As A Cavalryman Remembers*, Idaho, 1944, pp. 140–
144.

Both regular and volunteer U.S. units saw action during the Insurrection, and the course of the war saw a variety of U.S. martial arms employed. These South Dakota cavalrymen carry the .30-40 Krag carbine.

Col. Irving Hale, 1st Colorado Infantry, carries a Colt single-action .45, the issue pistol before the Colt .38.

surrection. While Theodore Roosevelt called the fighting in Cuba "The Splendid Little War," he made no such observation about the long, bitter Philippine fighting. Americans were able to sustain their almost naive enthusiasm for the little war with Spain in 1898 because of its short duration and spectacular victories.

But this enthusiasm was soon cooled by the protracted, grim war fought in the islands. Before 1898, few Americans even knew that the Philippines existed. But they soon learned. For the first time in American history, large numbers of U.S. servicemen were sent halfway around the globe to dodge hostile bullets. As in a later war, their battles erupted deep in jungles, over mountain peaks, through obscure bamboo villages, and across nameless rice paddies. In War Department annual reports there is even talk of "filipinization."

The land war started in February 1899 in Manila and kept on interminably for 14 weary years. The climactic battle of Bud Bagsak, fought high on a mountaintop in 1913, ended the shooting war. There were sporadic outbursts after the Bagsak disturbance, but nothing that could qualify as a pitched battle. By the end of hostilities, slightly over 126,000 U.S. servicemen (one third of America's armed forces in this period) had been sent to the islands.[2] They fought more than 3,000

separate pitched battles and intermittent skirmishes, and engaged in numerous extended manhunts. Many of these encounters were small unit actions led by noncommissioned officers and lieutenants, a usual condition of guerrilla warfare.

Most regular American military units and many state volunteers saw Philippine service. The last volunteers were sent home in June 1901. This date closely coincides with the formation of the Philippine Constabulary, a provencial police force designed to take over policing duties from the U.S. troops. With the war declared officially over the next month, American troops were ostensibly out of a job. It was time for "filipinization." American fighting men stayed on, of course, to affect the transition. They were available to assist the Constabulary and to move on their own in case things got out of hand. It turned out that the greatest fighting and the most casualties were suffered after July 1901.

In the end, America became a world power as a result of the Cuban and Philippine wars. The Philippine Islands were under U.S. jurisdiction until 1946 when they were finally granted independence.

[2]Graff, Henry F. (ed.), *American Imperialism and the Philippine Insurrection: Testimony Taken From Hearings on Affairs in the Philippine Islands, Before the Senate Committee on the Philippines—1902*, Boston 1969, p. xiv.

In the summer of 1901, Americans in the theatre discovered that the 1½-year-old war had simply entered its third and most vicious phase. It had begun with open warfare between American troops and a clearly identifiable Philippine army. Then it shifted to organized guerrilla warfare waged by an "underground" army. From there, it deteriorated to the third phase, which alternated between police actions and open warfare, with Americans fighting diehard insurrectionists, bandits, pirates, slave runners, and other such recalcitrants. Both sides resorted to unconventional tactics, committing acts of retaliation and terror.

Although 70 medals of honor were awarded for action in the Philippine fighting,[3] only two Americans emerged as celebrated heroes, and only one of the two actually won the medal. Both help tell the .38's story. Curiously, the medal winner, General Frederick Funston, soon faded into obscurity. The other hero, John J. Pershing, went on to everlasting fame in World War I. Pershing's humane and sensible role in the Philippine War earned him the respect of Filipinos and Americans alike.

Gen. Funston, a one-time soldier of fortune, was something of an adventurer. He had two primary assignments in the islands: first as commander of the 20th Kansas Volunteer Infantry, and later as commander of the 3d Brigade, 4th District, Department of Northern Luzon. The 3d Brigade was a typical Philippine unit. It included the 22d Infantry and 24th (black) infantry regiments; part of the 34th Volunteer Infantry; Troop "G," 4th Cavalry, and the Macabebe Scouts, a native organization loyal to Americans.

Funston won the Medal of Honor in April 1899. Two years later, in the spring of 1901, he sprung a clever trap and captured the will-o'-the-wisp insurgent leader, Emilio Aguinaldo. His ruse was right out of a dime novel (still immensely popular at this late date) and gained him front-page attention. Funston disguised some Macabebes as insurgents while he and several American officers pretended to be their prisoners. They marched right into Aguinaldo's hideout and captured him handily.

Gen. Funston was heard from again briefly, first as commander of cavalry troops in San Francisco just after the 1906 earthquake and fire, and again during the chase for Pancho Villa in 1916. He died the following year. Pershing, by contrast, added to his Philippine notoriety while searching for Villa even though Villa eluded him. It is significant that Pershing began his military career as a cavalryman while chasing Geronimo. The experience Pershing gained as a horse soldier in the American Southwest and later against the Sioux in

South Dakota, held him in good stead in the Philippines. The American Indian Wars served as good preparation for the Philippine War.

The infantry, as in all wars, was the mainstay in the Philippines. But the cavalry—that special breed of men—was used extensively wherever the infantry operated and in many places where it did not. As pointed out by contemporary commanders, cavalrymen could arrive on a battlefield relatively fresh after a long march whereas infantry, trudging along in the oppressive heat or through the deep mud of monsoons, often arrived bone tired. Gen. Funston reported that wherever cavalry was in short supply, infantry was mounted. "In order partly to make up for the lack of cavalry, so necessary in this sort of war, horses had been obtained some months previously and at all garrisons there had been organized small detachments of mounted infantrymen, these proving most useful."[4]

This was not a new concept; mounted infantrymen had been used in most American wars. Today, the practice is continued with "mechanized" infantry.

Surprisingly, latter-day military historians have largely overlooked the horse soldier's role in the Philippine fighting. This is all the more surprising since their employment is mentioned prominently in contemporary literature. By June 1901, eight regular cavalry regiments had arrived in the islands. In 1911, Pershing was military governor of Moro Province, which included the island of Jolo. He wrote the War Department, "Jolo is the strategical site for (a proposed army post) in the Sulu Archipelago . . . mounted troops can go anywhere on the island and they exert more influence over the Moros than dismounted troops."[5]

General Hugh L. Scott, a commander and governor of Jolo Island, served at the same time as Pershing and Funston. As a second lieutenant years earlier, he had joined the 7th Cavalry soon after the Little Big Horn battle. Scott noted that the American use of cavalry caught the Filipinos by surprise. On Jolo, he pointed out, the Spanish had not used mounted troops against the natives. So the Jolo tribesmen were "dumbfounded" at first when U.S. Cavalry swooped down on them unexpectedly. Says Scott, "They got very uneasy, not knowing when it was going to happen. They said, 'The governor strikes like lightning, and no man knows where or when.' "[6] In Vietnam, 63 years later, the army used its air cavalry, remounted in helicopter gunships, to attain precisely the same results.

In 1902, as in the previous five decades, the horse

---

[3]Schott, Joseph L., *Above and Beyond: the Story of the Congressional Medal of Honor*, New York, 1963, p. 72.

[4]Funston, Frederick, *Memories of Two Wars—Cuban and Philippine Experiences*, New York, 1911, p. 377.

[5]O'Connor, Richard, *Black Jack Pershing*, New York, 1961, p. 96.

[6]Scott, Hugh L., *Some Memories of a Soldier*, New York, 1928, p. 360.

cavalry depended heavily upon its revolvers. In fact, they were the army's prime user of its newly-adopted Colt .38 caliber sidearm. They had turned in their famous long-barreled Colt .45 revolvers back in 1893. And thereby hangs a tale within a tale.

As in all other wars, reputations of both men and arms were made and broken in the Philippines. In the army's eyes, the .38 Long Colt cartridge survived the 1898 War with high marks. But it soon suffered such a profound blow in the Philippine fighting that even today Army Ordnance technicians balk whenever someone proposes re-adopting the .38 caliber. By coincidence, the demise of the .38 cartridge in the army coincided with their diminishing reliance on the revolver. It took many years for Army Ordnance to become disillusioned with the .38; they did so long after everyone else had. But in all fairness to them, the evidence against the cartridge was not at all clear at first—it had led a rather checkered history.

Late in 1898, following the Cuban fighting, the army began to assess its arms and equipment. One review board's task was to consider several questions submitted to it by the Chief of Ordnance regarding the Cavalry's .38 caliber revolver.[7] This November 1898 board, composed of an ordnance officer, an artillery officer, and two cavalry officers, was convened at the order of the Secretary of War.

Since the cavalry used more handguns than any other branch of the U.S. armed forces, Army Ordnance and the War Department generally listened closely to mounted officers' opinions about handguns. One source further clarified the 1898 board's job as being "to inquire into the question of a revolver most suitable for the Cavalry arm of the U.S. Army."[8] Presumably, Cavalry concern helped to initiate this inquisition.

As it turned out, the Revolver Board's final conclusions, issued in the latter part of December 1898, would soon return to haunt them all again and again. The Board found that the .38 "has given quite general satisfaction . . . the stopping power of the caliber .38 bullet is thought to be sufficient (at handgun ranges), and there do not appear to be sufficient reasons to demand a change in caliber, there having been of late years no service experience which would develop facts to justify a recommendation and change."[9]

They were referring, of course, strictly to the revolver's performance in Cuba and the Northern Philippines, and they were quite right. They had enough data to substantiate their claim, examples similar to the 5th

The Moro tribesmen of the Sulu Archipelago used fanatical courage and hit-and-run tactics with incredible success against American forces.

Cavalry's Memorial Day experience or the one below. This .38 caliber success story occurred in the spring of 1900.

Colonel George A. Dodd and 87 men of Troop F, 3d Cavalry, were scouting northwestern Luzon in search of scattered bands of insurgents. Ahead of them friendly Filipinos hacked a trail through the dense undergrowth and jungle. (Dodd would later win his brigadier's star chasing Villa and his men in Mexico).

By April 25, 1900, Dodd's troops had already had two sharp fights with insurgent bands and on this particular morning, they were on a hot trail. About daylight, they arrived at the town of Aligangan where they surrounded 300 Filipinos. Dodd's men opened fire with their Krag carbines and began closing in. The na-

[7]Bady, Donald B., *Colt Automatic Pistols*, California, 1973, p. 20.

[8]Graham, Ron; Kopec, John; and Moore, C. Kenneth, *A Study of the Colt Single Action Revolver*, Texas, 1976, p. 474.

[9]Ibid, p. 474, and Op. Cit., Bady, p. 20.

Blades such as these in the hands of determined warriors wreaked havoc on the American troops. Far right is a kris with sheath. *(Courtesy Bob Docker)*

tives were armed as usual with a combination of firearms and a miscellany of edged weapons. When the Filipinos attempted to break out of the trap, the fighting became hand-to-hand.

All around the perimeter, troopers dropped their carbines and blazed away with their .38 caliber revolvers. After an hour and 15 minutes, Dodd's only reported casualty was a sergeant; he had been struck on the head and shoulders with a spear. Dodd later claimed 125 enemy accounted for—120 killed, five captured.[10]

There is ample evidence that when used under less-than-extraordinary conditions, the .38 cartridge was altogether adequate. But when the American military forces moved south into Mindanao and the Sulu Archipelago, they found extraordinary conditions—they found the Moro.

The southern Philippine Islands were inhabited by Mohammedan Filipinos called Moros by the Spanish. "Moro" is a Spanish term derived from the word "Moor." The Moros were a unique, warlike people whose incredible endurance, reckless bravery, and superhuman acts under fire are the stuff of a fighting man's nightmares. Their collisions with American forces became legendary. It was the Moro who shocked the army into finally retiring its .38 cartridge. Their culture, alien to Americans, was at least six centuries old. Spain had failed in her forcible attempt to change it. The U.S., using both force and diplomacy, would succeed.

Against these people the .38 never really had a

chance. General Pershing served two tours in the Philippines from 1899 to 1903, then again from 1909 to 1913. In 1909, he wrote about what has probably become the most recorded aspect of the fighting in the Philippines.

Writing to a friend on Dec. 24, 1909, Pershing recounted how the wife of an American officer had written home about her life in the Philippines.[11] She passed on a story about a captain who at close range fired all six .38 caliber revolver rounds into a charging Moro. Without so much as slowing down, the Moro ran right up to the captain and chopped him to pieces with a bolo. The Moro then "started on his way rejoicing," according to the account, "when a guard finally finished him with a .45 caliber bullet."

General Scott mentions several such incidents in his memoirs. He told of a Moro who was shot through the body by "seven army revolver bullets" yet continued on with enough strength and energy to "shear off the leg of an engineer soldier more smoothly than it could have been taken off by a surgeon."[12]

When the Filipino insurgents in Luzon and the other northern islands changed over to guerrilla fighting in the last months of 1899, they were short of firearms and ammunition. They soon learned to avoid toe-to-toe slugging matches with the better-armed and better-organized Americans, and to launch surprise attacks and carefully planned ambushes. The Moros, too, adopted these methods. Using these tactics, the Filipinos' few firearms, bolo weapons, spears, and clubs could be used with devastating effect.

To counter this kind of fighting, the army fell back on its Indian fighting experience concluded just nine years before.[13] In fact, many army leaders who served in the Philippines gained extensive guerrilla fighting experience while battling Chiefs Red Cloud, Crazy Horse, the remarkable Joseph, Geronimo, and other crafty Indian leaders.

It was early in 1902 that the Moros of Mindanao and the Sulu Archipelago became increasingly hostile toward the Americans. The Philippines were formally annexed to the U.S. in 1899 after a lengthy, heated public debate. The Moro Province, embracing the islands of Mindanao and Jolo, was created June 1, 1901, to be administered by a civil government backed up by the military. The first U.S. troops had landed on Mindanao in 1899, so they had time to study their adversaries. In an August 1899 dispatch, John Bass,

[11]Smythe, Donald, *Guerrilla Warrior: The Early Life of John J. Pershing*, New York, 1973, p. 161.

[12]Scott, Op. Cit., p. 316.

[13]Matloff, Maurice (general editor), *American Military History*, (Army Historical Series), Washington, D.C., 1969, p. 338.

[10]Wilcox, Marrion, *Harper's History of the War in the Philippines*, New York, 1900, p. 406.

correspondent for *Harper's Magazine*, provided this illumination:

> "Like a Western mining camp of old, Sulu is full of adventure. A native is quick to draw his knife, just as an American desperado was to draw his revolver. The knives in their hands are very deadly weapons at close quarters, especially the "barong," whose weight—in some cases five pounds—combined with the excellent balance, makes it especially effective.[14]"

Scott called the barong "a razor-edged cleaver" with which Moros would cut a man's body in two using a single stroke and then test the blade against the bone by chopping their victims to bits.[15] The Moros used several types and sizes of bladed weapons, all of them deadly, all possessing different names, and all identified specifically with Moros. A 1934 publication lists and describes these blades.[16] The word *bolo* is the general term used to describe any sword or long knife used in the Philippines.

Two Moro blades are mentioned again and again— the *campilan* (also spelled *"kampilan"*), and the more famous *kris,* sometimes written *"cris"* or *"creese"* after the Spanish. The *campilan* is a long Malayan sword with a carved, forked hilt made of wood. The *kris,* of Malay and Java extraction, is an ancient weapon distinctive with its blade wide at the hilt and sometimes waved, but usually straight. These weapons are often found beautifully carved and inlaid with precious and semiprecious materials.

Most sources agree that at the turn of the century, the southern islands were populated by more than 100,-000-plus Moros, many of whom were upset and already disputing the presence of the United States. Their numbers constituted only about four percent of the overall native population, the Christian Filipinos accounting for 92 percent.[17] Much of the trouble between Americans and Moros came about from the Americans' attempts to stop Moro raids and piracy and from American exploration of the interior of the Moro Province. One author noted, "The region of Mindanao and Sulu is one of the oldest battlegrounds in the world."[18] The Moros were veteran fighters.

The Moros stood apart, even in their dress. Typ-

The Philippine Insurrection had tremendous influence on selection of a U.S. service pistol. The Colt 1902 automatic, top, was under testing but was redesigned to the .45 caliber Model 1905, center, after the .38's failure in the Philippines. The Colt Model 1909 revolver in .45 was adopted as a stopgap measure until the 1911 automatic .45 was adopted.

ically, the men wore tight-fitting, striped trousers of many colors, and a short coat with gold or silk embroidery, set off by a colorful turban. Invariably, they wore a large edged weapon proudly thrust into a knotted silk girdle about the waist. Some observers noted boys of 10 wearing bolos. The Moro's blade, according to one soldier, "makes him the proudest, most independent man that walks the earth or rides the sea . . . always rubbing the blade or polishing the handle, it is the one article of value that he possesses."[19]

[14]Wilcox, Op. Cit., p. 245.

[15]Scott, Op. Cit., p. 283.

[16]Stone, George C., *A Glossary of the Construction, Decoration, and Use of Arms and Armor in All Countries and in All Times. . .* , 1934.

[17]Grunder, Garel A., and Livezey, William E., *The Philippines and the United States*, Oklahoma, 1951, p. 137.

[18]Hurley, Vic, *Swish of the Kris: The Story of the Moros*, New York, 1936, p. 13.

[19]Hagadorn, Charles B., "Our Friend the Sultan of Jolo," *The Century Magazine*, Vol. 60, No. 1, May 1900, p. 27.

Moro society can best be likened to the feudal society of Western Europe during Medieval times. Moros resided in independent, small fortresses called "cottas." Regional rulers were Sultans. The ruling elites within the forts—the "dattos"—held life-and-death power over their subjects and slaves. Most Moro warfare against American troops was directed by the dattos. They ruled with complete authority, based loosely on Islamic law.

A key factor in the last phase of the island fighting was the Moros' Mohammedan religion. The Mohammedan faith bred the *"juramentado."* As pointed out by a scholar, "The custom of *juramentado* had its origin in the *jihad*—the holy war of Islam against Christians. A *juramentado* was a frenzy-driven religious fanatic."[20]

A number of things could cause a Moro to become a *juramentado*—despondency, a desire to straighten up a bad life, a belief that someone was interfering with his religion, or a simple desire to enter Mohammedan heaven. The quickest way to attain Mohammedan heaven was to kill a Christian; or better yet, several Christians! Before stalking his prey, the *juramentado* was purified and prepared by a priest. His head and eyebrows were shaven and he donned a white gown. Then he went forth seeking victims.

The .38 cartridge had problems with both the garden variety Moro as well as the inspired, *juramentado* "supermoro." Gen. Scott speculated that the Moros seemed to have different nervous systems from Americans "for he carries lead like a grizzly bear and keeps coming on after being shot again and again. The only weapon that seems adequate to stop him immediately in his tracks is a pump-gun loaded with buck-shot."[21]

General Leonard Wood would probably have agreed with Scott. An incident from Wood's diary serves as a graphic example of why American servicemen lost faith in the .38 cartridge. On April 5, 1904, Wood and his troops were campaigning against Moros on Jolo. As they trudged through a stretch of tall grass that morning, a *juramentado* burst out and flew directly at the nearest flank man. Momentarily startled, the soldier reacted quickly. Snapping up his Krag rifle, he rapidly slammed five .30 caliber bullets into his assailant. Wood noted that the attacker was armed with a huge *campilan,* and had his clothes girded up and his hair tied up.

The Moro came bounding on, apparently oblivious to the newly-acquired lead in his system. He was cutting figure eights in the air, and "making a most impressive sight." Wood and his aide, Capt. Langhorne, drew revolvers but held their fire, afraid of hitting other soldiers ranged between themselves and the onrushing Moro.

The native charged up to his astounded target under

a hail of rifle fire from nearby soldiers, and was able to cut the intended victim's blanket roll and shirt (without inflicting a wound) before going down. Wood, admiring the "pluck" of the hapless native, observed that "it seemed a pity to have to kill so brave a man."[22] Need one wonder how the .38 slug would have performed?

There are reports that American troops early began fashioning dum-dum bullets for use against Moro opponents. They simply cut an "X" into the soft lead tip of the slug causing the bullet to mushroom on impact and measurably increase stopping power.

Yet Gen. Scott, who served in the islands from 1903 to 1906, tells of two *juramentado* incidents which add to the plus side of how the .38 performed. Throughout Scott's Philippine tour, regular troops who were authorized a sidearm were usually issued the Colt double-action .38 revolver. Scott relates that a *juramentado* sneaked his *barong* into the city of Jolo by way of the sewer system. Then he sat down and patiently waited for an unsuspecting Christian to happen by.

Sure enough, two American soldiers soon came sauntering along. The *juramentado* leaped up, brandishing his *barong*. The soldiers, caught off guard, turned and ran. They fled into a billiard saloon and circled the table with the wild man just behind them. They had their revolvers out, but could not use them because of innocent bystanders. In moments, they dashed back outside with the Moro in hot pursuit. They whirled on him in the street and quickly finished him with four bullets.[23]

A second similar incident involved three *juramentados* who entered the market at Jolo and sliced up three Filipinos. While this was going on, a troop of cavalry loped into view on their way to revolver practice. Golden opportunity! Looking up, the *juramentados* must have seen 50 or so blue-shirted tickets to paradise, delivered on the hoof! They immediately charged, waving their bolos. The troopers broke formation, dispersing, unholstering their revolvers, and maneuvering to get clear shots. Seconds later, the street echoed with exploding Colts. Only one of the attackers got close to a soldier, and he lived long enough to slice a stirrup.[24]

But such demonstrations as these were overshadowed by the spectacular failures of the .38 caliber bullet. Even though it is difficult to find eyewitness accounts to substantiate this statement, it is clear from official military correspondence that a significant segment of the army had become disenchanted with the .38 Colt cartridge. This dissatisfaction became apparent less than a year after the 1898 Revolver Board announced that the

20Orosa, Dr. Sixto Y., *The Sulu Archipelago and Its People*, The Philippines, 1970; original edition, 1923, p. 80.

21Scott, Op. Cit., p. 316.

22Hagedorn, Hermann, *Leonard Wood, A Biography*, Vol. II, New York, 1931, p. 44.

23Scott, Op. Cit., pp. 315, 316.

24Ibid, p. 318.

.38 Long Colt "has given quite general satisfaction."

Even at that, the .38 Long Colt died a slow death. As the Philippine campaigns progressed, field commanders began to send in more and more disparaging reports about its inadequate stopping power. As a result, Springfield Armory began a new series of tests in November 1899—a year exactly from the last Revolver Board. These tests continued until February 1900, but nothing was resolved.

The 1903 annual report of the Chief of Ordnance is revealing. Under ".38-Caliber cartridge," he noted: "Complaints have been received concerning the .38-caliber ball cartridge used in the Colt's double-action revolver . . . From the complaint (sic) received in regard to the action of the cartridge in service it is believed that attention has not been given to the adjustment of the tension screw for regulating the pressure of the mainspring, and consequently the required blow is not delivered to the primer."

The Ordnance Chief waved aside all complaints about lack of stopping power and insisted that the real problem lay in misfires due to a soft hammer blow! He reported further that his department was concentrating on improving the primers. It was this sort of attitude which slowed the changeover to a larger military handgun caliber at a critical time. But from the Ordnance standpoint, far removed from the scene, the field reports must have appeared simply fantastic. Unless seen first hand, it is somewhat difficult to swallow stories about little brown men absorbing prodigious amounts of lead like sponges with little or no effect. Ordnance could, of course, have gone to the scene.

In the Ordnance Department's 1904 annual report, the Chief of Ordnance was still preoccupied with improving .38 caliber primers. He announced that a satisfactory primer had finally been adopted for the .38. Overseas, the complaints continued.

During the previous year, 1903, Army Ordnance had adopted the final model of the Colt double-action .38 revolver in what can only be described as "tinkering" instead of improving. The 1903 "improvements" included slightly "shrinking" the inside of the six-inch barrel in an attempt to increase accuracy, and slightly narrowing the grips. Between 1892 and 1908, when Colt ceased production of the model, the Army ordered 68,500 double-action .38s.[25] After 1908, the Army bought no more .38 Colt revolvers.

Finally, in April 1904, the U.S. Cavalry listed specifications it considered essential for a new handgun and a different cartridge. Army Ordnance had been testing Colt's new .38 automatic pistol since 1900, but neither it nor the Cavalry considered the design to be acceptable by 1904.

General Funston saw one of the new .38 Colt automatics in action. During January 1901 (two months before he captured Aguinaldo), Funston rode with a mounted infantry patrol in Northern Luzon. With the group was Major W. C. Brown, inspector general of the 3d Brigade. Fifteen years later, he chased Pancho Villa with the 10th Cavalry. Brown had recently received one of the new automatics for trial. The patrol was soon exchanging shots with a group of Filipino insurgents. The insurgents finally broke contact and melted away, leaving their casualties on the field.

One of the dead was a noted Filipino ex-bandit and insurgent officer, Tagunton, shot through the heart. Upon examination, they found a distinctive steel jacketed bullet, one of Maj. Brown's. Funston claimed that Brown had fired from a distance of 75 yards.[26] But the automatic still had bugs to be worked out.

Colt tried to interest Ordnance in a .41 caliber cartridge that it had been developing, but Ordnance soon rejected it—about the same time that it rejected the .38.

In its 1904 specifications, the Cavalry described the design it wanted in either a semiautomatic pistol nor a double-action revolver. Of the two designs, neither was radical or new—both descriptions fit designs which had been in existence for some years. But the cartridge requirement—even though a return to the tried-and-proven .45—was significant. And by 1904, the Cavalry was adamant about it—it refused to consider anything other than .45 caliber.

The Cavalry specified three requirements for its proposed cartridge: (1) Caliber not less than .45; (2) Initial velocity not less than 725 feet per second (fps). (3) weight of the bullet not less than 250 grains.[27] The .38 Long Colt bullet, by comparison, moved along at 750 fps in its black powder load, and weighed 150 grains. In effect, the Cavalry was calling for a return to practically the same bullet which they used from 1873 to 1893: .45 caliber, 230-grain, initial velocity 730 fps, according to the 1874 army manual.

After the Cavalry published its requirements, tests were arranged. The object of the tests were to once and for all determine which cartridge had the best overall characteristics and stopping power for army use. The practical result of the 1904 tests would be a new handgun specifically for the Cavalry and the Light Artillery (the "light" or Horse Artillery had always been just behind the Cavalry as a heavy handgun user). But it was understood that whatever combination of handgun and cartridge the Cavalry and Artillery found acceptable, would be adopted armywide and probably servicewide.

Accordingly, in 1904 the Ordnance Department de-

[25]Serven, James E., Colt Firearms From 1836, La Habra, Calif., 1972, p. 239.

[26]Funston, Op. Cit., pp. 381, 382.

[27]Bady, Donald, "The .45 ACP Cartridge," American Rifleman Magazine, Vol. 105, No. 3, March 1957, pp. 22, 23.

tailed two officers to conduct the tests: a medical officer, Col. La Garde, and an ordnance officer, Col. John T. Thompson, who is better remembered as the guiding spirit behind the Thompson submachine gun. They ran exhaustive tests using a number of cartridges on targets which included human cadavers and live cattle awaiting slaughter. In the end, they recommended the .45.[28]

A year later, in the spring of 1905, Colt's Firearms Company produced its first prototype of the .45 automatic pistol. Six years after that, this John Browning design evolved into the world-famous Model 1911 Colt automatic. It is a recorded fact that the .45 revolver bullet (like its automatic counterpart) sometimes possessed superior stopping power in comparison to the army's .30-40 Krag rifle or carbine. It was the old .45 revolver cartridge that continued to embarass the .38 cartridge in the islands. Gen. Hugh Scott once again provides the evidence:

Early in 1904, while serving as governor of Jolo, Scott received word that a powerful Moro ruler, Pan-

glima Hassan, was contriving to capture and loot the walled city of Jolo, Scott's headquarters. By and by, Hassan showed up with a large force of armed men and tried to enter the city by using a ruse. Scott confronted Hassan and his ruse with a healthy number of American troops and a machine gun. The ruler looked about and decided that he really didn't want to loot Jolo after all. Not long afterwards, Hassan was arrested, jailed, and made to pay a fine. He was soon released and admonished to break up his gang. Instead, he increased it.

It wasn't long before Hassan's men fired on one of Scott's surveying parties and began to shoot up detachments of Scott's troops. They also began to attack other Moros. Thus began the manhunt after Hassan. He was soon captured again, but immediately escaped with Scott losing two fingers in the process. The manhunt continued for many miles over many days and many

[28]McConaughy, Miriam, *History of Rifles, Revolvers, and Pistols: Army Ordnance, 1917–1919*, Ordnance Publication No. 1865, Washington, D.C., 1920, p. 22.

In a drawing by Gilbert Gaul, California troops under Col. Duboce drive the Filipinos out of the rebel stronghold of Paco early in 1899. The conventional warfare ended quickly, replaced by nerve-wracking guerrilla fighting.

nights. At last, Gen. Scott cornered his quarry. An informant advised Scott that Hassan was hiding in the extinct volcanic crater of Mount Bagsak, later to be the last battleground of the Philippine fighting.

Hassan and two companions were inside a hut well within the 400-yard crater. Thick jungle growth lined the inside bottom of the cone. It was just before dawn. Scott and 400 men including dismounted cavalrymen peered over the lip of the volcano, their Krags ready. Far below, they could see a light come on in the hut. Then they could clearly hear someone singing, the man's voice walking sweetly on the cool morning air.

Just as the sun started to paint the eastern sky, three shadowy figures emerged from the structure and began

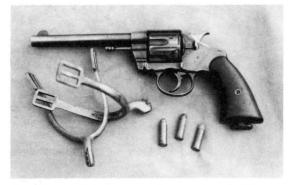

The ill-fated Colt double-action Army revolver in .38 Long Colt was the standard Army sidearm from 1892 until its replacement by the .45 automatic in 1911.

Gun crew members from the Sixth Artillery watch the effect of their shells in Pasay, 1899. Their sidearm was the .38 Colt revolver.

to labor up the murky crater wall. They skirted a number of shallow ravines and continued on silently. As they neared the top, Scott's men could see that all three men were armed. When the lead man reached the rim, he paused to survey his immediate front, perhaps from primal instinct.

It was his last act. A single shot boomed out across the tense calm and rolled up the sky. The figure threw up his hands, flinging his rifle away, and took a spectacular head first plunge fully 600 feet into the depths of the cone. A split second later, every Krag in the vicinity shattered the air, the angry muzzle flashes stabbing, converging on the two remaining men, now easy targets.

Both men went down under the storm, one of them quite dead before he touched the ground. The other, Hassan himself, rolled into a nearby ravine bordered by trees and brush. He had hung onto his Krag rifle despite his wounds.

Hassan returned the fire, wounding one cavalryman who had exposed himself carelessly. The other soldiers dodged for cover and blasted the ravine. After a while, a lone sergeant began working his way up close to Hassan's position, and the soldiers' fire slackened. When Hassan finally noticed the man, he swung his rifle around, but a bullet smashed his rifle's bolt. Hassan quickly drew his barong and went for his antagonist. The non-com stood up with his Colt .45 revolver, took careful aim, and crashed a single bullet through Hassan's ears. That ended the fight.

Scott sent down his surgeon, escorted by several soldiers. On close examination, Hassan's body was found to have 32 Krag bullets in it, but only the 33rd bullet—the .45—had actually brought him down.[29]

By 1907, Cavalry demands for the .45 caliber, especially for use in the Philippines, had become very loud. In its April 1907 summary, a pistol test board made several recommendations, four of which are pertinent here: "1.) Sufficient Colt revolvers, .45 calibre be issued to troops in the Philippines. 2.) Sufficient Colt automatic pistols, .45 calibre, be issued to arm three troops of cavalry for service test of not less than one year ... 4.) One troop of cavalry at each post where the automatic pistols are issued should be furnished with Colt revolvers .45 calibre for comparative purposes. And 5.) The pistols and revolvers should be issued to the exclusion of the present weapon (Colt .38 revolver) which should be turned in."[30]

It was the strongest statement against the .38 yet issued. But opposition to the Cavalry's wish to return to a .45 revolver sometimes came from high places—in 1907, it came in the form of a negative endorsement

[29]Scott, Op. Cit., pp. 298–349.

[30]Bady, *Colt Automatic Pistols*, Op. Cit., pp. 163, 63.

This poster, "Knocking Out the Moros," by artist H. Charles McBarron Jr., depicts Infantry troops fighting their way up Mount Bagsak in 1913, the last major battle of the long campaign. The officer is shown with a brand new Colt 1911 .45 automatic. Without question a very few of the first 1911's saw service in the Philippines.

from the War Department's new General Staff,[31] indicating at least in part why the horse soldiers were fighting an uphill battle. So, back in the Philippines, they continued to make do with what they had: the General Staff had opposed recommendation #1.

Even though Gen. Scott never identified precisely which Colt .45 revolver his sergeant used on Mount Bagsak, it was undoubtedly one of the two models already in the islands. The ones on hand were the old Model 1873 single-action revolvers with either 5½- or 7½-inch barrels, and the 1902 modified Colt double-action revolver with 6-inch barrel and distinctive oversize trigger and triggerguard.

As with the .38, it is difficult to find eyewitness accounts of how the older .45 revolvers actually performed on the battlefield. One of the few reports in print is provided by Gen. Funston. He relates the story of a skirmish that occurred April 23, 1900, in Northern Luzon. Funston, another officer, and 18 mounted Philippine Scouts, were out looking for trouble northwest of San Isidro.

They soon found it at a rickety bamboo bridge. On the other side of the bridge, which crossed a broad and deep ravine, two Filipino insurgents ran away across a field. As they neared the far edge of the field, 400 yards away, a dozen of their comrades stepped out of some heavy brush, formed themselves into line, and opened an ineffective fire.

Funston quickly ordered his lone officer to advance with part of their force through the ravine in a move to flank the Filipinos' position. Funston, himself, galloped the rest of his detachment out across the bridge, one at a time so as not to collapse it. On the far side, he brought his Scouts into line. They paused momentarily to draw revolvers. Funston's own sidearm was a "45-calibre Colt." The Scouts, too, had Colt .45 single-actions.

Funston gave the order, and they spurred their mounts. He personally went after a rifle-wielding insurgent soldier, but rode within four feet of an insurgent officer. The officer raised his sidearm and fired directly into Funston's face, stinging him with sparks, but otherwise causing no harm. Almost simultaneously,

31Ibid., p. 163.

Captain John J. Pershing, later a general and one of the few real heroes of the war, in the advance against Fort Bacolod, April, 1903. *(National Archives photo)*

Funston fired back, "the heavy bullet cutting (the officer's) left hand practically off at the wrist." He concluded with the statement, "Except for one shot fired from a carbine, all our work was done with a revolver."[32]

None of Funston's men were injured, but the Filipinos suffered eight dead (including the officer who was hit again) or dying.

Notwithstanding the above, in 1907 the U.S. Army's official sidearm was still the double-action Colt .38 revolver. But relief was forthcoming as illustrated in a series of remarkable letters between a former army Indian scout and the Ordnance Department. Chief Iodine was interested in obtaining the latest army handgun. On January 4, 1908, he queried the Department to this effect. He also asked about the experimental Colt .45 automatic.

An Ordnance major informed him that the .38 was still regulation and that he could not predict when and if a .45 would be adopted. Two years later, the Chief wrote again. Basically, he repeated his request. This time, Col. Thompson, who was still with the Ordnance Department, answered him. The letter is dated June 29, 1909. Thompson wrote that "the Colt's revolver, caliber .45 model of 1909 is being procedured (sic) for issue only to troops in the Philippine Islands and none of these revolvers will be available for issue or sale to troops in the United States. There is no authority for the exchange of Colt's revolvers, caliber .38, for Colt's revolver, caliber .45."[33]

So two years after the Board's 1907 recommendation for issue of .45 revolvers in the Philippines, and five

years after the Cavalry's determination to return to a .45 caliber hand arm, long-suffering horse soldiers at last began to receive a .45 caliber handgun—the Colt "New Service" double-action revolver with 5½-inch barrel. Colt began production of this revolver in 1897, and the army had been testing it ever since—usually as a "control" to the various prototype automatic pistols. With slight changes, the "New Service" revolver became the Model 1917 and served on as a "substitute standard" arm in both World Wars.

Between February 1909 and December 1910, the Ordnance Department purchased and issued 18,303 Model 1909 Colts to troops in the Philippines and possibly elsewhere. The Marine Corps received 1,200 of the total number manufactured.[34]

Still, the .38 caliber Colt continued on as the regular issue sidearm. The Model 1909 was simply a limited-issue weapon obtained by the army primarily to offset the on-again-off-again .38. But it also served another purpose—it was the Cavalry's attempt to sidestep adoption of an automatic pistol.

It is significant that in 1907 the U.S. Cavalry specifically requested a .45 *revolver* at a time when Army Ordnance was quite clearly on the verge of adopting the .45 automatic. Since the army's first Colt .38 automatic trials in 1900, Cavalry officers had expressed an abiding distrust of this type of arm. Between 1900 and 1909, this distrust melted into dislike, and the dislike finally boiled over into a stubborn rejection.

So it was that in March 1910, on the eve of the War Department's adoption of the Colt automatic, Colt representatives presented their most recently modified .45 automatic to a Cavalry board. The board's conclusions were in part: "It may be said that the sentiment of Cavalry officers is generally against the adoption of an automatic pistol for the United States Cavalry ... it is recommended that there be no longer any hesitation in deciding between the automatic pistol and the revolver, caliber .45, as the issue of the latter weapon will be generally acceptable to the service and the Board recommends that it be done. . . ."[35]

In the War Department Annual Reports for 1910, Volume III, the following statement is found under "Department of Mindanao, (The Philippines), Revolvers—The substitution of the caliber .45 Colt's revolver for the caliber .38 is a distinct improvement. The kind of gun more than compensates for the extra weight."

But the Cavalry was living in Never-Never Land. In 1911, Army Ordnance and the Secretary of War forever ended the horsemen's love affair with the revolver. A

[32]Funston, Op. Cit., pp. 338–342.

[33]Moore, Kenneth, "Chief Iodine, Indian Scout," *Arms Gazette* Magazine, Vol. 5, No. 2, November 1977, pp. 42, 47.

[34]Kuhn, Lt. Col. R. C., ".45 Martial Revolvers," *The Gun Report* Magazine, Vol. 6, No. 12, May 1961, p. 41.

[35]Bady, *Colt Automatic Pistols*, Op. Cit., p. 187.

board of officers and the Chief of Ordnance recommended the adoption of the Model 1911 Colt .45 automatic and the Secretary of War approved their recommendation in March 1911. Just as the Army had occasionally followed the Cavalry's lead in adopting a hand arm, so the Cavalry now had to follow the Army's.

In Volume I of the 1913 War Department annual reports (year ended June 30, 1913), published in 1914, the Chief of Ordnance noted that a "sufficient number" of Model 1911 automatics had been issued to every branch of the service—except Cavalry. He further noted that the Cavalry had just begun to receive their issue—last.

By 1913, the Cavalry saw the light. This fact was reported in a different chapter of the above 1913 volume: "The question of the retention of the automatic pistol has received much attention during the past year. The majority of Cavalry officers favor its retention and consider it a valuable and necessary addition to the cavalryman's weapons."[36]

But the .38 Colt wasn't dead yet. It had one final military duty to perform in the Philippines. In 1909, while the Cavalry was busily casting away their .38s, another outfit was busily gathering them up. They must have been true believers in the .38 cartridge. The 1909 War Department annual reports tell the tale:

"Information has been received that 10 Colt's revolvers, caliber .38, and holsters, will be issued to each scout company, and instructions have been given to turn in all Colt's revolvers, caliber .45, with holsters and cartridge boxes, upon receipt of the caliber .38 revolvers, after which the caliber .45 revolvers will no longer form part of the equipment of Philippine Scouts."[37]

The .38 had received a reprieve. In 1898, it was given a new lease on life, then in 1909, just as the end seemed imminent, a reprieve. But as far as the Regular Army was concerned, this was to be the last gasp—the .38 Long Colt cartridge was on the brink of oblivion. Only once more did the Army rescue it from mothballs: during the great pistol shortage just after America's entry into World War I. Gen. Pershing allowed its limited issue strictly as an emergency measure to rear echelon troops in France. Then the Army let it go.

So the Philippine Scouts holstered their rejected .38 Colts and plunged into the final days of the island war and the final days of the Army's .38 revolver.

All throughout the Philippine fighting, the Scouts were an organic part of the U.S. Army. They were strictly a military outfit composed of native Filipinos led by American officers. The first unit of Scouts was

formed in February 1900, built around the earlier Macabebe Scout organization.[38] The Macabebe Scouts, named after the province in which they were recruited, were organized in September 1899 and led by Lt. Matthew A. Batson of the 4th Cavalry. From the beginning, the Scouts were employed as Infantry. But the lieutenant soon organized at least a battalion of the Scouts as Cavalry. Some Scouts, like the American troops, served as Mounted Infantry.

By 1902, Philippine Cavalry was an operational part of the Scouts. They had their own distinctive crossed-sabre insignia with the letter "P" attached[39] and they were provided for in Army regulations published in 1902. The Philippine Scouts were organized with two principal objects in mind: "To furnish an efficient body of native troops at comparatively small cost, and to save American troops a part of the great losses they incur when in the field in tropical countries."[40] They were also more familiar with the countryside and with Filipino dialects than Americans, were first-rate fighters, and proved invaluable again and again. The Scouts were never a part of the Philippine Constabulary although they were sometimes called to assist the Constabulary with police duties.

They survived well into the Twentieth Century. In 1939, the organization numbered about 5,000 and was called the 26th Cavalry. In 1942, they fought Japanese troops in a 140-mile rear-guard action while covering the American withdrawal to Bataan.

By 1913, the Scouts had long since become a recognized military force in the islands. As of June 30, 1913, they numbered 180 officers and 5,403 enlisted men present for duty.[41] This size had remained relatively constant over the years. They were organized into 12 battalions of four companies each and four "independent" companies totaling 52 companies altogether stationed throughout the islands. This accounts for a fair number of Colt .38s returned to the field in 1909.

The last big clashes in the southern Philippines were the direct result of Gen. Pershing's order to disarm the Moros. He issued the order on September 8, 1911, and Moro reaction was swift and violent. Many decided to fight rather than turn in their beloved bladed weapons and firearms. So for two more years, disorganized Moro bands and staunch individualists fought Pershing's troops in helter-skelter skirmishes. After much grum-

36 War Department Annual Reports, 1909, Vol. III, Washington, D.C., 1909, p. 170.

37 Wilcox, Op. Cit., p. 333.

38 Sexton, Capt. William T., Soldiers in the Sun: An Adventure in Imperialism, Pennsylvania, 1939, p. 266.

39 Laframboise, Leon W., History of the Artillery, Cavalry, and Infantry Branch of Service Insignia, Missouri, 1976, pp. 94, 95.

40 War Department Annual Reports, 1909, Volume III, Washington, D.C., 1909, p. 172.

41 War Department Annual Reports, 1913, Volume I, Washington, D.C., 1914, pp. 220 and 222.

bling and several serious shooting incidents, it all came to a head atop Mount Bagsak (Bud Bagsak), island of Jolo. Early in June 1913, a disgruntled Moro leader named Amil gathered a large force and fled to the 2,200-foot-high extinct volcano. Amil took refuge in several intersupporting cottas around and about the sprawling Bagsak crater.

Pershing opposed him with six American infantry companies of the 8th Infantry Regiment, two mountain gun detachments, a medical detachment, a demolition squad, and several companies of Philippine Scouts. He also took along a detachment of 50 cavalrymen of the 8th Cavalry to be used primarily as a scouting and a reserve force. As it turned out, the battle of Bud Bagsak developed into a series of uphill infantry actions. The strongest cotta, Bagsak itself, was on the highest part of the crater, the last 100 yards of which was nearly perpendicular.

To get to it, Pershing had to first conquer the other strongpoints. Using a combined 8th Infantry and Philippine Scout combat team, he began his preliminary attacks on June 11. The mountain artillery was manhandled up the mountains for close support. Then they began to systematically take the strong points.

On the morning of June 12, a large force of Moros poured out of one of their fortresses shrieking and screaming. They were dressed in "their best finery." But times had changed. American infantry and the Scouts were armed largely with .30 caliber Model 1903 Springfield rifles. Officers and noncommissioned officers in branches other than Cavalry or the Scouts were armed with the new Colt .45 automatic. The Moros approached to within less than 50 yards after disappearing into a deep ravine. The Springfields opened a loud, ragged fire. Not a single native gained the defenders' positions.

Key parts of the operation entailed scaling heights.

Twice—on the first day, then again on the third day—the Philippine Scouts were sent scrambling up sheer cliffs. Then they dropped down behind the Moros, catching them by surprise. The fighting was at close quarters and hand-to-hand. There is no doubt that the .38s were fired in anger.

On the fourth day, June 14, Pershing sent some of his cavalrymen and Philippine Scouts to reconnoiter the main Bagsak cotta. By June 15, Pershing felt he was ready to launch his final attack. Two companies of Scouts, the 51st and the 52d, composed largely of Moros, were to go up first. The Scouts moved out when they received the signal. They made good progress until they reached the first of three lines of trenches. The Moro defenses included a series of bamboo fences constructed to prevent an enemy from outflanking them.

Eight to 10 bamboo blockhouses, complete with protective trenches, covered the heights. Throughout the Scouts' early run, they were covered by the mountain guns and small arms fire from friendly troops. But once they reached the trenches, the covering fire was lifted and they were on their own. They were met by a crescendo of rifle fire supported by a cloud of flying spears and bolos. Hand-to-hand fighting became general.

Pershing later wrote his wife that this fighting was "the fiercest I have ever seen." About the middle of the afternoon, a demolition squad was sent up, but it was not used. The troops scorned the War Department's brand new, weak hand grenades in favor of homemade grenades—four sticks of dynamite lashed together. These made short work of the Moro earthenworks (except when an alert native heaved the explosives back!).

The battle lasted nine hours, the Philippine Scouts finally overrunning the last of the defenses of Bud Bagsak late in the afternoon. When the sun went down that evening, the Philippine war was finally, decisively, over—as was the checkered career of the .38 Colt.

For many American troopers, the Punitive Expedition began as a grand adventure—the last great Cavalry campaign, and a test for unseasoned men and equipment. The ultimate glory was as dubious as the outcome. *(National Archives photo)*

CHAPTER FOURTEEN

THE .45 AUTO WITH PERSHING IN MEXICO

By Colonel Charles Askins

BUCK SERGEANT ELLERY WATERS, "C" Troop, 13th Cavalry, was sergeant of the guard and he made his rounds of the five guard posts on horseback. This was not unusual, for the Post No. 3 was four miles from Columbus and at 2:30 a.m. he expected his inspection to be the last before breakfast. He found everything in order, all his men alert and with nothing untoward to report. He turned and rode along the five-strand barbed-wire fence back to the little encampment of "C" Troop. The horse soldiers were encamped at a windmill a half-mile west of the El Paso & Western depot in Columbus.

Waters—14 years in the Cavalry with service in the Philippines and years of duty on the Tex-Mex border—stepped down from old Eagle, his favorite mount, just as the company street filled with riders. The horsemen fired busily, mostly with six-shooters, but a few with rifles. A machine gun, more than a mile away on a low hill east of Columbus, gave forth with a long series of *pak-pak-pak* bursts—a pause, undoubtedly while the crew changed magazines—and then it commenced again. None of the fire fell near the cavalrymen.

Ellery Waters, 37 years old, a veteran of innumerable brushes with the fanatic Moros of Mindanao, brushed the flap on the GI holster upward and fetched forth the automatic pistol which he had been issued only a month before. It was the .45 Cal Model 1911 pistol. It was loaded with seven cartridges and Waters had two clips in reserve. He stood in the entrance to the guard room and he milked off the first clip, reloaded and let go with the second; finally, since the riders still milled and fired, he loaded up with his third and last magazine and let go with it. "I was maybe a mite afeered these bastards were cowboys from the Diamond As jist hoorawing us but when the bullets started popping the tents I knowed

fer sure they wasn't jist playing. I aimed to kill 'im."

Sergeant Waters had fired away a whole year's allotment of ammunition. He hadn't scratched a target. For all that his shots were among the first ever fired in combat from the .45 automatic pistol. The time was March 9, 1916, and the place was Columbus, New Mexico. The attackers were guerrilla followers of the leading terrorist of that day, Francisco "Pancho" Villa. This revolutionary, a bandit, outlaw, robber, and murderer, had two months before taken 17 Americans off the Noreste de Mexico passenger train just outside Chihuahua City and lined them up and shot all of them. This had incensed the American nation but the U.S. Government under Woodrow Wilson had done nothing. Villa then conceived the raid on an American city. His scheme was to incite the United States to an invasion of Mexico. Villa had aspirations toward the presidency of Mexico and he wanted to create a situation of high tension between the American administration and the provisional presidency of Mexico. The ever-so-shaky President, Venustiano Carranza, simply could not muster sufficient forces to entrap and finish off Pancho Villa. The wily chieftain, Villa, in an attempt to compound Carranza's problem, staged the hit-and-run raid on the tiny border town.

The U.S. Regular Army at the moment of the Villa intrusion numbered 76,480 officers and men. There were 23,000 of the brand new .45 Model 1911 pistols in the supply pipeline. This was more than enough pistols to arm all officers and ranking NCOs. For all that there were many NCOs who were still packing the old Colt .45 Model of 1909, a relic of the Philippines Insurrection. The supply procedures were slow and uncertain; too, there were many old-timers who had no confidence in the "new-fangled" automatic. "I ain't

The U.S. Cavalry on the march after Pancho Villa. Though Cavalry tactics were little changed from the 19th Century, the weaponry was from the modern era—1903 Springfield rifles, machine guns on pack mules, and the new Colt pistol.

gonna pack it," an old line sergeant told his company commander. "I ain't got no confy-dence in them new-fangled pistols."

Sergeant Ellery Waters, later killed in the Meuse-Argonne offensive, was one of the doubting Thomases. "If'n I'd had my ol' .45 I'd got me sum of thim greasers," he afterward commented when questioned as to why he fired 21 shots at a closely bunched gaggle of horsemen and had not nicked man or mount.

The U.S. Cavalry scarcely covered themselves with glory at Columbus. Six troopers were killed and 14 wounded; the civilian casualties amounted to nine killed. The "El Paso Times," in a lurid story on the morning of the 10th of March, said the New Mexico hamlet was struck by 1,500 Villista raiders and that American forces had killed "more than 100" of the banditti. This was a small exaggeration. The truth is the 62 troopers of "C" Troop did not draw any blood. If any raiders were pinked it was done by the local citizenry who did some desultory firing. After Sgt. Waters pooped off all his ammo from the brand new and just battle-tried .45 auto he ran over to the orderly room where all the arms for the garrison were locked up. He had the key. After he got the place unlocked he waited for First Sergeant Norwell Burns to unlock the circular rifle racks. Once this was done and a handful of troopers had dashed inside (the orderly room was a shack

purloined from the El Paso & Western railroad) he, along with the First Sergeant "injuned" over to the supply room where the ammo was also under lock and key. The troop was badly understrength; supposedly composed of 160 men, there were only 62 present. Of these only about half the unit filed into the orderly room and picked up a rifle.

A search was made for the supply sergeant, a trooper named Hampton Armitage. He had the key to the concrete blockhouse which served as the supply repository. He could not be found (he turned up next morning and said he had been kidnapped. The truth was he was hiding under the El Paso & Western water tank). Waters and Burns broke down the door and issued bandoleers of the .30-06 cartridges.

The Villistas, there were 185 of them, were under the command of a subchieftain of the leader, Colonel Julian Cardenas. This commander had split his forces, leading about 100 of his horsemen on the left flank while he directed the remaining 85 raiders off on the right flank under the command of Colonel Candelario Cervantes. Cardenas and his bravos sited an old Chauchat 8mm light machine gun from a low hill about 600 meters from the Columbus main street, a location which permitted them to sweep the single street.

The raid, which lasted for two hours, resulted in the burning of three buildings including the railroad sta-

Prior to the Columbus raid, Pancho Villa, left center, met with General Black Jack Pershing, center right, on the International Bridge at El Paso. First Lieutenant George Patton is looking over Pershing's left shoulder.

tion, the looting of three stores, and the theft of seven Cavalry horses. Then the Villistas rode southward.

Villa, let it be noted, was a hundred miles below the border chuckling at his own temerity. He said to his chief bodyguard, Rodolfo Fierro, "Now let's see what the gringos do." The Americanos took action, but not too promptly. It was full a week before the Army reacted and had troops into Mexico in pursuit of the elusive raiders. During the interim, Black Jack Pershing, veteran of Indian fighting, the Philippines clean-up campaign against the militant Moros, and commander of the Cavalry post of Fort Bliss, Texas, was rushed out to Columbus and told to pursue the dastardly invaders if he must to the very environs of Mexico City itself.

It took a bit of doing and two outfits arrived without their bedrolls but finally on March 15, the 13th, 7th, and 11th Cavalry Regiments together with an entire battalion of pack artillery, the 1st of the 4th Field, along with two batteries of the 6th Field Artillery got into Mexico. They were accompanied with a Quartermaster Wagon Train, with a second contingent following the day after. At Palomas, six miles below Columbus, the garrison commander, a Carranzista (the Federals were known as followers of the provisional *presidente*, Carranza) stepped bravely forth and in stuttering Spanish told the advance detachment of the 7th Cavalry that it could not proceed. At his back were 17 quaking *peones*,

armed with Henry, Mauser, Winchester Model 66, and Lebel rifles. These intrepid soldiery literally faded into the surrounding mesquite when First Lieutenant Jeffery Hodges hauled forth his shining new .45 Model 1911 and in very intemperate and profane Yankee said, "Get your Goddamned ass out of the road, you Mexican sonofabitch." Needless to say while Porfirio Dominquez did not understand the words the muzzle of the big pistol spoke a universal language. He moved aside with an alacrity he had not displayed in many a long day. The punitive expedition was under full steam. To the west was the second contingent consisting of mostly the 10th Cavalry. This force was under the command of Colonel W. C. Brown, although General Pershing elected to enter Mexico with this groupment.

The first gringo soldier to set foot over the international frontier was First Sergeant William P. Hawkins. At his belt he carried not the .45 Model 1911 but an earlier pistol, the .45 Model 1907. The first of the big pistols had been the Model 1905; the Model 1907, of which only 207 were ever made, was purely at the behest of the Army, which accepted 201 of them for further field test. The remaining six pistols were retained by the Colt Company. At any rate Hawkins, a 23-year veteran of the Cavalry, had been issued the obsolete test model in 1908 and had clung to it with all the obstinancy of the old soldier.

The Model 1905, and later the Model '07, were rather crude prototypes of the final pistol, the Model 1911. The earlier guns had a grip-to-barrel angle of very nearly 90 degrees. This was an abomination, for when the pistol was pointed quickly the muzzle aimed at an opponent's knees. There was no safety whatever, and of course no grip safety. The hammer was what we refer to today as the burr type. The front sight, a very low rounded half-moon, was machined as an integral part of the slide. The Model 1907 was a slight improvement. It had a sort of grip safety; however, the grip-to-barrel angle was still the same—a most critical feature. There was a cartridge indicator atop the slide which showed if there were a round in the chamber. This was an excellent feature and more's the pity this was abandoned when the Model 1911 finally appeared on the scene. The '07 had a built-on lanyard ring.

These were the days when every properly accoutered cavalryman swung a saber at his belt. Movement orders for the cavalry regiments were explicit that the sword would be left in garrison. At the same time the order stipulated that all ranks would be armed with the pistol. If the new Model 1911 was not available, then the Model 1909 revolver, .45 caliber, would be issued in lieu thereof. Even so many troopers arrived in Columbus *sans* any sidearm except the 1905 bayonet. Throughout the Mexican campaign the pistols were continued of issue as these became available. Supply procedures were slow in those halcyon days. Nevertheless, by the end of the march virtually all the 10,000 troops were armed with the service pistol. The Great War, 1917–18, which immediately followed the Pershing Expedition, saw virtually all combat troops armed with the Model 1911 or the limited standard Model 1917 revolver.

Pancho Villa, who had not been within a hundred miles of Columbus, laughed at the fumbling efforts of the Yanqui soldiery to catch up with him. At Guerrero he split his miniscule army (he had 400 ragtag peasantry armed with a miscellany of weapons and mounted on scarecrow ponies) and sent off two detachments to attack the village of Miñaca and the other to hit the sizeable pueblo of Guerrero. The canny chieftain held back a fourth contingent as a sort of mobile reserve. Both attacks were successful; the Villistas found the federal garrisons sound asleep (including the sentries) and captured both towns. Ambition stirring within him, the wily leader turned on his left flank and struck at San Ysidro.

This time the Carranzistas were alerted and they drove off the bandits. Villa, watching the action from a nearby low ridge, saw his noble revolucionarios were getting a drubbing so he ordered Col. Rodolfo Fierro, ordinarily his bodyguard, to gallop down with 50 of the *"Dorados"*—the Golden Ones—and turn the flank of

Pershing used several Dodge touring cars like this one on the 1916 Expedition. The trooper is using a field portable Aberdeen Chronograph unit.

the *federales*. This they did quite successfully but during the melee Villa took a 7mm bullet through the calf. It missed the bone but bled so alarmingly that it appeared the old bandit might die. He was carried into a private home in Guerrero and a local medico was summoned. He dressed the wound, staunched the bleeding and was summarily shot by Fierro for his pains.

The 7th Cavalry (the outfit that was with Custer at the Little Big Horn) was nearest Guerrero when word reached Colonel George Dodd that Villa had been wounded near San Ysidro. The doughty cavalryman gave the command to gallop and his regiment covered 55 miles during 17 continuous hours of marching.

The pooped-out horses and riders approached the pueblo of Guerrero at daylight. When the Mexican outposts saw the U.S. Cavalry coming down on them dispersed as skirmishers and with the jaded horses at the high trot they all departed for Yucatan and points farther south. Villa may have still been in hiding in the town at the moment. Later, it is established, he was moved to a cave in the Sierra Madre and remained there for three weeks recuperating.

The pursuit of his valiants went on for 10 miles and the gringo Cavalry rode down and killed 37 Villistas. "I got me three of them pepper-bellies with my new autter-matic," Wade Fitzgerald, First Sergeant of "B" Troop, commented afterward.

General Pershing, who had moved into the pueblo of Bachiniva and established his headquarters there, called in Major Frank "Tommy" Tompkins and ordered the cavalryman to take "K" and "M" Troops of the 11th Cavalry and ride hard for Parral. "Our best intelligence indicates that Villa is in hiding either in the town or nearby. His leg is still not healed and it just may be you can come up with him there." Major Tompkins and his troopers rode off in a cloud of dust. The fact that Parral was 95 miles southward did not disturb the commander,

The ragtag army of General Pancho Villa on the march. Militarily they didn't look impressive, but they managed to keep one step ahead of Pershing's forces throughout the campaign. Villa himself rarely rode in the Dodge touring car, preferring to ride with his troops on his favorite horse, *Cojones*.

Pancho Villa is remembered alternately as a bandit and a patriot; in fact he was probably a little of both. Villa, center, and General Fierro, left, have been in conference with U.S. General Scott. *(National Archives photo)*

The original .45 automatic pistol was the Colt Model 1905. Though it achieved commercial success, it failed the 1907 military trials. It did, however, serve as the inspiration for further development, eventually culminating in the Colt 1911. Weaknesses to be corrected included a poor grip angle and complex double-link locking system.

but just to be sure he was not into a situation beyond his strength the Commanding General, Black Jack Pershing, ordered Colonel William X. Brown of the 10th Cavalry and Major Robert T. Howze of the 11th Cavalry to tag along behind the hard riding Tompkins.

The Mexicans by this time were quite hostile and the column was under a desultory sniper fire. In Sabinal, a pueblo enroute, Tompkins broke off a detachment of his riders and they swung around on the flank and came into the town from the back side. There they surprised a score of *campesinos* busily engaged in plopping shots into the gringo horse column. Seven were killed before the remainder could flee into the nearby mountains.

At San Borja, a Carranzista, Gen. Jorge Cavazos—he had routed the Villistas at the time Villa took the round through his leg—intercepted the hard-riding 11th and informed Tommy Tompkins that word of his coming had gotten to Parral and that the town was making ready a dirty surprise for him. The Chihuahua city was old Villa stamping ground and his amigos there were legend. As a matter of fact when the punitive expedition set foot over the border there was an under-

standing between the provisional Mexican government and President Wilson that our forces would not enter any towns and would not utilize the Mexican rail network. Tompkins pulled up short and went into camp at Santa Rosalia some dozen miles short of the city.

The next day out came a questionable character who spoke plausible English and said he was Captain Antonio Mesa and that he was from the garrison commander. He said the *jefe* wanted Major Tompkins to understand that he could enter Parral for the purpose of buying rations and securing corn for his overworked mounts.

With this assurance from General Ismael Lozano, the local Carranzista chief, the Cavalry mounted up and moved into Parral. Tompkins pulled up in front of the garrison headquarters and was immediately surrounded by a thousand armed and exceedingly ugly locals. The general, when told that his right-hand bower, Captain Antonio Mesa, had extended an invitation to enter Parral, looked nonplussed and said, "But I have no officer on my staff by that name." It was obvious the Americans had blundered into a hornet's nest.

Villa's forces were virtually without artillery. The barrel for this three-inch howitzer came from a memorial in Guatemala; the carriage was handmade!

The Punitive Expedition was the last time Indian scouts were used by the army. These Apaches are carrying 1903 Springfields in their saddle scabbards.

Tommy Tompkins gave the order to move out, and to cover his rear he dropped back with a guard he had designated to cover the retreat. The Mexicans started firing and horses began to drop. All the pack animals were killed or wounded before the troopers reached a railroad embankment on the northwest extremity of the city. Here the soldiers dispersed and took up positions fronting the Mexicans. First Sergeant Jay Richley poked his head up over the embankment and took a bullet through the right eye. Two other troopers had been wounded during the retreat. Because of his orders not to fire on civilians, Tompkins up until that moment had forbidden his men to return the fire.

He ordered his bugler to blow recall and when his people assembled behind the embankment he commenced an orderly withdrawal in the direction of Santa Cruz de Villegas. Here he moved into a perimeter defense and ordered his troopers to resist any further attacks from the Mexicans. By this time Pfc. Albert Erickson had been killed and six troopers wounded.

Major Tompkins sent three troopers off to find Col.

Brown and ask for reinforcements. When the message reached the CO of the 10th he immediately sent forward a skeleton squadron of black troopers (the 10th Cavalry was all black) and when these additional forces pulled into the perimeter the Mexicans backed off about a half-mile and sat their horses, amusing themselves with a haphazard fire from their .44 Winchester carbines.

Captain Aubrey Lippincott, a white officer assigned to the 10th, and very probably the best rifle shot in the Cavalry of that day, eased himself up on the roof of a nearby adobe *jacal*, laced himself into his Springfield sling, ran the sight up to 800 yards, rested the 1903 rifle over the parapet of the adobe dwelling and on the very first round neatly shot a Mexican right out of his Chihuahua saddle. The distance was all of a half-mile. This exhibition had a most remarkably quieting effect on the milling, shouting horsemen. By ones and twos and threes they drifted off into a nearby arroyo, the wash leading back toward Parral, and the beleaguered U.S. Cavalry was left quite alone.

Black Jack Pershing a week later dispatched Major Arlen Howze at the head of six troops of Cavalry plus a machine gun platoon toward Cusihuriachic. The American headquarters was literally afloat with rumors of where Villa was in hiding. This insignificant village was the focus of a number of these *"cuentos,"* and by hard galloping, the Americans were in Cusihuriachic by daylight. As so often happened, the story there was that Villa and his rowdies were at Rancho Ojos Azules (Blue Springs) some 20 miles beyond the pueblo.

On went the horse soldiers. When about a half-mile from the rancho headquarters the Villista pickets saw the approaching soldiery and, firing wildly, fell back on their main force. Howze, before he approached the headquarters, had split his force and sent three troops, including the machine gun platoon, around behind, on the side toward the Sierra Madre. Without taking time to dismount his men he gave the command to charge and with the rifles still in the boots, the cavalrymen unholstered the "new-fangled .45 autt-ermatics" and galloped down on the wildly stampeding *valiantes* of the outlaw Villa.

It was a pigeon shoot. The Americans killed 60 Villistas and wounded 72. These gringo soldiers were all old hands. Scarcely a man in the Cavalry of that day but had put in two and some three enlistments. They were well-disciplined, cool, able fighters and this was revenge for the drubbing Tommy Tompkins had gotten at Parral. It represented the best success of the whole Pershing campaign. Major Howze, from a long line of military people, went on to command a division in World War I. A stadium at Ft. Bliss is named for the family.

Probably the most famous member of the Punitive

Expedition, besides the illustrious commander, Pershing himself, was an insignificant lieutenant named George S. Patton, Jr. This shavetail at the time was anything but famous. As a matter of fact he was something of an upstart and none too well disciplined. It was only some 30 years later that he really made his mark in military annals. George Patton may very well be the most outstanding Army commander of World War II but in 1916 he was nothing more exemplary than an aide— but an aide to Black Jack himself, which was a most promising beginning.

Patton, assigned to the 8th Cavalry at Fort Bliss, was utterly downhearted when he learned that the 7th, the sister regiment, would be taken with Pershing on the invasion of Mexico. Taking the bull by the tail he walked over to Pershing's quarters after duty hours, knocked on the door as bold as brass and when the enlisted orderly answered the bell he told the corporal. "I must see the General. It is extremely important." Now, in those long-forgotten days, mere lieutenants had virtually no conversations with general officers. Not even during duty hours—much less in the evening and in the old lion's den besides!

Black Jack strode into the room and thundered, "What in the hell do you think you are doing here? Who gave you permission to come to my quarters after hours? I am going to have you disciplined!"

Not in the least intimidated, Patton spoke, "Sir, I

Six American troopers were killed in Villa's raid on Columbus. The bandits' casualties were light.

want to go with you on this march into Mexico. I will accept any assignment. Just please permit me to make up your forces."

The next morning Patton found that not only was he transferred from the 8th Cavalry to the 7th but Pershing had made him his personal aide!

There were virtually no passenger autos with the American forces. There were some very old and badly worn trucks, far too few, and two rickety airplanes, but Pershing, by right of rank, had several Dodge touring cars. The invasion had been held up in its inception

The colorful Tommy Tompkins, later a colonel, leads his men out of Mexico after the chase after Villa was called off. Although Villa was shot in the leg and his activities greatly disrupted during the long chase, he stayed ahead of the cavalry, and relatively little was accomplished.

when the CG's Dodge broke down. But now deep in the land of "blanketed thieves and hooded whores" as the American soldiery referred to the place, First Lt. Patton at the behest of his boss, had not only the Old Man's Dodge but two others in trail and he and 16 troopers were well below the pueblo of San Antonio del Valle, searching for a supply of corn for the half-starved cavalry mounts.

The convoy reached and passed through Rubio, a collection of adobe *jacals,* and took the single track toward the considerable ranch headquarters called Rancho San Miguel. In the rear seat of the General's Dodge, beside the exuberant Patton, sat one of the most illustrious soldiers of fortune of that day. This was Emil Holmdahl. Whether a German, a Swede, or a Norwegian, the man was always careful never to say, but the facts were he had fought all over the world. He had been in the Boxer Rebellion, in the Boer War in South Africa, and now, somehow, he had attached himself to the Pershing headquarters and at the behest of Black Jack, who, it is rumored, told him, "Go along with that irrepressible aide of mine and see he does not get his ass shot off," Holmdahl rode with a Springfield between

his knees and the new-fangled .45 Colt auto at his hip.

The hacienda sat on a high hill, devoid of cover, and it is likely the site was selected strictly for defense. At any rate it was impossible for even a single peon with a single burro to approach down the only dusty road without being seen for long minutes from the house.

The house, a low rambling structure made entirely of adobe, was surrounded by a formidable wall. This wall was 12 feet in height and entry was gained only through a broad arched *entrada.* All the place needed was a moat and a drawbridge to present the picture of a medieval castle. As Patton and his party drew up at the great arched passage they noted four *campesinos* beside the wall butchering a beef. The lieutenant alighted and so did Emil Holmdahl; the other soldiery, after the fashion of the army of that day, remained seated until told to alight.

About that time a gaggle of horsemen spewed out of the arched gateway, firing busily as they galloped down on the startled Patton and his companion. The shots, all from pistols, kicked up the dust at Patton's feet, rang off the sides of the auto and wounded the driver, Private Lunt, in the calf.

Mexican revolutionary snipers in action during an attack on Juarez, Chihuahua. These soldiers are armed with both the Model 1894 Winchester in .30-30 caliber and the older '92 Winchester in .44-40 caliber. Winchester rifles were one of the favored arms among Villa's forces. *(Courtesy University of Oklahoma Library)*

The Colt 1911 .45 automatic pistol was
the final result of years of testing and
development. In the 1911 service trials,
it performed flawlessly through a 6,000-
round endurance test and was
subsequently adopted by the armed
forces. The Cavalry objected to an
automatic pistol, but was overruled. By
1916 most units had been issued 1911's.

George Patton had been looking for this sort of encounter. He dipped down, knocked the flap upward on
the GI issue holster, and came out with the brand new
.45 pistol. He was firing at about 10 paces and with his
first 230-grain slug he got the leading rider through the
right arm; on the second shot he did better—he shot this
Villista through both lungs. The third rider was
unseated when Patton hit his horse in the neck. The
fourth rider, by this time quirting his mount to get out
of there, was struck just above the saddle cantle, the
bullet rupturing his liver.

The first rider, still sitting his saddle, took the reins
in his teeth, changed the quirt to his left hand, and proceeded to pour the leather to his mount. But he was not
quite fast enough. Holmdahl, the old hand at such af-
frays, rested his body over the hood of the Dodge,
swung the Springfield along with the hell-for-leather
Mexican and dumped him out of the saddle at not less
than 300 yards. His bag was an interesting one; the
rider was Colonel Julian Cardenas, he who had led the
raid on Columbus.

George Patton, who was later to shoot the high pistol
score in the Pentathlon event of the 1924 Olympics, was
quite proud of himself. He tied the dead Villistas on the

running boards of the three Dodges and trundled them
back to Expedition headquarters to show off to General
Pershing.

There was an Engineer company with the Pershing
forces and a number of detachments. These fellows
were supposed to build bridges, improve the roads and
establish water points. Too, along with other duties,
they were supposed to map the roads. Of course all the
roads were ox-cart single-track dirt trails; the Mexicans
had no autos, and just what was to be accomplished by
tracing these meandering passages is a good question.
Be that as it may, Corporal Davis Marksbury rode
away from the Namiquipa headquarters one day with
12 troopers. Their mission, according to Aubrey
Humphrey, the Engineer captain in charge of the 71st
Engineer Detachment, was to map the road toward Los
Tanques de Cordoba.

The party, riding in a closely bunched formation of
twos, had just ridden into a canyon called Los Alamos
(cottonwoods) when they were charged by a company of
at least 20 Villistas. The Mexicans had waited until the
troopers were within 60 yards of the clump of trees
where they were waiting in ambush. The guerrillas
were upon the cavalrymen before they could scarcely

A few old-timers might have preferred their obsolete Colt Single-Action Army revolvers or the .38 Colts that found disfavor in the Philippines, but the new automatic gave a good account for itself in Mexico, and was carried by almost all mounted troops. It would see even more widespread use in France a year later. *(National Archives photos)*

draw Springfield rifles from their saddle scabbards.

Corporal Marksbury, leader of the detachment, was shot from the saddle. The 7mm bullet penetrated his throat and he died instantly. Three other American soldiers were wounded, one of them shot through the body. For all that, Pfc. George Hewlett, who neither dismounted nor attempted to draw his Springfield from beneath his leg, plucked the .45 Model 1911 from his belt and at a distance of 50 yards shot the leader of the Villistas through the head. It was a lucky shot and Hewlett never claimed it was otherwise. However, he swung over to the rider beside the chieftain and knocked him from the saddle as well. The bullet hit his left shoulder and spilled him to the ground.

It has always been a matter of discussion whether it was Julian Cardenas or Candelario Cervantes who led the raid on Columbus. It was found when the Engineers got things sorted out that Pfc. Hewlett had killed Colonel Cervantes with his first round from the new-fangled pistol. Lt. George Patton had taken care of Col. Julian Cardenas; Pfc. Hewlett accounted for Cer-

vantes. The ledger was beginning to level out at last.

Pershing was crippled by a lack of communications. His far-flung forces were mostly out of touch and with inadequate radios, his air force was reduced to two flimsy Jennies, and most of his intelligence was lies from the local inhabitants. For all that he was quite aware that there was a rising storm of resentment against the Punitive Expedition. Carranza, the provisional president, sent word through a local commander, General Jorge Trevino, that he could not move his forces either south or east or yet west. If he ware to march it must be northward toward the U.S. boundary. Black Jack considered this rank impertinence and informed the *presidente* that he took his orders from the U.S. War Department and would move wherever it appeared most likely he would encounter Villa.

Word, and there were literally scores of rumors daily, reached Pershing that at Villa Ahumada, a sizable town about a hundred miles south of El Paso, the Carranzistas had amassed 10,000 troops and planned to harass the Americans across all of the State of Chihuahua.

Mexican Rurales.

The gray-clad Mexican *Rurales* were a mounted government police force, generally loyal to the central government and hence against Villa, although sides tended to change. These troops are armed with Remington rolling block carbines and shortened versions of the U.S. Model 1860 saber. *(National Archives photo)*

Pershing, by this time inured to the exaggerations of the local intelligence, discounted the 10,000 Carrinzistas by 10 and sent off to Villa Ahumada "C" Troop of the 10th Cavalry. This was a troop from the only Negro regiment in the U.S. Army. The 10th had been created during Indian fighting days and Pershing had at one time been the regimental commander. In command of the troopers galloping off toward the Carranza camp was Captain Charley Boyd.

This fellow had a reputation for being a trouble-maker. He had been for 18 years an enlisted man, and had been thrice courtmartialed. Just how he ever surmounted his somewhat checkered background and was finally commissioned is difficult to explain. He had conducted himself rather well during the Spanish-American dustup and as a result must have been commissioned. Now as an over-age-in-grade sort of re-tread he was troop commander in the 10th.

Pershing had scarcely seen the last of the dust settle

from the fast moving black unit when he decided, just to be on the safe side, he would reinforce it. He dispatched Capt. Lewis Morey and the "K" Troop of the 10th. Finally, 24 hours later, he put the 1st Battalion of the First Infantry on the road toward Villa Ahumada. It was under the command of Major Martin Crimmins, who it should be noted, was the only mounted officer with the foot sloggers.

The ride from Casas Grandes, the Pershing head-quarters, to Villa Ahumada, was about 100 miles. The first night Boyd and his dusky troopers pulled up at the Rancho Santo Domingo where the ranch foreman, Bill McCabe, made the horsemen welcome. The ranch belonged to an American syndicate and was constantly plundered not only by the bandit Villistas but also by the Carranzistas.

Charley Boyd, an aggressive sort much given to loud talk and pugnacious threats, told McCabe, "There's supposed to be 10,000 chile-pickers in Villa Ahumada

Time out for some local brew! The trooper at left carries an old 1909 Colt revolver. *(National Archives photo)*

This Villista has obtained a modern Mauser military rifle, probably 7mm. *(National Archives photo)*

Villa's armored train carried the bandit leader and his troops between Juarez and Mexico City.

jus waiting fer us. I ain't skeered of 'em. I've got 51 troopers here, but that'll be enough."

More to the point, McCabe told the somewhat erratic officer, "I wouldn't ride through Carrizal just up ahead if I were you. My vaqueros were in town just today and they say the Mexicans know you are coming and they aim to ambush your force." Boyd exploded. "I ain't goin' 'round no damn Mex pueblo on this march. We'll drive right on through and if'n they wants a fight they'll damn well git it!"

Before evening, "K" Troop, with Lewis Morey in command, rode into the Rancho Santa Domingo. By right of seniority Boyd was the ranking officer. Morey had only 36 troopers with him, a total force between the two troops of 87 soldiers.

Despite his loudmouth threats to plunge right through every village, town, and hamlet along his line of march, he pulled up on the outskirts of Carrizal and the local *commandante* came out to *hablar.* While Boyd

argued with this worthy he noted about 300 Carranzistas were moving in on his little force from both flanks. He broke off the pow-wow and commanded his troopers to dismount. The horses were sent back toward Rancho Santa Domingo. Boyd waved his black troopers forward, planning to take cover against the sides of an irrigation ditch.

The Mexicans by this time had set up two old Hotchkiss machine guns on a slight ridge which gave them an excellent command of the situation.

The second burst from the nearer machine gun hit three troopers and Boyd was shot in the right hand. He scooped up his pistol from the dirt with his left hand and with some half-dozen troopers charged down on the old Hotchkiss gun. When he was almost atop the weapon he took a bullet through the head. This panicked his soldiery who turned and fled back to the cover of the irrigation ditch.

Before so recklessly charging the machine gun, Boyd

had ordered Capt. Morey to move out toward his right flank and keep that sector covered. With Boyd's death, command of "C" Troop fell upon the shoulders of First Lt. Algernon Adair. This officer immediately took command and, rallying his men, overran the Hotchkiss position. By this time his men had been firing so wildly they were running dangerously short of ammunition. Adair directed that those dead and wounded troopers were to be stripped of bandoleers. At about that moment he took a 7mm slug through the body. This left the troop in command of First Sergeant Alwyn Bloodgood, a veteran of the 10th.

Captain Morey was wounded and, with their officers all casualties, the rout commenced. Those who had somehow retained their mounts galloped off toward Rancho Santa Domingo. Those who were afoot threw away their rifles and ran into the mesquite.

Bill McCabe reported to the Inspector General when the subsequent investigation was made that troopers from "C" and "K" Troops drifted back to the ranch singly and in twos and threes. Virtually none of them had retained their arms and most were still in a state of fright and shock. It was the worst defeat for American forces of the punitive expedition.

There were 40 casualties with a total of 17 dead to include the officers. There were 23 prisoners; these were foot-marched to the railroad and loaded aboard cattle cars and transported to the Chihuahua State prison where they were held until the U.S. State Department could gain their release.

The activities of the expeditionary force wound down after the debacle at Carrizal. Although Pershing remained in Mexico for months afterward there were no sizeable contacts. Villa laughed at the efforts of the Americans and indeed the campaign of Carranza and his cohorts to subdue him. He finally accepted a sort of

Pancho Villa and his favorite horse, *Cojones*, pose at a friend's house in Juarez.

amnesty from the provisional government and was handed, gratuitously, a large ranch in Chihuahua. Journeying into town one day in his own Dodge car he was liberally sprayed with hot lead from a dozen assassins, in the pay of well-established enemies. Thus came the end of his evil trail.

The .45 Model 1911 pistol, while enjoying only a modicum of useage, had acquitted itself most handsomely. So well indeed, that when General Pershing, in writing his After Action report on the Punitive Expedition, recommended that the pistol be issued to all the combat ranks. Black Jack subsequently commanded all our forces during World War I and it is interesting to realize that while not all ranks were armed with the Model 1911 there was finally a grand total of 60 percent of our troops who packed the pistol.

Mexico served not only as a training ground for the soon-to-come First World War, but as a proving ground for Colt's Model 1911—still our service sidearm 65 years later. The desultory campaign in the Mexican deserts also witnessed the passing of the Cavalry as a viable combat arm.

Sergeant York became unquestionably the best known American hero of the First World War, winning not only our highest decoration, the Congressional Medal of Honor, but also the French *Croix de Guerre* with palm. (*National Archives Photo.*)

CHAPTER FIFTEEN

ALVIN YORK— CITIZEN SOLDIER

By Garry James

O N JUNE 28, 1914 Archduke Franz Ferdinand, heir to the throne of the Austro-Hungarian Empire, and his wife, Sophie, climbed ponderously into the back seat of an open touring car. Despite warnings of an assassination attempt, the archduke insisted upon continuing his motorcade through the streets of Sarajevo, the capital of Bosnia.

As the automobile passed the city's central police station a figure dressed in a black coat and hat emerged from the crowd and threw a hand grenade at the royal couple. The missile landed in the folded top and then bounced into the street where it exploded beneath the rear wheels of a following vehicle.

After ascertaining the extent of the damage, Franz Ferdinand commented: "The fellow must be insane, let us proceed with the program."

A short distance from the site of the bomb attack the car came to a stop as some confusion had arisen as to the planned route. At this moment another desperate figure darted into the street, drew a revolver and fired at the pair from almost point-blank range.

Blood spurted from between the archduke's lips as his wife fell forward and across his lap.

Some 6,000 miles away a lanky, red-headed mountaineer sighted down the barrel of his Kentucky rifle and unerringly shot a fox through the head. He retrieved the dead animal and put it into a sack along with several others. At $35 a pelt, he'd done a good day's work, and though he'd rather shoot and hunt than do almost anything else, it was time to head back to the cabin.

Sophie died almost immediately, and the archduke lay in the governor's residence gasping for his last breaths. The assassin's bullet had severed his jugular vein, and with it the hope of peace in Europe.

The Tennessean whistled a gay tune as he set to skin-

ning his quarry. The mountains were his home and his love, and nothing could induce him to leave them— nothing, perhaps, except two wild shots fired by a young Bosnian rebel.

Alvin York, destined to be the most highly decorated and famous American soldier to emerge from World War I, was born in Pall Mall, Fentress County, Tennessee, in 1887.

He was the third in a family of eleven children, eight boys and three girls. York's father was an itinerant blacksmith who preferred the open hunting grounds of the Valley of the Three Forks of the Wolf to the confining atmosphere of the forge.

His love of shooting and of the outdoors was quickly absorbed by young Alvin who eschewed the rigors of the classroom for the more practical occupation of putting meat on the family table.

York's chosen hunting gun was his father's flintlock "Kentucky" longrifle, a type which was favored by most of the other mountain people as well. He found that he had a natural eye for shooting and was the frequent winner at the numerous turkey and beef shoots held in his vicinity.

His hunting was generally for red and grey foxes, for those animals' pelts brought the most money. Other popular game included wild hogs, squirrels, raccoons, mountain cats, deer, and bear, although even in York's time the latter were beginning to get scarce.

York adored his father, and when he died in 1911, the boy in his own words, "sorter went hog wild." Alvin took to gambling, drinking and general hell-raising around the rustic drinking shacks called "blind tigers" by the locals, on the Tennessee-Kentucky state line.

Knife fights, whoring and the drinking of 75-cents-aquart moonshine were all popular activities at these dens, and York did his best to take full advantage of all of them.

He was wont to carry a small nickel-plated "Saturday-night-special" revolver in his trouser pocket, and as he would ride his mule home from his nocturnal forays, liked to take pot-shots at neighbors' geese, turkeys, fenceposts and weather vanes, which, despite his inebriation, he seldom missed.

York admitted that the only book he had read up to this time was a biography on Frank and Jesse James, and its influence was responsible for much of his wildness. Fancying himself quite a backwoods pistolero, he would spur his mule into a full gallop and shoot at, and hit, targets firing from either hand.

York's visits to the state line became more and more frequent and of greater duration. When he would arrive home early in the morning he would find his mother waiting up for him, afraid that he might have been hurt or killed.

She would remind Alvin of how his father never drank, swore or gambled, and added that she worried about the disposition of his immortal soul should he be killed during one of his misadventures.

York began to take her admonitions to heart and would wander at great length through the hills reflecting on his wild life style. Finally, ashamed, he decided to resort to prayer and visited a fundamentalist church in Wolf River, where he had long discussions with the preacher, eventually coming to the conclusion, "When you miss the finer things in life you might just as well be a razorback out in the mountains for all the good you are to yourself and anyone else."

Totally forsaking his old ways, he joined the Church of Christ in Christian Union. The sect had few rules or rituals, with its members adhering to strict views that the Bible is the revealed word of God and that its precepts should not be deviated from.

Like many a repentant sinner, Alvin York embraced his new-found religion fervently. He helped to teach the children's Sunday school and even took singing lessons so that he could lead the hymns. Soon the parishoners were calling him the "singing elder."

About this time he began to take renewed notice of a girl he had grown up with, much to the chagrin of her parents, who were wary of York's bad reputation. The couple began to meet on the sly, Gracie going out to milk the cows and Alvin just happening by on the way to one of his hunting expeditions.

Things were finally beginning to take shape for Alvin York, and his life was settling down to one of purpose and contentment—then the Germans invaded Belgium.

It was some time before the news of the war in Europe filtered into Pall Mall, and even when it did, the inhabitants felt that it had little to do with them. York

continued his courting, hunting and church-going, not giving the faraway fray much of a thought—even when the United States declared war in 1917.

Although many of the young men in town were now hot to "jine up," York began to have serious misgivings about the propriety of killing another human being. It was all very simple—the Bible says "Thou shalt not kill." When York received his notice to register for the draft he was in a quandry. As he later noted in his autobiography: "Everything was going from under me. Fight! Kill! And I'd been converted to the Gospel of peace and love, and of 'Do good for evil.'"

The minister of York's church was also the local registrar, and he helped his parishoner to file a petition as a conscientious objector on the grounds that he was a "member of a well-recognized sect or organization. . . . whose existing creed or principles forbade its members to participate in war in any form and whose religious

In a space of 90 days, 16 encampments like this were constructed for the training of the new National Army, composed of thousands of recruits like York.

After his historic fight, Sergeant York posed at the foot of the hill where the action took place. York brought in 132 prisoners. (*National Archives Photo.*)

principles are against war or participation therein. . . ."

The draft board was less than impressed with this avowal and countered with, "Denied, because we do not think 'The Church of Christ in Christian Union' is a well-recognized religious sect . . . Also we understand it has no special creed except the Bible, which its members more or less interpret for themselves, and some do not disbelieve in war—or least there is nothing forbidding them to participate."

York appealed the decision, and was again turned down. Accepting the inevitable, he made his way to Pall Mall to register. Soon thereafter he was called to the county seat for his physical, and on November 14th received a notification card telling him to report to his local board. The next day he was on his way to Camp Gordon, Georgia.

York was assigned to Company G, 328th Infantry, 82nd Division, nicknamed the "All-American Divi-

sion," because it was made up of men from every state in the Union. For the first time in his life, York was forced to associate not only with people from big cities and other states, but with large contingents of new citizens who could barely speak English. He had little respect for his new associates, few of whom even knew what end of a rifle the bullet came out of. A mild xenophobia developed which blossomed into a thriving homesickness. He was now in even deeper despair.

Alvin could stand it no longer and finally went to his company commander, a fellow Southerner, and told him of his trepidations concerning fighting. His sincerity impressed the captain, who made arrangements for the mountaineer to talk to the battalion commander, Major Buxton, a Rhode Island Yankee.

The officer was immediately struck with York's candid nature and spent a long evening with him discussing the Bible. Buxton would quote a passage condoning

Like the soldier above, York was issued a new 1917 U.S. Enfield when he arrived in France. By the war's end most combat troops also carried the Colt .45 pistol.

Though the American troops were unseasoned, they were fresh and eager for action; by early November 1918 the Allies stood on the banks of the Rhine.

York's patrol faced well-entrenched German machine gun positions; York's uncanny accuracy in picking off the gunners claimed victory from certain disaster.

The 1917 U.S. Enfield, caliber .30-06, was produced in great quantities in 1917–1918 to augment the slower production of the 1903 Springfield rifle. Over two million were manufactured.

war, and York would counter it with one censuring it. After both men had exhausted their arguments the Tennessee private returned to his bunk even more perplexed than ever.

He applied for a pass to go home and think things over and was allowed to return to Pall Mall for 10 days. Released from the confines of the camp, York began to reason more clearly, and decided to take the matter directly to the ultimate authority. After much prayer, he felt he had "received the word" and had been given the assent to "go to war and even kill and yet (God would) not hold it against me."

Alvin went back to camp much relieved, and although the old fears and doubts were still lurking beneath the surface, he was able to sublimate them to his military duties and training.

Immediately York established himself as a crack shot with his .30-06, 1903 Springfield. He owned that the rifle, while not as accurate as his "hog gun" out to 100 yards, was superior at greater ranges. When he first received his '03 he was particularly disgruntled at having to remove the gobs of cosmoline filling every aperture, and noted in his diary, "Well, they give me a gun and oh my that old gun was jes full of Greece and I had to clean that old gun for enspection. So I had a hard time to get that gun clean."

On April 21, 1917, York and his comrades were moved to Camp Upton, New York, preparatory to being sent overseas. After several days of drilling, the men were loaded onto a converted Swedish freighter and set off for Europe. Alvin proved to be a somewhat indifferent sailor and was glad when the troopship arrived in Liverpool a fortnight later.

The men were immediately whisked aboard trains and taken to Southampton where they were again put on board ships bound, this time, for Le Havre, France.

At Le Havre, York's Springfield was replaced with a new Model 1917 Enfield and he was ominously issued with a gas mask.

After more training, reviews, and considerable hiking, the unit was ordered to the front lines. York kept his Bible handy, just to reassure himself that he was doing the right thing.

Now a corporal, he received his baptism of fire in the Montsec sector where he was in charge of an automatic squad armed with French Chauchat machine guns—a weapon for which York had slight regard. "They were big and clumsy. They were too heavy. They were not

accurate or silent. You never could be sure you hit what you fired at no matter how good a shot you were. All you could do with them was make a lot of noise."

After further seasoning at St. Mihiel, York's unit was loaded onto a narrow-gauge railroad and taken to a disembarkation point where they were transported, via French buses, to the Argonne Forest.

The Allies had received quite a pounding from the German guns. Large areas of the woods had been destroyed and the ground, muddied from a constant drizzle, was littered with dead horses and other debris of battle. York described the scene as the "Abomination of Desolation."

On October 8th, following fierce fighting, the men were moved to Hill 223 which would be the staging point for an attack on the Decauville Railroad, some three kilometers distant.

The troops were supposed to have been given a supporting artillery barrage, but as often happens, orders became confused and the men had to go over the top without it.

As soon as they began their move the Boche machine gunners opened up and pinned the advancing Americans to the ground. The Spandaus were in an elevated position and hundreds of Yanks fell within moments of emerging from cover, while the others were afraid to lift their faces out of the mud.

Following their platoon sergeant's improvised plan, Sergeant Bernard Early and three squads, one led by York, made their way toward the machine gun emplacements on the left front.

The 17 doughboys managed to work their way behind German lines, and though they couldn't see the guns, they were at least able to move in the direction of the sound of the fire.

As they jumped a small stream the squads surprised a number of German orderlies, stretcher bearers and runners, who immediately surrendered. Without warning, German machine guns opened up and severely wounded Sergeant Early and the two other corporals, and killed or wounded six of the squad members. The prisoners hit the ground along with the other Americans, and both were raked with a withering fire from the Spandaus. York was caught in the open about 25 yards from the gun pits. Looking back and seeing the wounded, he now realized that he was in command, and more or less on his own.

Carefully, York eased his rifle forward and as soon as

a German gunner raised his head, he fired. The man disappeared behind the parapet. As one of his comrades exposed himself to see where the fire was coming from, the corporal shot him too. Heads kept appearing and York kept ticking them off in the manner of the turkey shoots he was so fond of back in Tennessee.

As soon as he was able, Alvin raised himself from the prone to the standing position where he could shoot offhand, his favorite hold.

By this time he had gone through several five-shot clips of ammunition and was beginning to run low. Suddenly, a German officer and five men leaped from the emplacement and charged York with their bayonets fixed.

As he had only a couple of rounds in his rifle, he drew his M1911, .45 Colt pistol, pointed it and felled the rearmost of his assailants, followed by the fifth, fourth, third, second and finally the officer. York had used this technique while hunting wild turkeys at home. If he shot the ones farthest away the gobblers nearest to him would not become alarmed and fly away.

He continued shooting at the machine gunners with his Enfield, while shouting at them to surrender. Finally, a German officer signalled that he wanted to talk. At first he thought York was British, and exclaimed, "Good God" when he turned out to be a Yank. The officer turned his pistol over to York and agreed to surrender his men if he would stop shooting. Alvin nodded and covered the prisoner with his .45 while about 50 men emerged from the pit. One soldier tossed a hand grenade at York's head, and though it missed him and wounded one of the prisoners, the mountaineer shot his assailant to insure that the rest of the Germans would come along quietly.

When the captives had assembled, York called back to his men to move out. One private told him that with so few guards it would be impossible to get the Germans back to the American lines. Overhearing the conversation, the Boche major questioned York as to how many men he really had, the corporal replied, "aplenty."

He had the prisoners carry the wounded, and forced the major, at the point of his Colt automatic, to head the column. As it worked its way back through the enemy trenches other machine gunners moved around to rake the line. York cooly told the major to order these men to surrender or he would blow his head off. By the time they reached the battalion headquarters the Americans had accumulated 132 prisoners. Later when he reported to the brigade commander, General Lindsay, the general commented, "Well York, I hear you captured the whole damned German army." With characteristic understatement York corrected him. "Nossir, I only have one hundred and thirty-two." Later, when asked how he accomplished his feat he replied casually, "I surrounded 'em."

For his heroism, York was awarded the Congressional Medal of Honor, the French Legion of Honor, the Croix de Guerre with palms, the Medaille Militaire and the Italian War Cross as well as 50 other decorations. General Pershing called him the "outstanding civilian soldier of the war," and French Commanding General Ferdinand Foch proclaimed, "What you did was the greatest thing accomplished by any private soldier of all the armies of Europe."

On his arrival in New York, Alvin was given a lavish ticker-tape reception, replete with a suite at the Waldorf-Astoria. He was besieged with offers to go on lecture tours, endorse products and act in movies, all of which he politely declined with the cryptic comment, "Wouldn't I look funny in tights."

York returned to his mountains, presumably to enjoy the quiet life, however he soon realized that his notoriety made this impossible, and he succumbed to offers to go on a lecture tour. The money he received for his efforts all went to the Alvin York Agricultural Institute, an organization he established to introduce modern farming methods to his area, and to a Bible school.

In 1941 a film on his life, "Sergeant York," starring Gary Cooper netted his institute and school almost a quarter of a million dollars, and garnered an Oscar for Cooper.

When World War II began, York made many public appearances to boost morale and sell war bonds. In 1945, considering his job finally done, he returned to the mountains and a longed-for retirement.

In 1954 he was staggered by a cerebral hemorrhage, and then slapped with a bill by the government for $25,000 in back taxes. As he had given practically all his earnings to his institute and school and was now "riding the bed," he was forced to rely on public donations to pay the debt. As one of the townsfolk put it, "By God, it ain't easy to be a hero now with all these taxes."

It was never easy to be a hero. And Alvin York epitomized the breed—the quiet American who simply did his duty as he saw it.

BIBLIOGRAPHY

1. *AMARILLO GLOBE NEWS*, Amarillo, Texas, Golden Anniversary Edition, August 14, 1938.

2. Baca, Elfego, *A POLITICAL RECORD OF ELFEGO BACA AND A BRIEF HISTORY OF HIS LIFE*, 1944.

3. Bady, Donald B., *COLT AUTOMATIC PISTOLS*, Alhambra, Calif., 1973.

4. Bady, Donald B., *"THE .45 ACP CARTRIDGE,"* The American Rifleman Magazine, Vol. 105, No. 3, March, 1957.

5. Barnard, Henry, *ARMSMEAR*, Hartford: Mrs. Samuel Colt, 1866.

6. Beale, Gen'l. R.L.T., C.S.A., *HISTORY OF THE NINTH VA. CAVALRY.*

7. Beckett, V.B., *BACA'S BATTLE*, Stagecoach Press, 1962.

8. Boatner, Mark M. III. *ENCYCLOPEDIA OF THE AMERICAN REVOLUTION*, New York, David McKay Co., 1966.

9. Breihan, Carl W., *"ANNIE OAKLEY—LITTLE SURE SHOT."* Oldtimes Wild West, October, 1979.

10. Brenner, Anita, *THE WIND THAT SWEPT MEXICO*, University of Texas Press, 1943 & 1971.

11. Burke, John, *BUFFALO BILL, THE NOBLEST WHITESKIN.* G. Putnam, 1973.

12. Carriker, Robert C., Editor, "THOMPSON McFADDEN'S DIARY OF AN INDIAN CAMPAIGN," 1874, Southwestern Quarterly, Vol. LXXV, No. 2, Pg. 212–218, October, 1971.

13. Century Magazine, *"BATTLES & LEADERS OF THE CIVIL WAR."*

14. Chamberlain, Samuel, *MY CONFESSION*, New York: Harper & Brothers, 1956.

15. Chrisman, Harry E., *LOST TRAILS OF THE CIMARRON*, Denver Sage Books, 1961.

16. Cloman, Lt. Col. Sydney, *MYSELF AND A FEW MOROS*, New York, 1923.

17. Cody, W.F., *AN AUTOBIOGRAPHY OF BUFFALO BILL.* Cosmopolitan Book Corp., 1920.

18. Coe, George W., *FRONTIER FIGHTER*, Houghton Mifflin Company, 1934.

19. Commager, Henry S. and Morris, Richard B., *THE SPIRIT OF SEVENTY-SIX.* New York, Harper & Rowe, 1958.

20. Cook, Fred J., *WHAT MANNER OF MEN—FORGOTTEN HEROES OF THE AMERICAN REVOLUTION:* New York, William Morrow & Company, 1959.

21. Cook, James H., *FIFTY YEARS OF THE OLD FRONTIER.* Yale University Press, 1923, & University of Oklahoma Press, 1957.

22. Cowles, Virginia, *THE KAISER.* Harper & Rowe, 1963.

23. Cranbrook, James, *"THE GUNS OF ANNIE OAKLEY."* Guns Magazine, May, 1956.

24. Crichton, Kyle S., *LAW AND ORDER LIMITED.* The Rio Grande Press, 1970, originally printed 1928.

25. Davis, Burke, *LAST CAVALIER.*

26. Davis, Burke, *TO APPOMATTOX.*

27. Davis, William, *CIVIL WAR TIMES ILLUSTRATED.*

28. Dearborn, Henry, *JOURNALS OF HENRY DEARBORN, 1776–1783*, Cambridge, John Wilson & Son, 1887.

29. Dickert, D. Augustus, *HISTORY OF KERSHAU'S BRIGADE.*

30. Dixon, Olive K., *LIFE OF BILLY DIXON, PLAINSMAN, SCOUT AND PIONEER.* Dallas, P.L. Turner & Co., Revised Edition, 1927.

31. Dunaway, Rev. Wayland F., *REMINISCENCES OF A REBEL.*

32. Edwards, John N., *SHELBY & HIS MEN.*

33. Evans, Clement, *CONFEDERATE MILITARY HISTORY* (12 vols.).

34. Fellows, Dexter, *THIS WAY TO THE BIG SHOW.* The Viking Press, 1936.

35. Ford, John Salmon, *RIP FORD'S TEXAS.* Austin, University Of Texas Press, Memoirs of "Rip" Ford, c. 1885.

36. Freeman, Douglas S., *LEE'S LIEUTENANTS.*

37. Freeman, Douglas S., *R.E. LEE* (4 vols.).

38. French, William, *SOME RECOLLECTIONS OF A WESTERN RANCHMAN.* Argosy-Antiquarian Ltd., 1965, first printed 1927.

39. *HISTORICAL REVIEW OF NEW MEXICO*, Volume XXI, University of New Mexico, 1946.

40. *AN ILLUSTRATED HISTORY OF NEW MEXICO*, The Lewis Publishing Co., 1895.

41. Fuller, Maurice G., *SOUTHERN LIFE IN SOUTHERN LITERATURE.*

42. Funston, Frederick, *MEMORIES OF TWO WARS—CUBAN AND PHILIPPINE EXPERIENCES.* New York, 1911.

43. Gard, Wayne, *THE GREAT BUFFALO HUNT, ITS HISTORY AND DRAMA AND ITS ROLE IN THE OPENING OF THE WEST.* New York, Alfred Knopf, 1960.

44. Gates, John M. *SCHOOLBOOKS AND KRAGS: THE UNITED STATES ARMY IN THE PHILIPPINES, 1898–1902.* Connecticut, 1973.

45. Graff, Henry F. (ed.), *AMERICAN IMPERIALISM AND THE PHILIPPINE INSURRECTION: TESTIMONY FROM HEARINGS ON AFFAIRS IN THE PHILIPPINE ISLANDS BEFORE THE SENATE COMMITTEE ON THE PHILIP-PINES—1902.* Boston, 1969.

46. Graham, Ron, Kopec, John; and Moore, C. Kenneth, *A STUDY OF THE COLT SINGLE ACTION ARMY REVOLVER.* Texas, 1976.

47. Greer, James Kimmins, *COLONEL JACK HAYS.* New York, E.P. Dutton & Company, Inc., 1952.

48. Hagadorn, Charles B., (Adjutant, 23d U.S. Infantry), *"OUR FRIEND THE SULTAN OF JOLO".* New York, The Century Magazine, Vol. 60, No. 1, May, 1900.

49. Hagedorn, Hermann, *LEONARD WOOD, A BIOGRAPHY*, Vol. II. New York, 1931.

50. Havighurst, Walter, *ANNIE OAKLEY OF THE WILD WEST.*

51. Hawsley, Ashley, Jr., *WHO FIRED THE FIRST SHOT?*

52. Henry, Robert Selph, *STORY OF THE CONFEDERACY.*

53. Holbrook, Steward N., *LITTLE ANNIE OAKLEY AND OTHER RUGGED PEOPLE.* Macmillan, 1948.

54. Huddleston, Joe D., *COLONIAL RIFLEMEN IN THE AMERICAN REVOLUTION.* York, Pennsylvania, George Shumway, 1978.

55. Hurley, Vic., *SWISH OF THE KRIS: THE STORY OF THE MOROS,* New York, 1936.

56. Johnson, Byron A., *THE ROUSING LIFE OF ELFEGO BACA,* The Albuquerque Museum, 1981.

57. Keating, Bern, *THE FLAMBOYANT MR. COLT AND HIS DEADLY SIX-SHOOTER.* New York, Doubleday & Co., 1978.

58. Keller, Allan., *MORGAN'S RAID.*

59. Knox, Bill, *THE MIRACLE OF THE RIDGEPOLE,* Southwest Heritage, Vol. 1, No. 2, Pg. 37–50, 1967.

60. Kopec, John A., *A STUDY OF THE COLT SINGLE ACTION REVOLVER.* Taylor Publishing Co., 1978.

61. Koury, Michael J., *ARMS FOR TEXAS.* Fort Collins, The Old Army Press, 1973.

62. Krick, Robert, *LEE'S COLONELS.*

63. Kuhn, Lt. Col. R.C., *.45 MARTIAL REVOLVERS.* The Gun Report Magazine, Vol. 6, No. 12, May, 1961.

64. La Bree, Ben., *CONFEDERATE SOLDIER IN THE CIVIL WAR.*

65. Laframboise, Leon W., *HISTORY OF THE ARTILLERY, CAVALRY AND INFANTRY BRANCH OF SERVICE INSIGNIA.* Steelville, Missouri, 1976.

66. Lane, Jack C., *ARMED PROGRESSIVE: GENERAL LEONARD WOOD.* San Rafael, Ca. 1978.

67. Lossing, Benson J., *THE PICTORIAL FIELD BOOK OF THE REVOLUTION; or, ILLUSTRATIONS BY PEN AND PENCIL OF THE HISTORY, BIOGRAPHY, SCENERY, RELICS AND TRADITIONS OF THE WAR FOR INDEPENDENCE.* 2 Vols: New York, 1851.

68. McCarthy, John L., *ADOBE WALLS BRIDE,* the story of Billy and Olive King Dixon. San Antonio: The Naylor Co., 1955.

69. McConaughy, Miriam, *HISTORY OF RIFLES, REVOLVERS, AND PISTOLS: ARMY ORDNANCE, 1917–1919.* Ordnance Publication No. 1865, Washington, D.C., 1920.

70. Manarin, Louis & Wallace, Lee., *RICHMOND VOLUNTEERS 1861–1865.*

71. Matloff, Maurice (gen. ed.), *AMERICAN MILITARY HISTORY,* Army Historical Series, Washington, D.C., 1969.

72. Momtross, Lynn, *THE STORY OF THE CONTINENTAL ARMY, 1775–1783.* New York, Barnes & Noble, 1952.

73. Moore, C. Kenneth, *"CHIEF IODINE, INDIAN SCOUT."* Arms Gazette Magazine, Vol. 5, No. 2, November, 1977.

74. Mullin, Robert N., *THE BOYHOOD OF BILLY THE KID,* Texas Western Press, New Mexico Magazine, September 1959; April 1960, May, 1960.

75. Munson, John W., *REMINISCENCES OF A MOSBY GUERRILLA.*

76. O'Connor, Richard, *BLACK JACK PERSHING,* New York, 1961.

77. O'Neal, Bill, *ENCYCLOPEDIA OF WESTERN GUN-FIGHTERS,* 1979.

78. Orosa, Dr. Sixto Y., *THE SULU ARCHIPELAGO AND ITS PEOPLE,* The Philippines, 1970, (originally published in New York, 1923).

79. Parsons, John E., *SAM COLT'S OWN RECORD.* Hartford: The Connecticut Historical Society, 1949.

80. Parsons, John E., *THE PEACEMAKER AND ITS RIVALS,* William Morrow and Company, 1950.

81. Pate, J. Nell, *"THE BATTLES OF ADOBE WALLS."* Great Plains Journal, Vol. 16, No. 1, Pg. 2–39, 1976.

82. Porter, Millie Jones, *MEMORY CUPS OF PANHANDLE PIONEERS.* Clarendon, Texas, Clarendon Press, 1945.

83. Price, William H., Civil War Research Assoc. Service, *CIVIL WAR HANDBOOK.*

84. Rathjen, Frederick W., *THE TEXAS PANHANDLE FRONTIER.* Austin: University of Texas Press, 1973.

85. *REPORT OF THE CHIEF OF ORDNANCE,* Washington, D.C., 1903.

86. *REPORT OF THE CHIEF OF ORDNANCE,* Washington, D.C., 1904.

87. Richardson, Rupert N., *THE BATTLE OF ADOBE WALLS, 1874 BATTLES OF TEXAS.* Waco, Texas, The Texian Press, 1967.

88. Rodney, George B., *AS A CAVALRYMAN REMEMBERS,* Idaho, 1944.

89. Russell, Don, *THE LIVES AND LEGENDS OF BUFFALO BILL,* Norman, 1960.

90. Schaefer, Jack, *HEROES WITHOUT GLORY.* Houghton Mifflin Company, Time, September 10, 1945.

91. Schott, Joseph L., *THE ORDEAL OF SAMAR.* New York, 1964.

92. Scott, Hugh L., *SOME MEMORIES OF A SOLDIER.* New York, 1928.

93. Scott, Maj. John., *PARTISAN LIFE WITH MOSBY.*

94. Sell and Weybright, *BUFFALO BILL AND THE WILD WEST.* Oxford University Press, 1955.

95. Serven, James E., *COLT FIREARMS FROM 1836.* La Habra, California, 1972.

96. Sexton, William T., *SOLDIERS IN THE SUN: AN ADVENTURE IN IMPERIALISM.* Pennsylvania, 1939.

97. Sibley, Marilyn McAdams, Ed., *SAMUEL H. WALKER'S ACCOUNT OF THE MIER EXPEDITION.* The Texas State Historical Association, 1978.

98. Smythe, Donald, *GUERRILLA WARRIOR: THE EARLY LIFE OF JOHN J. PERSHING.* New York, 1973.

99. Sparks, Jared, *THE WRITINGS OF GEORGE WASHINGTON*, 12 vols: Boston, Little, Brown & Co., 1858.

100. Stackpole, Gen. Edw. J., *FREDERICKSBURG CAMPAIGN.*

101. Stanley, F., *THE TEXAS PANHANDLE, FROM CATTLEMEN TO FEED LOTS* (1880–1970). Privately published, 1971.

102. Stone, George C., *A GLOSSARY OF THE CONSTRUCTION, DECORATION AND USE OF ARMS AND ARMOR IN ALL COUNTRIES AND IN ALL TIMES.* New York, 1934.

103. Swartwout, Annie Fern, *MISSIE, AN HISTORICAL BIOGRAPHY OF ANNIE OAKLEY.* The Brown Publishing Co., 1947.

104. Thatcher, James, *MILITARY JOURNAL OF THE AMERICAN REVOLUTION.* Hartford, Jurlbut, Williams & Co., 1862.

105. Thompson, John W., Jr., Capt. U.S.M.C., *JEB STUART.*

106. U.S. Govt. Printing Office, *OFFICE RECORDS OF THE WAR OF REBELLION*, (index).

107. Wallace, Lee., *VIRGINIA MILITARY ORGANIZATIONS 1861–1865.*

108. *WAR DEPARTMENT ANNUAL REPORTS, 1909*, Volume III. Washington, D.C., 1909.

109. *WAR DEPARTMENT ANNUAL REPORTS*, 1910, Volume III, Washington, D.C., 1910.

110. *WAR DEPARTMENT ANNUAL REPORTS*, 1911, Volume I. Washington, D.C. 1912.

111. *WAR DEPARTMENT ANNUAL REPORTS*, 1913, Volume 1. Washington, D.C., 1914.

112. Warner, Ezra J., *GENERALS IN GRAY.*

113. White, Lonnie J., *INDIAN BATTLES IN THE TEXAS PANHANDLE, 1874.* Journal of the West, Vol. VI, No. 2, April, 1967, Pg. 278–309.

114. White, Lonnie J., Editor, *OLD MOBEETIE 1877–1885.* Panhandle News Items from the Dodge City Times. Canyon, Texas: The Panhandle-Plains Historical Society, 1967.

115. Wilcox, Marrion, *HARPER'S HISTORY OF THE WAR IN THE PHILIPPINES.* New York, 1900.

116. Williamson, James J., *MOSBY'S RANGERS.*

117. Wilson, R.L. and Phillips, P.R., *PATTERSON COLT PISTOL VARIATIONS.* Dallas: Jackson Arms, 1979.

118. Wilson, R.L. and Sutherland, R.Q., *THE BOOK OF COLT FIREARMS.* Kansas City, Published by R.Q. Sutherland, 1970.

119. Wilson, R.L., *THE COLT HERITAGE.* New York: Simon & Schuster, 1979.

120. Wolff, Leon, *LITTLE BROWN BROTHER.* New York, 1961.

121. Wright, Albert H., *THE SULLIVAN EXPEDITION OF 1779*, 4 parts in 1 volume. Ithaca, New York, A.H. Wright, 1943.

122. Yost, Nellie Snyder, *BUFFALO BILL—HIS FAMILY, FRIENDS, FAME, FAILURES AND FORTUNES.* Swallow Press, 1979.

ABOUT THE AUTHORS

CRAIG BODDINGTON was born in Kansas City, Kansas, in 1952. He graduated from the University of Kansas with a degree in English, and was a Marine Corps infantry officer. He is currently serving as a captain in the Marine Corps Reserve. Boddington has published outdoor and firearms-related articles in most of the U.S. outdoor and sporting journals, and is an avid hunter with several African safaris to his credit. He is presently Editor of Guns & Ammo Specialty Books, Petersen Publishing Company, and Executive Editor of *Petersen's HUNTING* magazine. He and his wife reside in Los Angeles.

JOE HUDDLESTON was born in Carthage, Tennessee, in 1937. He graduated from Texas Christian with a degree in psychology and was commissioned in the U.S. Army. During his army career he served as Ordnance Officer Chief, Conventional Weapons Branch, Aberdeen Proving Ground; was the Military History Instructor at Northeast Missouri State University; saw service in Vietnam, and was advisor to the Royal Thai Army. He was also commander of the Marksmanship Training Unit at Fort Meade. He is currently a major in the U.S. Army Reserve and curator of the 101st Airborne Division Museum at Fort Campbell, Kentucky. He authored *Colonial Riflemen in the American Revolution*, and his hobby is making and hunting with Kentucky longrifles. He resides in Clarksville, Tennessee with his wife and three daughters.

MERRILL K. LINDSAY is one of America's foremost firearms historians, with membership in more than a dozen international societies in the historical arms field, including the Company of Military Historians. He is the winner of the Townsend Whelen Award for "a major contribution to arms and arms literature." Mr. Lindsay is an arms consultant to a number of museums, a member of the Visiting Committee of the Metropolitan Museum of Art, President and Director of the Eli Whitney Museum, Inc., and an advisor to the U.S. Historical Society. He has authored a number of books on historical firearms, including *100 Great Guns* (Walker & Co.), *The Kentucky Rifle* (Arma Press), and, most recently, *The Lure of Antique Arms* and *The New England Gun, the First Two Hundred Years*, both published by David McKay. His recent findings about Alexander Hamilton's trick pistols have created quite a stir in historical circles, as the roles of Hamilton and Burr now need to be reversed and that bit of history rewritten.

ARTHUR J. RESSEL's background in Hawken lore and especially factual information on the rifles has been gleaned from over 30 years of interest, association, and collecting artifacts from the fur trade era, especially the Hawken rifles themselves. Mr. Ressel is the owner of The Hawken Shop in St. Louis, boasting the largest collection of original St. Louis Hawken rifles in the world. In his continued research on the mountain men and their arms and equipment, his travels have enabled him to carefully examine more than 50 prime examples of Hawken craftsmanship.

R.L. WILSON is currently Historical Consultant, Colt Firearms Division, and is a freelance consultant and author in the arms field. His career began in 1959–1963 with intern positions at The Armouries, H.M. Tower of London, the Corcoran Gallery of Art, and the Wadsworth Atheneum. He is on advisory boards or serves as consultant on arms and armor subjects to the Metropolitan Museum of Art, the Buffalo Bill Historical Center, the Remington Arms Company Museum, the Eli Whitney Museum, and the U.S. Historical Society. He is also Honorary Curator of Firearms, Kansas State Historical Society, and a consultant to private collectors. Funded by grants from the Buffalo Bill Historical Center (Kinnucan Chair) and the James H. Woods Foundation, he is currently working on a definitive study of the Winchester 1 of 1,000 rifles. He has authored some 14 books on firearms, including his most recent, *The Colt Heritage*. Born in Minnesota, he studied history and art at Carleton College, and now resides in Connecticut with his wife, two sons, two daughters, and his father-in-law.

WILLIAM A. ALBAUGH III was born in Baltimore, Maryland, in 1908. He attended Friends School and studied at Randolph-Macon College, Ashland, Virginia, and New York University. He studied law for a year under Gordon Ambler in Richmond. During World War II he served as an officer in Naval Intelligence, seeing action in both the Atlantic and Pacific theaters. He continued intelligence work for the government until his retirement in 1973, upon which he moved to Tappahannock, Virginia, where he now resides. His interest in the Civil War, and especially the Confederate side, stems from his childhood, and was stimulated by having ancestors who carried arms for the South. His first writing on the subject appeared in the 1930's. Since then he has had articles published in a wide variety of periodicals, and he has written 10 books on the Confederacy and their arms and armaments. He is currently a contributing editor for the North/South Trader, a periodical devoted wholly to the Civil War.

ROY MARTIN MARCOT was born in Virginia in 1946, and has been involved with firearms since an early age. He was active in competitive N.R.A. rifle and pistol shooting from the age of 13, and is a Certified Rifle and Pistol Instructor and recipient of the "Instructor's Training Award" for his involvement with youth firearms instruction. Mr. Marcot has been researching Spencer repeating rifles since 1978 and has written several articles on the subject for various antique firearms magazines. He is the recent recipient of a Kinnucan Arms Chair grant from the Winchester Museum to continue his studies about the Spencer firearm and its inventor Christopher M. Spencer. He is in the final stages of completing a definitive book on the subject. Mr. Marcot is a certified Safety Professional and works as a Loss Prevention Manager for a large national insurance company, and he is currently a captain in the U.S. Army Reserve. He, his wife, and two sons reside in Irvine, California.

JIM EARLE, a native Texan, has spent his professional career as an engineering professor at Texas A&M University. His avocation has long been researching the history of the Old West, and he has written numerous books and articles on the gunfighters, lawmen, and outlaws of the American West. A number of books on the subject have been published under his imprint, the Early West Series of College Station, Texas. He has been a cartoonist for *The Battalion*, a College Station newspaper, where his character, Slouch, has appeared since 1953 on a daily basis. He has also authored eight engineering textbooks and 31 laboratory manuals. He and his wife, Theresa, reside in College Station, Texas, where she shares his interest in the Old West by collecting and dealing in rare western books.

JACK LOTT was born in Maryland of pioneer Anglo-Scotch-German stock. His interest in hunting and firearms stems from his father's tales of the pine woods and swamps of the Deep South, and he has been a wanderer of the woods, hills and deserts since childhood. At an early age his family moved to California, where he attended Beverly Hills High School and Los Angeles City College. He has long been a professional gunsmith and collector of fine firearms and sporting books, with emphasis on the early African explorers and hunters. Frederick Russell Burnham's book, *Scouting on Two Continents*, inspired him to go to Rhodesia, and he has visited Africa off and on since 1959. Africa continues its fascination for Mr. Lott, especially collecting papers and artifacts from the pioneer era. A lifelong admirer of Burnham, his collection includes Burnham's personal

firearms and many of his papers and artifacts. Mr. Lott's articles on hunting and firearms, both modern and historical, have appeared in many firearms and outdoor periodicals. In addition to gunsmithing, Mr. Lott is a precision machinist and toolmaker, and currently resides in Los Angeles.

LEE A. SILVA, a native Californian, was born in 1936. His father operated a cattle and quarter horse ranch on the Colorado River, and he was raised around guns and hunting from the time he was born. As a teenager he guided corporate executives, baseball players, and such on duck and goose hunts, and was upset at the apathy towards conservation. Subsequently he majored in Wildlife Conservation at San Jose State College, ultimately graduating with a business degree. He came to Hollywood to study acting and writing, and was a commercial salvage and abalone diver. In Hollywood he appeared on the western series "Rawhide," as well as various daytime dramas. He later appeared in his own singing act in Las Vegas, playing in many of the top clubs before returning to Hollywood to write. A student of the Old West throughout his varied career, he published his first article in 1970 and since then has written three novels and numerous stories and articles on the Old West and firearms that played a part in that era. He is currently residing in Los Angeles and writing in addition to continuing his career as a country-western singer.

JAMES BELLAH was born in New York City of an old family tracing its roots back to the Mayflower. He graduated from the University of California and has been an actor on stage, radio, and television. He served in the Army and was Senior Information NCO at Camp Moore, Honshu, Japan, and also taught English in Tokyo. He is currently a major in the California State Military Reserve, serving as a Public Affairs Officer. His writing career has included newspaper and magazine journalism, and he is currently a full-time novelist and part-time journalism instructor. His writing has included screenplays for motion pictures, television, more than 30 short stories, numerous feature articles, and over 40 books. The West Coast Review of Books awarded his novel *Stood A Man* a "Porgey" Gold Medal for 1980 for the best novel based on fact. His short story "Jason Glendauer's Watch" won the Western Writers of America's Golden Spur for the best short story of 1979. His latest book, a historical novel entitled *Imperial Express*, will appear early in 1982. He resides in Tarzana, California, in a house that is reminiscent of a bygone era.

ANGELA HYNES was born in England and studied English Education at London University. She came to the United States as Publicity Manager for the recreated version of Buffalo Bill's Wild West. During two years in that position she toured the world with the show and began her career as a writer. She is currently a full-time freelance writer, with articles published in British and Australian magazines as well as in the U.S.

RICK HACKER was born in 1942 and has been involved with hunting and shooting sports since he was 16, and his love of history and historical firearms has developed from that hobby. He has been a published author for more than half his life, selling his first story to *Boys Life* at the age of 17. Since then he has written two screenplays, several short stories, and numerous articles on firearms, hunting, and American history for most of America's outdoor and firearms journals. He is in the process of completing his first book, *The Muzzleloading Hunter.* An avid outdoorsman and big game hunter, he has always felt a close identity with Theodore Roosevelt, and over the years he has accumulated a sizable collection of T.R. memorabilia, including several original letters, some of which are quoted herein for the first time. Mr. Hacker was raised in Phoenix, Arizona, where he attended Arizona State University, majoring in advertising and broadcasting. He currently resides in Los Angeles with his wife.

LEE RUTLEDGE resides in his home town of Riverside, California, where he was born during World War II. He traces his interest in the serious study of military and arms history to the 4th grade, an interest that was heightened by his time in the U.S. Army during the mid-1960's. A former newspaper reporter and a former assistant librarian, Mr. Rutledge is now a freelance writer concentrating primarily on American military subjects.

COLONEL CHARLES ASKINS is one of the old-timers in the outdoor and firearms writing field. Currently the senior field editor of the *American Rifleman*, he has served on the staff of most firearms journals. He has authored eight books on guns, shooting, and hunting, and has published more than 1,000 stories and articles. A former Forest Ranger, U.S. Border Patrolman, and retired Regular Army officer with 33½ years service, Askins says, "I fought two major wars and any number of skirmishes with the .45 Auto. There isn't any other handgun quite as good." Three times winner of National championships, five times Texas champion, presented the Outstanding American Handgunner Award in 1974, Askins holds 534 medals and 117 trophies for his pistol prowess. The colonel has made 25 African safaris, five shikars to Asia, and has hunted every continent except Australia. He currently resides with his wife in San Antonio.

GARRY JAMES was born in Los Angeles in 1944 and received a BA in journalism from California State University, Northridge. He has collected and studied antique firearms since the age of seven. He has served as technical adviser in motion pictures, edited numerous books on firearms, and written countless articles for historical and firearms-related publications. He is an Arms and Armour consulting expert for Sotheby, Parke, Bernet, and is currently working on a book on 19th Century British firearms. Mr. James, his wife, and their one daughter reside in Northridge, California.